COD

ZANE GREY

ZANE GREY

CODE OF THE WEST

HODDER PAPERBACKS

*The characters in this book are entirely imaginary and
bear no relation to any living person*

FIRST PUBLISHED JULY	1934
NEW EDITION (RESET)	1955
HODDER PAPERBACK EDITION	1962
SECOND IMPRESSION	1969

Made and Printed in Great Britain for
Hodder Paperbacks Ltd.,
St. Paul's House, Warwick Lane,
London, E.C.4, by
Hazell Watson & Viney Ltd.,
Aylesbury, Bucks

SBN 340 00482 7

1

Of the many problems that had beset Mary Stockwell during her two years of teaching school in the sparsely settled Tonto Basin of Arizona, this last one was the knottiest, the one that touched her most keenly. For it involved her little sister, Georgiana May, who was on her way to Arizona to be cured, the letter from their mother disclosed, of a slight tendency towards tuberculosis, and a very great leaning towards indiscriminate flirtation.

This day Mary was unusually tired. She had walked all the way up to the little log school-house on Tonto Creek—six miles—and back again to the Thurman ranch at Green Valley, where she boarded. Her eighteen pupils, ranging from six-year-old Mytie Thurman to sixteen-year-old Richard, had broken all records that day for insubordination. Then the hot sun of the September afternoon and the thick dust of the long dry road through brush and forest had taxed her to extreme weariness. Consequently she was not at her best to receive such a shock as her mother's letter had given her.

"Well, there's no help for it," she thought wearily, taking up the letter again. "Georgiana is on her way—will arrive in Globe on the ninth. Let me see. Goodness, that's to-morrow—Tuesday. The mail stage leaves Globe on Wednesday. She'll get to Ryson about five o'clock. And I can't get away. I'll have to send someone to meet her. . . . Dear little golden-haired Georgie!"

Miss Stockwell seemed divided between distress at this sudden vexatious responsibility and a reviving tender memory of her sister. What would she do with her? How would the Thurmans take this visit? Georgiana had looked very much like an angel, but she most assuredly had belied her appearance. Taking up the letter again, the perplexed schoolmistress hurried to that part which had so shocked her and scattered her wits:

". . . Dr. Smith says Georgie's right lung is affected, but Dr. Jones, whom father swears by, says Georgie had just danced and gadded herself into a run-down condition. But I think Dr. Smith is right. I never could bear that man Jones. You remember Mrs.

Jones—what airs she put on. Anyway, Georgie is in a bad way, besides being possessed of a variety of devils.

"Daughter, you've been away from home going on six years, and part of the time you've been living in the backwoods. You've been better off, thank Heavens, but you're buried alive as far as knowing what's come over the world. Since you left we've had the Great War, and then after-the-war, which was worse. I'm sure I don't know how to explain what has happened. At least I can give you some idea of Georgiana. She is now seventeen, and pretty. She knows more than you, who are twice her age. She knows more than I do. Whatever the modern girl has developed Georgie has it. It seems to me that no one can help loving her. This is not a mother's foolish vanity. It's based on what I see and hear. All our friends love Georgie. And as for the boys—the young men—they are wild about her, and she does her best to keep them that way. I hate to admit it, but Georgie is an outrageous flirt.

"But to come to the point—Georgiana absolutely will have her own way. All these modern girls are alike in this respect. They say we parents are 'out of date,' 'we do not understand.' Perhaps they are right. Father thinks Georgie has not been held back by any restraint or anything we have tried to teach her. But worried and sick and frightened as I am about Georgie, I can't believe she is really *bad*. I realise, though, that this may be merely a mother's faith or blindness or vanity.

"Georgiana has graduated from high school. We want her to work. But she will never work in Erie, and perhaps any hard application now—if Georgie could perform such a miracle— might be worse for her health.

"Friends of ours, the Wayburns, are motoring to California, and offered to take Georgie West with them. You may be sure we grasped desperately and hopefully at the idea of sending her. That thrilled her. We are not so well off as formerly. But we made sacrifices and got Georgie all she wanted, and we will arrange to pay her board indefinitely out there. Maybe the West you tell so wonderfully about will cure her and be her salvation. Most assuredly her coming will be a trial for you. But, daughter, we beg of you—accept it, and do your best—for Georgie's sake."

The second perusal of that amazing letter left Miss Stockwell saddened and thoughtful, but free of her former perplexity and worry. Her mother had done her best. If Georgiana could stand the rugged, virile, wild Tonto Basin, she would not only regain her health, but she would grow away from the falseness and over-sophistication that followed the war. Buried in the wilderness as Miss Stockwell had been, nevertheless she had kept up an active interest in the outside world. And all that periodicals could supply of information concerning news and progress of the times she had assimilated. Not improbably, she understood better that precocious new American type—the modern girl—than did her mother. She welcomed the coming of her sister. It might be difficult for her, but that did not matter. It could not help but be good for Georgiana.

Then suddenly she was confronted with another aspect of the case—the effect Georgiana would have on this environment, on the Thurmans, and all these good, simple primitive people who must come in contact with her sister. She had grown fond of the Tonto and its rugged simplicity. She had long been conscious of how she was helping the children, and through them their parents. Was there not a deeper and more personal reason why she had become content with life there? A warmth tingled in her cheeks as she shirked the query. But in regard to Georgiana—there was bound to be an upheaval at Green Valley. Georgiana might pursue the audacious tenor of her frivolous life back there in Erie, but she could not do it in Arizona. Miss Stockwell vaguely realised how impossible it would be, though she could not then tell just why.

But the thought brought home to her a true appreciation of the boys and young men with whom she had become acquainted. The sons of the three Thurman families she knew especially well, for she had lived a year in their homes. Young men all, mostly in their early twenties, they were; though Enoch Thurman was over thirty, and Serge, his cousin, was a few years younger. All of them were hard riders of the high bare ranges of the Tonto. Only one of them had a wife. And sweethearts were so scarce that the boys were always fighting over one. They drove cattle in all seasons, helping one another, hewed timber, tilled and harvested fields of corn and sorghum, hunted the bears and lions that preyed on their stock. And the money they earned, which was not much, they gave to their mother. Seldom did any of them ride farther from their homesteads than Ryson. The lure of city life had not penetrated here. Several of the Thurmans had been in the training-camps during the war, and one of them, Boyd Thurman, the best rider, roper, axe-man, and hunter of the lot, had seen service in France. He had returned uninjured, and seemingly unchanged by all he had gone through. That fact, more than any Miss Stockwell could name, marked the individuality of the Thurmans and the character of the Tonto. Old Henry Thurman was wont to brag: "Nary a black mark ag'in' Boyd—in camp or war!"

During her years of teaching in the Tonto, Miss Stockwell had never seen a Thurman, or any of their relatives, under the influence of liquor. They did not lie. If they made a promise it would be kept. Clean, fine, virile, manly young giants they all seemed to her. They smoked cigarettes, of their own making, and they would fight at the drop of a sombrero. They were cool, easy, tranquil, contented young backswoodsmen, strong and resourceful in the open, full of a latent fire and reserve force seldom called upon. They loved jokes, tricks, and dances. Among these hardy and daring young mountaineers a girl of Georgiana's kind would be like a firebrand in the grass of the prairie.

The sharp clip-clop of trotting horses outside on the road interrupted Miss Stockwell's meditations. The riders were returning from the range. She thought it would be well for her to go out at once and make arrangements with one of the boys to go to Ryson next day to meet the stage.

"I wonder what Georgie will think of this ranch," mused Miss Stockwell, as she went out.

The old ranch-house, part logs and part frame, moss-covered and weather-beaten, with its rambling additions shaded by trees, had grown to be a picturesque and satisfying sight to her. But at first it had struck her, as had almost everything, as crude and primitive, and suggestive of raw pioneer life.

She walked to the back of the house, through the yard, where chickens and calves and dogs had free access, to the corrals.

The adjoining corral was large, and always, in spite of its space, had been a bewildering place to Miss Stockwell. One corner was heaped full of old wagons, buggies, farm implements, and worn-out autos, so that it was merely a junk-heap. A long, rambling barn ran the whole length of the corral, and in fact constituted the barrier on that side. Like the house, additions had been built to it from time to time, so that it seemed a jumble of peaks, roofs, lofts, and wide-open doors showing broken stalls. The corral was crowded with dusty, rolling horses. These features, perhaps, were what usually bewildered Miss Stockwell, though she liked to see the sweaty horses roll.

Miss Stockwell found the riders, nine of them, grouped before one of the wide doors of the barn. She had a singular feeling that these young Westerners had suddenly become more important and significant to her.

In a group these boys all looked strangely alike. It was necessary to pick one out and study him individually to see where he differed from his comrades. They were all tall, lean, rangy, with the round powerful limbs, the small hips, the slightly bowed legs of the born horseman. If they were of different complexions it could not be discerned then, for each of them was black from dust and brush. They wore huge sombreros, mostly black, some of them grey, and all were old, slouched, and grimy. Blue jeans, jumpers, and overalls seemed the favourite garb. Several had discarded their chaps, to reveal trousers stuffed into high-topped, high-heeled boots, shiny and worn, bearing long spurs with huge rowels.

They responded to Miss Stockwell's greeting with the slow, drawling Texas speech that never failed to please her.

"Boys, I want one of you to do me an especial favour," she said.

Enoch Thurman came from behind the group. He was the chief of this clan, a lofty-statured rider, the very sight of whom had always fascinated her.

"Wal, Miss Mary, if it's takin' you to the dance, I'm shore puttin' up my bid," he drawled. He had wonderfully clear light-grey eyes, and the piercing quality of their gaze was now softened by a twinkle. A smile, too, changed the rigidity of the dark lean face.

It occurred to Miss Stockwell that from the date of Georgiana's arrival she would have to attend the dances. The prospect was alarming. The few functions of this kind in which she had participated had rendered her somewhat incapable of teaching the next day. For these boys had kept her dancing unremittingly from dark till dawn.

"I accept your kind invitation, Enoch, but that's not the favour I mean," she said, with a smile.

Then Boyd Thurman lunged up, smiling. He was stalwart, big-shouldered, of strong rugged face, hard as bronze, and his blue eyes were as frank as a child's. He tipped back his sombrero, showing a shock of tow-coloured hair.

"Teacher, what is this heah favour?" he inquired.

"Reckon we're all a-rarin' to do you any favour," said Wess Thurman. He was a cousin of Boyd's and Enoch's, twenty-two, with the Thurman stature and wide-open eyes.

"It's to go to Ryson to-morrow to meet my sister," responded Miss Stockwell.

The announcement was not a trivial one in its content. Indeed, it seemed of tremendous importance. The boys reacted slowly to its significance.

"To-morrow," spoke up Enoch regretfully. "Wal, I'm shore sorry. But I can't go, Miss Mary. We rode Mescal Ridge to-day, an' I drove some yearlin's inside our drift fence. They belong to that Bar XX outfit, an' shore there's no love lost between us. I'm drivin' them off our range to-morrow."

Judging from the eagerness of the rest of the boys, with the exception of Cal Thurman, they all preferred meeting Miss Stockwell's sister to driving cattle. And for several moments it appeared that Enoch would not have much help on the morrow.

"Goodness! I don't want you all!" she protested. "One of you will do. If it's such an occasion, you might draw lots."

But this suggestion did not meet with the approval of the majority. They argued about it. Miss Stockwell had long been used to their simplicity, their earnestness and loquacity, and when opposed their singular perversity to one another's ideas and persistence in their own.

"Say, can she dance?" suddenly inquired Serge Thurman, brother of Wess. He was a yellow-haired young giant, sunburnt, with eyes reddened by heat and dust and wind. Serge was the most gallant, as well as the best dancer, of all the Thurmans. His query opened up a new train of thought, manifestly of intense interest to the boys.

Miss Stockwell had to laugh. Assuredly, the advent of Georgiana would be worth seeing. "Why, I'm pretty sure she dances," she replied thoughtfully. It began to dawn upon her that she might repay these Thurmans for some of the innocent little tricks they had played on her.

"Now, Miss Stockwell, what's this heah sister of yourn like?" queried Pan Handle Ames. He was one of the several men employed by Enoch, like most of them of Texas stock, and a rider of the desert Pan Handle of Texas before he came to Arizona. He had a homely face and serious air. And his question precipitated such renewed interest that it seemed absolutely vital to the issue.

The teacher studied these friendly, queer young men, laughing to herself, thrilling for them, and slowly yielding to machinations of her own. How likeable they were! They would spend hours over this simple matter, unless she settled it.

"I'll tell you, boys," she asserted. "I have a picture of her. I'll fetch it—and then you can decide who really *wants* to meet her."

That, at last, was one thing they approved of with instant unity.

Miss Stockwell hurried to her room, and with growing consciousness of her opportunity, searched in her effects for the picture of a maiden aunt who was noted for her plain, severe face. She felt a twinge at the thought of the use she meant to make of this likeness of the good aunt whom she loved, but did not let such trepidations dissuade her from her purpose. Armed with the photograph, she hurried back to the group of boys in the corral.

"There!" she exclaimed, holding it out.

All of them but Cal Thurman crowded round her, eager to see the likeness of her sister. Cal seemed amused at their actions. . . . He was Enoch's youngest brother, a boy of nineteen, and apparently the only one of the clan not particularly interested in girls.

There was a moment of strained, silent attention, then one of them burst out:

"Aw, Miss Mary, she ain't a bit like you."

"Not much," said Serge decisively, with a finality the teacher did not fail to note.

"Wal, is *this*—is she really your sister?" queried Enoch slowly, as if trying to remember. "Shore I thought you once showed me a picture."

"Ahuh!" added Pan Handle Ames. "Nice sweet-appearin' lady." He said it with aloof nonchalance, with obvious insincerity.

Then, as a group, they became silent, rather awkwardly and slowly realising that the situation had subtly changed. They backed away from the teacher's side and assumed former lounging positions, most of them calmly resorting to the inevitable cigarette. Enoch regarded his clan with undisguised mirth. They had placed themselves in an embarrassing position.

"Wal, I reckon you-all are rarin' to chase them Bar XX steers in the mawnin'," he drawled, with dry sarcasm. Enoch knew his clan.

The riders had drifted imperceptibly as if by magic, back into that cool, easy serenity that usually characterised them. No hint of embarrassment or concern or consciousness of Enoch's half-veiled scorn showed in look or action.

"Enoch, you cain't drive that bunch of yearlin's without me an' Boyd," asserted Serge calmly.

Boyd nodded his assurance of this, and his big eyes shone with a glare as he spoke. "Reckon thet new Bar XX foreman won't like you any better, Enoch. An' considerin' how much thet was, he's goin' to be riled when he finds out. He's always achin' to start a fight. An' if you don't drive thet bunch off our range he'll swear we're rustlin'."

Enoch took this seriously, as if there was a good deal in it.

"Boyd, I was only doin' Bloom a favour," he replied. "It was near dark when we rounded up that bunch. An' his outfit is ridin' Mescal Ridge to-morrow."

"Shore. But my advice is to get them cattle on his range before the day's busted," went on Boyd. "An' it mightn't be easy to find them all."

Enoch then turned to Miss Stockwell with more of a serious consideration of the matter. "Miss Mary, I'm needin' Serge an' Boyd to-morrow, an' so none of us can meet your sister. But shore any of the rest of my obligin' an' lady-killin' outfit can get off for the day."

"Thank you, Enoch," replied the teacher, and thus fortified by his permission, she turned again to the boys to inquire sweetly: "Now, which one of you will do me this favour?"

As her gaze surveyed them all collectively they remained mute, thoughtful, very far away; but when she singled out Pan Handle Ames to look directly at him, he drawled:

"Miss Mary, air you forgettin' how I drove you home from the school-house one day?"

"Indeed I'm not!" returned Miss Stockwell, with a shudder. 'Driving automobiles is not your forte."

"Wal, it shore ain't. But all the same, I'd 'a' got you home if the car had held together," replied Pan Handle, and then settled back coolly to enjoy his cigarette. He knew he was out of the reckoning.

Then it seemed incumbent upon the others to face Miss Stockwell, ready to answer her appealing and reproachful gaze, when it alighted upon each of them.

Dick Thurman was the youngest of the boys, and he was still in school. "You know, teacher, I'd go, if it wasn't for lessons. I'm behind now, you say, an' father keeps me busy before an' after school."

Lock Thurman was the dark-skinned, dark-eyed and dark-haired member of the family, a young man of superb stature, and the quietest, shyest of all the clan.

"Lock, please, won't you go?" asked the teacher.

He shook his head and dropped it, to hide his face. "I reckon I'm afeared of women," he said.

"Huh! Why don't you say you're afeared of thet there girl of yourn—Angie Bowers?" retorted his brother Wess.

"I ain't no more afeared of her than you are of her twin sister Aggie," responded Lock.

"Wal, when you cain't tell which is Angie an' which is Aggie— all the time mixin' up your gurls—you oughta be scared. What'll you do if you ever git married?" spoke up Serge.

This might have led to another argument had not Miss Stockwell broken in upon them by appealing to Wess.

"Teacher, I just hate to tell you I cain't go for your sister," replied Wess, in apparent deep sincerity. "I got a lot to do to-morrow, an' shore need that day off Enoch said we could have. My saddle's got to be mended, an' my boots need half-solin', an' father's at me to begin docterin' the dog's feet—for we'll be chasin' bear soon—an' mother wants a lot done—an' I just cain't go to Ryson. Ask Arizona there. He can leave off cuttin' sorghum for to-morrow."

Thus directed, Miss Stockwell turned to the young man designated as Arizona. If he had another name she had never heard it. He was the only one of small stature in the group, a ruddy-faced, blinking-eyed rider, with a reputation for humour that his appearance belied.

"Aw, Miss Stockwell, I'm 'most sick because I cain't oblige you," asserted this worthy, in the most regretful of voices. "But old Hennery gave me plumb orders to cut thet sorghum before it rains."

"Wal," spoke up Wess, "it hasn't rained for a month an' it'll go dry now till October."

"Nope. It's a-goin' to rain shore aboot day after to-morrer. See them hazy clouds flyin' up from the south-west. Shore sign of storm. You get Con to go."

Con Casey, the comrade now referred to by Arizona, was a newcomer to the Thurman range, an Irishman only a few years in America and not long in the West. He was the most earnest and simple-minded of young men, and a source of vast amusement to his comrades. They liked him, though they made him the butt of their jokes and tricks.

When the teacher appealed to Con he sat up, startled. His solemn freckled face lost its ruddy colour, his big pale-blue eyes dilated and stared. There was no mistaking his sincerity or his fright.

"My Gawd!" he ejaculated, in deep solemn tones. "Miss Stockwell, shure I niver was alone wit' a woman in me loife."

The boys guffawed at this, and cast sly banter at him, but there was no doubt that they believed him.

Miss Stockwell wore a manner of great anxiety which was really not in strict harmony with her true feelings. She was enjoying the situation hugely, and saw that it would probably work out exactly as she had hoped. Then what a climax on the morrow, when Georgiana appeared on the scene!

Tim Matthews, another rider, added his ridiculous excuse to avoid meeting the teacher's sister; and the last one, excepting Cal Thurman, nonchalantly made a statement that he was not very well and might soon be having the doctor of the village.

At that Cal slouched up with all his five-foot-eleven of superb young manhood and surveyed his brothers and comrades in amused derision.

"You're a lot of boobs, I'll tell the world," he said.

Miss Stockwell thrilled at this, and felt the imminence of something she had hoped for. This nineteen-year-old son of Henry Thurman's was, in her opinion, the finest of the whole clan. He had all the hardiness, simplicity, and ruggedness of the Tonto natives, and somewhat more of intelligence and schooling. He seemed more modern and was fairly well read. Cal had spent his last year of school under Miss Stockwell and he had been a good student. His grandfather had been a Texan and a Rebel noted for his wild fiery temperament, which, according to family talk, Cal had inherited.

"Teacher, I'll be glad to go meet your sister," he declared, turning to her. "I was only waitin' to see how they'd wriggle out of it."

"Thank you, Cal. I'm certain you won't be sorry," replied the teacher gratefully. She was, indeed, pleased, and now began to revolve in mind just how to prepare Cal for the advent of Georgiana. Certainly up to that moment it had not occurred to her to go on with the deception.

"She's to come on the stage from Globe?" inquired Cal, as he walked with Miss Stockwell towards the corral gate.

"Yes. To-morrow."

"What'll I take—the buckboard or car?"

The teacher thought that over a moment.

"It's an awful old clap-trap—that bundle of rusty iron," observed the teacher, remembering her few experiences in the family automobile. "I don't believe it's as safe as the buckboard."

"Sure I'll get her here safe," replied Cal, with a laugh.

By this time they had reached the corral gate, which he opened for her. Suddenly loud cries of mirth resounded from the boys back by the barn. The teacher turned with Cal to see what had occasioned them such amusement. Some of them were standing with their heads close together and were apparently conversing earnestly. Their very air intimated deviltry and secrecy.

Cal gazed at them suspiciously, and a darker fire gleamed in his eyes. He had a smooth, almost beardless face, clear brown tan, and less of the leanness and craggy hardness that characterised his brothers' features. He looked something better than handsome, the teacher thought.

"Say, that outfit is up to tricks," he muttered. And he pushed back his huge sombrero to run a sinewy hand through his brown hair.

"Tricks?" echoed Miss Stockwell, vague. Had she better not divulge her own duplicity?

"Sure. Just look at Tim. He's plannin' something now. He always wags his head that way when he's . . . Aw, I can read their minds."

"What are they going to do?" inquired Miss Stockwell curiously.

"They'll be in Ryson to-morrow when I meet your sister," he answered grimly.

"What! They will?" cried the teacher, almost too eagerly. Cal looked at her dubiously, and again he brushed back his hair. He wanted, and meant, to be obliging, but evidently he did not have any delightful anticipations at the prospect before him. Almost like a flash came the inspiration to Miss Stockwell to go on with the deception and not enlighten Cal as to the truth regarding Georgiana. He would be all the more amazed and dazed when the realisation burst suddenly upon him. Georgiana, too, would make the best of it.

"Let me see that picture you showed the boys—so I'll know her," said Cal.

Miss Stockwell handed it to him without a word. Cal gazed at it for a moment.

"Can't see any resemblance to you," he remarked, presently. "She's homely, an' you're good-lookin'."

"Thank you, Cal," replied Miss Stockwell demurely. "I appreciate your compliment. But you didn't have to say so just because you found my—my sister plain."

"Say!—I mean it, teacher. Why, Enoch thinks you're the best-lookin' woman he ever saw. An' sure he's a good judge."

Miss Stockwell felt a little warmth on her cheek that was not all the westering sun. She liked the boy's faith in Enoch. There was a singularly fine relation between these brothers, and one that augured well for the boy's future.

"Cal, I think I'd take the buckboard instead of that old car," suggested Miss Stockwell. She was thinking of the spirited black horses usually driven with the buckboard, and how much more they might appeal to a girl.

"Aw, she won't mind the looks of that old gas-wagon. An' sure I don't care," said Cal, with a laugh. "You see, the stage gets in late sometimes, an' if I take the car I can drive your sister out here quick, before dark. It's fifteen miles to Ryson, you know, an' would take me several hours with the team. I'd like to get home before dark."

"Why—so particularly? I've heard how you can ride the trails after night."

"Aw, that outfit will be up to some trick, an' between you an' me I'd rather not be caught along a dark road with that old—I mean—your sister," replied Cal, finishing lamely.

"Oh, I see," mused Miss Stockwell slowly, studying the perplexed face of the young man. "Very well, Cal. You do as you think best. But take a hunch from me, as you boys say. You won't be sorry I inflicted this job on you."

"Aw, now, teacher, I didn't mean you'd done that," he protested. "It's only Tim an' those darn' fools. They've got a chance to get even. You don't know what I did to them last dance."

"Well, I don't care what you did to them or what they do to you —to-morrow. You're not going to be sorry you went. You might be very glad."

"Why?" he asked, with a dawning of curiosity. He eyed her in confidence, yet withal as a boy who realised an unknown quantity in women. He had not the slightest idea what she meant, yet he had acquired an interest apart from his kindliness or desire to oblige her. "Maybe she's rich an' will give me a new saddle or somethin'," he remarked jokingly.

"Maybe. She'll give you *something*, that's certain," replied Miss Stockwell mysteriously.

She left him at the corral gate, holding it open for her, a pleased and rather vaguely expectant smile on his face as he turned to look back at his scheming comrades.

2

NEXT morning when Cal presented himself at the breakfast table, fully two hours later than the usual time for the riders, he was filled with dismay to discover that several of his comrades had not gone off about their range tasks.

"Howdy," was Pan Handle's greeting.

"Mawnin', Cal," drawled Arizona.

"Wal, Cal, you shore bit the hay last night," said Wess dryly.

"Reckon it's bad fer you to have meetin' ladies on yore mind," added Tim Matthews solicitously.

"Ahuh!" growled Cal as he eyed his friends distrustfully.

During warm weather the Thurmans served meals on the porch that connected the adjoining sections of the large, rambling ranch-house. A roof of rough boards stretched rather low above the porch, and a stairway led from the floor up to a hole in the attic. Here some of the riders slept. Cal, who preferred the outdoors, had slept in a little log bunk-house of one room, which he had erected himself. With a knowing smile Cal passed the boys at the long table and proceeded to a bench against the log wall, where he filled a basin with water and vigorously washed face and hands. In fact, he splashed so violently and shook his tousled wet head so vehemently that he washed water clear to the table.

"Hey, air you a whale blowin'?" complained Pan Handle.

"Naw, he's only coolin' off his haid," observed Tim.

Cal went about his morning ablutions without paying any attention to his tormentors; and he broke his rule of shaving only once a week. This appeared to be of exceeding interest to the boys.

"Say, he's shavin'," ejaculated Arizona, as if that simple action was astounding.

"Reckon he wants to look handsome," observed Wess.

"Wal, he never could—no matter what a dude he makes of himself," added Pan Handle.

"Rarin' to go!" exclaimed Tim mockingly.

When Cal finally turned to the breakfast table the others had almost finished eating. Cal called into the kitchen: "Mother, won't you or Molly bring me somethin' to eat? These hawgs out here have grazed like sheep across a pasture."

"Cal," replied his mother, "you oughta get up in the mawnin'."

Then his sister Molly appeared, carrying several smoking dishes which she set down before him. She was a wholesome-looking girl of about seventeen, unmistakably a Thurman in features.

"Cal, can I go to town with you?" she asked appealingly.

"I should say not," he replied.

"But I want to buy some things," she protested.

"I'll buy them for you," replied Cal.

"Miss Stockwell left a list of things she wants."

"All right. Has she gone to school?"

"Yes. She went with father in the buckboard. She wanted to see you, but you weren't up. Said good-bye and you weren't to forget what she told you about meeting Georgiana."

"Now, Molly, cain't you see there ain't any danger of Cal's forgettin' his date with George-anner?" put in Wess facetiously.

Then Cal began his breakfast in silence, aware of the bland observance of his comrades, and he did not waste any time eating. Pushing back his empty plate, he looked square at them.

"Not ridin' to-day, huh?" he queried.

"Nope," replied Wess laconically.

"Nor tacklin' any of the lot of work that ought to be done?"

"Nope."

"Goin' huntin' with the dogs, maybe?"

"Reckon it's too dry an' hot to hunt. But I'm shore goin' soon as it rains an' gets cooler. Lots of bear this fall. An' a world of acorns up on the high ridges."

"Well, what are you goin' to do to-day?" deliberately questioned Cal.

"Reckon I'm takin' a day off," said Wess serenely.

"Goin' to Ryson?" went on Cal grimly.

"Shore. There ain't any excitement round heah. An' I've got a world of stuff to buy. Tobacco an' horseshoes an' cartridges, an——"

"I'll buy your stuff," cut in Cal.

"Couldn't think of trustin' you," returned Wess blandly. "Besides, I want to see Angie."

"She's not home, an' you know it," rejoined Cal. Then he directed his gaze at Pan Handle Ames. "Reckon you've important reasons to show up in Ryson—huh?"

"Cal, I jest naturally got to go. There's a lot——"

"Bah!" interrupted Cal as he rose to his feet, shoving the bench seat backwards. He did not need to hear more subterfuge or question Arizona or Tim. They were too casual, too unnaturally uninterested. He judged the enormity of their machinations by the singular blankness of their faces.

"Goin' to ride in on horseback?" concluded Cal, with a last glimpse of hopelessness.

"Nope. We're takin' the big car," said Wess. "You see, Uncle Henry wants flour, grain, an' a lot of supplies he ordered an' needs bad. Oh, we'll have a load comin' back."

"I wanted the big car," retorted Cal hotly. "Didn't father know I was goin' to meet a lady?"

"I reckon he did, for when we told him how bad we needed it to fetch back all the stuff, he said you could drive the Ford," replied Wess, with a composure that indicated supreme self-control.

"An' father's gone with the buckboard!" ejaculated Cal, almost showing distress.

"Yes, he's drivin' teacher to school, an' then he's goin' to Hiram Bowes's."

"Cal, seein' what a meekanik you air an' how you can drive, it seems to us heah thet you'll go along in the Ford like a turkey sailin' downhill," said Pan Handle Ames, with astounding kindliness and admiration.

Just then Tim doubled up and began to cough violently. Plain indeed were his heroic efforts to control mirth. Cal gazed at these four cronies in slow-gathering wrath. Finally he let go.

"Wess, I'll bet you a horse to a pouch of tobacco that you'll get licked for this job."

"Say! What job are you ravin' aboot? An' who's gonna lick me? You cain't, Cousin Cal."

"I'm not afraid to tackle it again, an' if I can't, by golly! I'll find someone who can," retorted Cal darkly.

With that he abruptly turned away from his tormentors and strode for the corrals. The profound silence left behind him was further and final proof of a remarkable self-control exercised by these trickers. It worried Cal, yet at the same time it began to arouse his antagonism. The task imposed upon him by the good school-teacher had assumed more than irksome possibilities. Manifestly it had furnished his cousin and comrade riders an unusual opportunity. But would they do anything really rude or unkind to Miss Stockwell's sister? Cal could not, even in temper, believe that they would. But they were equal to any stretch of the imagination as far as he was concerned, and they would do anything under the sun to make him miserable.

He went directly to look over the Ford car. It had seen three or four years more than its best days. But it miraculously held together and really did not look like the junk-heap it actually was. That was because Cal's father had covered it recently with a paint he wanted to get rid of.

Cal Thurman loved horses, and as a rider he was second only to his famous brother Boyd. But he hated automobiles and simply could not understand what made them run or stop or get out of order. As mathematics had been the only study Miss Stockwell could not make clear to Cal, so the operation of a threshing-machine or automobile or the age-old steam-engine at the sawmill, was the only thing about the ranch that Cal's father could not teach him. To be sure, he had tried to learn to drive an automobile, and had succeeded to some extent. But it took a mechanical genius to make this Ford go. This morning, however, the deceitful engine started with a crack and a bang, and, to Cal's amaze, in a moment was humming like a monster bee. Cal felt elated. He might fool that outfit, after all. Cal's mother was a slight, tall, grey-haired woman, with a wonderful record of pioneer service and sacrifice written on her worn face. The days of her ruggedness were past. She gave Cal money and instructions, and as he was about to go she called him back.

"Son, listen," she said, in lower tone. "Shore them tow-haids air up to some mischief. Now don't forget your manners, whatever they do. It speaks well for you that you offered to meet teacher's sister. Carry it through, Cal. In my youth the Thurmans of Texas knew how to be courteous to a guest. We've most forgot it heah in this hard Tonto country. Shore I look up to you an' Molly."

"All right, Mother, I'll be good," replied Cal, with a laugh, and bounded out on the porch and off towards the corral. He wanted to avoid meeting his tormentors again, and was fortunate in this. Upon reaching the Ford, he was relieved and amazed to find the engine still running—not only running, but actually softly humming, with an occasional purr.

Cal got out of the corral and down on the valley road without being hailed from behind—a fact that he took as a good start to his adventure. Then he forgot the boys and lost himself in attention to the car and the sensation of driving along the shady, beautiful road. For some unknown reason the Ford ran better than it ever had run for Cal. As he hummed along between the green walls of juniper and live-oak trees he gradually forgot his uneasiness.

Four or five miles took Cal down out of the foothills into the level brush-covered valley lands that led to Ryson. Here and there, at long intervals, lay the ranch of a cattleman. All the old settlers in this country let their stock range over unfenced government lands. Most of them had homesteaded the one hundred and sixty acres allotted by the government, and whenever Cal rode through this district he was possessed of a stronger desire to settle on a place of his own.

"I'll homestead that Bear Flat, if father will let me, this very fall," he soliloquised. "Wess has his eye on Mesa Hill, an' I'll bet he's just waitin' to save enough money to marry one of them darn' twins—or maybe till he can find out which is Angie an' which is Aggie! But girls are the least of my trouble. No marrying for me. Give me my horses an' a dog an' a gun."

So young Thurman drove on along the road, with the dry, warm, fragrant breeze in his face, and his thoughts leisurely following idle, dreamy channels.

Several miles east of Ryson he turned a curve in the road to see a tall lanky young man plodding wearily along, bowed under the burden of a bundle wrapped in canvas. As Cal neared the fellow it became evident that he could hardly lift one foot after the other. His soiled, worn garb attested to the possibility of contact with brush and a bed on the ground. Cal slowed up, naturally expecting the man to turn and ask for a ride. But he did neither. Then Cal stopped and hailed him.

"Hey, want a lift?"

The young man raised a cadaverous pale face that quickly aroused Cal's sympathy.

"Thanks. I'll say I would," replied the traveller, and he lifted the bundle down from his stooped shoulders.

"Throw it in back an' ride in front with me," suggested Cal, eyeing him with growing interest. Upon closer view this individual appeared to Cal to be the most singularly built human being he had ever seen. He was very tall, and extremely thin, and so loose jointed that he seemed about to fall apart. His arms were so long as to be grotesque—like the arms of an ape—and his hands were of prodigious size. He had what Cal called a chicken neck, a small head, and the homeliest face Cal had ever looked into. Altogether he presented a ridiculous and pathetic figure.

"I was all in—and lost in the bargain," said he. The freckles stood out prominently on his wax-coloured skin. He was so long and awkward, and his feet were so huge, that Cal thought he was not going to be able to get into the front seat. But he folded himself in, and slouched down with a heave of relief.

"Lost? What place were you trying to find?" queried Cal as he started the car again.

"I've hiked from Phœnix. And a couple of days this side of Roosevelt Dam I butted into a gas station along the road—Chadwick. The man there told me I could get a job at the Bar XX ranch, and where to find the trail. I found a trail all right, but it led nowhere. I got lost and couldn't find my way back to Chadwick. Been ten days and nights."

"Huh! You must be hungry?"

"I'll say so."

"Well, you're way off the track. Bar XX ranch is east. You've travelled north. An' I happen to know Bloom, the foreman of that outfit. He doesn't want any men."

"It's kinda hard to get a job," replied the fellow, with a sigh. "Made sure I could catch on in the Salt River Valley. But everybody's broke there, same as me, and I guess they'd just as lief not see any service men."

"You were in the army?" asked Cal, with a heightening of sympathy.

"No. I was a marine," replied the other briefly.

His tone of aloofness rather reminded Cal of Boyd upon his return from France. These service men who had seen service were reticent, strange.

"Marine? That's a sailor, huh? Did you get over?"

"I'll say so. I went through Château Thierry, and now, by God! I can't get work in my own country," he replied bitterly.

"Say, Buddy, if you're on the level you can get a job in the Tonto," returned Cal rather curtly. His companion vouchsafed no reply to this, and the conversation, so interestingly begun, languished. Cal thought the fellow seemed cast down by this remark. Meanwhile the car swung into the long stretch of grey road at the farther end of which lay the village of Ryson.

Ranches gave place to cottages, widely separated, and these in turn to the row of square-fronted, old, and weatherbeaten frame and stone structures that constituted Ryson. The one street appeared as wide as a public square. Along its quarter of a mile of business section could be seen several cattle, two horses, a burro, and some dogs, but no people. A couple of dilapidated automobiles marked the site of the garage, which had evidently once been a blacksmith's shop. The town seemed enveloped in the warm, drowsy, sleepy air of midsummer.

Cal stopped his Ford at the garage, not without a slight feeling of gratification at the amaze his advent would create. Upon the last occasion of his leaving the garage with this particular Ford one of the mechanics had remarked: "It's a cinch we'll never see this flivver ag'in!"

"Say, will you have dinner with me?" queried Cal of his silent companion.

"Will I? Boy, lead me on," replied the ex-marine. "I'll say you're a sport."

"Glad to have you," responded Cal. "But we're early. There's the hotel—that grey house with the wide porch. You can wait for me there."

"You'll find me anchored, and I'm hoping the dinner bell will ring quick," he replied, taking his bundle and shuffling away in the direction indicated.

The young man of the garage stood gaping. "Cal, what is thet you had with you?" inquired one.

"Where'd it come from?" asked another.

"It's a scarecrow hitched on to a coupla bean-poles," said a third.

Cal laughed and explained: "Oh, that's a chap I picked up on the road."

"Did he manipulate on this hyar Lizzie of yourn?" inquired the first garage man, indicating the Thurman Ford.

"No, he didn't," retorted Cal. "I'll have you understand *I* drove this car."

"Car? This ain't no car. It's a sheet-iron wagon with a milk-cap fer an engine."

"Ahuh! Well, you lay off her with your monkey-wrenches," returned Cal.

Leaving the car there, Cal proceeded into the big barn-like general store and post office, and set about the responsible and difficult task of selecting and purchasing the things enumerated by the womenfolk of the Thurman household. In his anxiety during the performance of this duty he quite forgot the dinner engagement he had made with the hungry traveller until he had completed the selection to the best of his ability. Then he carried the packages out to the car and deposited them on the back seat. "Reckon she'll have a lot of stuff to pack," he muttered, suddenly reminded of his expected passenger.

After this he repaired to the hotel porch, there to find the cadaverous individual waiting with hungry eyes.

"Say, I'm sorry I was so long, but I had a lot to do," said Cal. "Let's go in an' get it."

In the ensuing half-hour Cal was to learn that a kind action, however thoughtlessly entered into, could have singular effect, not only upon the recipient, but upon him who offered it. Naturally, being a range-rider, he had been many a time as hungry as a bear, but he had never seen a man apparently half-starved. How good this meal must have been to the fellow! Cal's curiosity followed his sympathy.

"My name's Cal Thurman," he said, at the end of the dinner. "What's yours?"

"Tuck Merry," was the reply.

"Say, that's a funny name. Merry! It sure doesn't suit you, friend. An' Tuck—never heard it before."

"It's a nickname. Almost forgot I had another. But it was Thaddeus."

"Huh? How'd you ever get called Tuck?" asked Cal curiously.

"I was in the marines. They're a scrappy bunch. An' every time I punched a buddy I'd tuck him away to sleep. So they nicknamed me Tuck."

"Well, I'll be darned!" exclaimed Cal in wondering admiration. Nothing could have been more calculated to arouse his friendliness. "You must have a punch?"

"Yes. It just comes natural," replied Merry simply. "I've got a couple of mitts, too. See there."

He doubled his enormous hands and showed Cal two fists of almost incredible size.

"Say!" ejaculated Cal, with shining eyes. Then an idea flashed like lightning through his mind, and he liked it. The instant it clarified and caught his fancy it grew and grew until it was positively thrilling. "See here, Tuck, you said you wanted a job?"

"I'll say I said so," returned Merry rousing to interest.

"Are you well? I mean, are you strong?" queried Cal hesitatingly. "You look like you'd fall in two pieces."

"I'm a deceiving cuss. Pretty much tuckered out now. But I was husky when I started West. A little rest and a mess-table like this would soon put me in as good shape as when I was one of Dempsey's sparring pardners."

"*What?*" cried Cal breathlessly.

"See here, matey. I was raised on the waterfront in New York. Do you get that? Was in the navy for years. Finally was boxing instructor. Then after the war I knocked around in sparring bouts. Last job I had was with Dempsey."

"Whoop-ee!" ejaculated Cal, under his breath. He slammed the table with his fist. The idea had assumed bewildering and exhilarating proportions. "Say, Tuck, I've taken a liking to you."

"I'll say that's the first good luck I've had for many a day," returned Merry feelingly.

"I'll get you a job—two dollars a day an' board—all the good grub you can eat," blurted out Cal, breathlessly and low. "Up on my father's ranch. It's Tonto country, an' once you live there you will never leave it. You can save your money—homestead your hundred an' sixty acres—an' some day be a rancher."

"Cal, I ain't as strong as I thought," replied Tuck weakly. "Don't promise so much at once. Just find me work an' a meal ticket."

"My father runs a sawmill," went on Cal. "He always needs a man. An' all us riders hate sawin' wood. That job would give you time off now an' then to ride with us an' go huntin'. I'll give you a horse. We've got over a hundred horses out home. . . . Tuck, the job's yours if you'll do me a little favour."

Tuck Merry held out his huge hand and said: "Mate, there ain't nothing I wouldn't do for you."

"Listen," whispered Cal intensely. "First, you're not to tell a soul that you were in the marines an' how you got that name Tuck an' was one of Dempsey's boxin' pardners."

"I get you, Cal. I'm dumb on the has-been stuff. I lose my memory."

Cal was now tingling with thrilling glee at the enormous possibilities of his idea.

"Tuck, I'm the baby of the Thurman family," he went on. "I've two brothers an' seven cousins, all of which think I'm spoiled. Father gave me more time for schoolin' an' I've had a little better advantages, maybe. An' these fellows all pick on me to beat hell. Now don't let me give you the idea there's any hard feelin'. Not at all. I sure think heaps of all the boys, an' as for Enoch an' Boyd, my brothers, I sure love them. But they all make life awful tough for me. Girls are scarce, an' when we have dances —which is often—there are not enough to go round. If I poke my nose into the school-house, where we have our dances, I sure get it punched. For that matter, fightin' is next to dancin' in the

Tonto. They sort of go together. Wess Thurman licked me bad not long ago. They've all had their fun with me, an', darn it, I've never licked a single one of them. They're older an' bigger. . . . Now what I want you to do is to lick all of them."

"Ain't you givin' me a large order, matey?" queried Merry, smiling for the first time.

"Not yet. Aw, Tuck, that'll be easy. Don't worry. They'll all *pick* the fights. You needn't do anythin' but wait, an' when one of them starts somethin' you just tuck him away."

"I'll do my best," promised Merry. "What else? What's the *large* order, if this one ain't much?"

"Now I'm comin' to hard feelin's," responded Cal, with more grimness than humour. "There's Bloom, foreman of the Bar XX ranch. Bad blood between his outfit an' the Thurmans. I'd like you to beat the daylights out of Bloom, an' a couple of others."

"Cal, I heard this was wild country, this Tonto. Isn't there liable to be gun-play?"

"Why, if you packed a gun it might be risky. But if you *don't* there's no danger. You'll fool these riders somethin' awful. I *know* it. I can just see what'll come off. They'll all make fun of you, an' Bloom an' his kind will insult you. All you'll need to do is to say: 'Mister, would you oblige me by gettin' off your horse,' an' he'll pile off like a fallin' log. Then you say: 'You see I don't pack a gun, an' if you're a gentleman an' not afraid, you'll lay off your hardware.' The rest, pard Tuck, will be immense."

"You're on. Pard she is," replied Tuck, offering his huge hand. There were a depth and a gravity in his acceptance of this gauge, and he crushed Cal's fingers in a tremendous grip. Cal jerked, writhed, and then sank down with a groan.

"Say, man! Let go!" he cried, and then, as his hand came free, limp and crumpled, he rubbed it and tried to move his fingers. "Sufferin' bobcats! I want to use this hand again." Then he laughed with grim glee. "Tuck, you're goin' to give me a lot of joy. Now let's see. You can go back to Green Valley with me. I'm to meet a woman, sister of our schoolteacher, an' take her home. I reckon you'll need to buy some things, unless you've got some Sunday clothes in that bundle."

"These are my swell togs," replied Tuck with a grin. "There's nothing in my pack but blankets, some odds an' ends, an' a pair of boxing-gloves."

"Huh! Then you can teach me to box?" queried Cal, with his glance dark and full of fire.

"Cal, in three months I'll have you so you can stand your nice relatives in a row an' lick them all one after another."

"Glory! Wouldn't that be great," ejaculated Cal. "But it's too good to be true. One a week would be good enough. Here's some money, Tuck. You go buy what you need. An' be sure you're hangin' round when that outfit rides in from Green Valley. They're up to some job."

"Pard Cal, I'll be there with bells on," replied the lanky Tuck.

Cal parted from his new-found friend and went out to take a message for his sister, an errand he had forgotten. His keen eye scanned the long, bare, dusty road that led eastward towards Green Valley. No sign of the boys yet! He did not wish them any very bad luck, but he hoped their car would break down. But he well knew that nothing short of a miracle could keep them from being on hand when the stage arrived. That thought prompted him to hurry with his errand, and then go back to the store to telephone. First he called up Roosevelt, to learn that the stage was ahead of time and had left there two hours earlier. Next he telephoned to Packard, a post office and gasoline station on the Globe road. His call was answered by Abe Hazelitt, a young fellow he had known for years.

"Hello, Abe. This's Cal—Cal Thurman—talkin'. How are you?"

"Howdy, Cal," came the reply, in Abe's high-pitched drawl. "Wal, I was shore fine jest lately, but now I'm dinged if I know whether I'm ridin' or walkin'."

"What's the matter, Abe?" asked Cal.

"Cal, I'm gosh-durned if I know. But the stage jest rolled in—an' somethin's happened."

"Stage? Ahuh!" replied Cal, with quickening of interest. "That's what I wanted to know about. On time, huh?"

"Way ahead of time. We all near dropped dead. Jake's drivin' like hell to-day, I'll tell the world."

"Jake drivin' fast?" echoed Cal. "Sure that's funny. What's got into him?"

"Reckon it's the same as what's got into me, Cal."

"Aw, you're loco. Abe, is there a lady passenger on the stage?"

Cal heard his friend chuckle at the other end of the wire, and then hesitate before replying. "Cal, listen to me whisper. . . . Yes, I should smile."

"That's good. She is a sister of our school-teacher, Miss Stockwell. I've been sent to meet her here an' take her out home. Abe, please tell her that Cal Thurman is waitin' at Ryson."

A long, low whistle came over the wire. Then: "My Gawd! the luck of some fellars!"

"Luck? Say, Abe, have any of the boys phoned you—Wess or Tim or Pan Handle?" queried Cal suspiciously.

"Nary one, Cal. You'll have her all to yourself. An' believe me——"

"Cut it out," almost yelled Cal. "I know what you mean by luck. Somebody had to meet her, an' that low-down outfit at Green Valley just quit barefaced when they saw her picture."

"They did! Wal, I'll be dinged! Say, Cal, mebbe you're barkin' up the wrong tree."

"Say, yourself!" retorted Cal testily. "You talk sort of queer. Abe, I'll ring off now, before you make me sore. You'll tell the lady, please?"

"I shore will. An' say—— Hold on, Cal. Don't hang up—— Hello!"

"Hello!" replied Cal. "I'm still on, but in a hurry."

A much lower-toned and hoarser voice continued breathlessly: "Cal, she was jest in here before you called. I seen her. She's wearin' socks! Anyway, I seen her bare knees—they're pink—an', so help me, Moses, they're painted! Cal, she's shore some——"

"*Shut up!*" roared Cal, in sudden fury at what he thought his friend's badinage. "You can't josh me. You're a liar, Abe Hazelitt. The boys have put you on."

"Naw, Cal, I hope to die," replied Abe, apparently bursting with glee. "I ain't been put on to nothin'. But I shore know what's a-comin' to you, Cal Thurman."

In mingled anger, fear, and consternation, Cal slammed up the receiver and rushed away from the telephone.

"Pink knees! . . . Painted! . . ." fumed Cal. "The idea! What that outfit can't think of is sure beyond me. . . . Abe, now, they rung him in on it. An' he knows what's comin' to me, huh? . . . All right, boys, I guess none of you savvy what Tuck Merry has up his sleeve. This is sure goin' to end in a fight."

CAL THURMAN did not have very much time to ruminate over the mysterious intimations that had been suggested by his talk with Abe Hazelitt on the telephone. For he had scarcely left the post office, to walk down the road towards the garage, when he espied the boys from Green Valley. They were grouped with the garage mechanics round his Ford car. If Cal had needed any more to rouse his ire, this fact was enough.

He approached them with long strides. Upon nearer view he found, to his amaze, that the boys were clean-shaven, and all had donned spick-and-span new suits of overalls, and wore their Sunday sombreros and shiny boots. Wonderful to see, Arizona, who was noted for his slovenly dress, appeared arrayed as the others, and he positively shone.

"Howdy, Cal! I'm shore congratulatin' you," drawled Wess, placidly indicating the Ford car.

"Pard Cal, yo're some driver," added Arizona.

"Good day, Cal. Looks like you was a-rarin' to go somewhere," put in Pan Handle.

"How air you, boy?" queried Tim serenely.

"Say, you seem mighty all-fired glad to see me," replied Cal sarcastically, running his keen gaze from one to another. They were cool, lazy, smiling, tranquil. Cal knew them. The deeper their plot, the harder they were to reach! Their very serenity was a mask hiding an enormous guilt. Cal shivered in his boots. How he wished this day was over! At the same instant a warmth stirred in him—the thought of Tuck Merry.

Cal pushed the boys away from the Ford car and began to prowl around it to see if they had done anything to it. Here he was almost helpless. He examined engine, tyres, wheel, and the various parts necessary to the operation of the car, but he could not be sure whether they had tampered with it or not. Certainly they had not had much time to do anything. Nevertheless, with the garage mechanics in the secret, they might have accomplished a good deal. Had he missed a bolt in this place? It was impossible to remember. Had he ever before noticed a crack in the floor extending across the front of the car? He could not recall it. The old Ford presented an enigma. Cal distrusted the looks of it, yet had no proof of his suspicions.

"Say, if you hombres have been monkeyin' with this car . . . !" he exclaimed, glaring darkly at them.

"Cal, you shore are a chivulrus fellar where ladies are concerned," drawled Wess, "but you ain't got any but low-down idees for your relations an' friends."

"Reckon you ain't insinuatin' I'd do some underhand trick?" queried Pan Handle reproachfully.

"Cal, you've been punched more'n onct fer insultin' remarks," added Tim Matthews meaningly.

"Aw!" burst out Cal, exploding helplessly. "You fellows can't pull the wool over my eyes. You're up to some deviltry, an' I'm bettin', from the looks of you an' your soft-soap talk, it's pretty skunky. . . . An' as for your punch, Tim Matthews, I'd like to know if you think you can go on punchin' me for ever?"

"Wal, mebbe for ever would be far-fetched," replied Tim dryly. "But jest so long as you live I shore will be able to punch you."

Cal gazed steadily into the grinning face of his friend.

"Tim, you're the big gambler of the Thurman outfit, aren't you?"

"Wal, I reckon thet distinctshun has been forced upon me," replied Tim, with nonchalance not devoid of pride.

"Ahuh! You know my black horse Pitch, don't you, an' how you've tried to buy, borrow, an' steal him?"

"I'm denyin' the last allegashun," retorted Tim testily.

"Well, I'm bettin' Pitch against your bronc Baldy that I lick you before I'm a year older."

All the boys stared, and Tim's lean jaw dropped.

"Boy, hev you been drinkin'?" he asked incredulously.

"Bah! You know I never drink," retorted Cal. "Are you on— or are you afraid to bet?"

"See heah, Cal," interposed Wess, "thet's a fool bet! You know you love Pitch an' he was Enoch's gift to you—the best hoss ever broke in the Tonto."

"Sure I know, an' you can gamble I wouldn't bet if I didn't know I could lick Tim," returned Cal.

Tim came out of his trance to seize his golden opportunity.

"Boys, I call his bluff. The bet's on—my Baldy ag'in' his hoss Pitch. An' all of you paste the date in your hats. Savvy? An', Cal, I hate to take your hoss, but my pride is ag'in' such fresh gab as yours."

"Pride goes before a fall, my friend Timothy," said Cal deliberately. "Now, boys, I call on you, too. An' listen. I know you're up to some tricks, an' that Tim is at the bottom of it. I want you all to be around when I lick him."

This sally brought forth loud laughter from all the listeners except Tim. He looked dubious and astounded.

"We'll shore be there, Cal," said Wess.

Without further comment Cal cranked the Ford, finding, to his secret amaze, that the engine again started with unusual alacrity, and then he climbed to the driver's seat. As he drove off towards the post office he expected much jest and laughter to be flung after him. In this, however, he was mistaken. Something was wrong with the car, surely. It ran too easily and smoothly, and it gave Cal the impression that it wanted to race. All at once he conceived an absolute conviction that the boys had tampered with it in some uncanny way. He drove to the post office and turned round, and stopped beyond the door near the porch. A number of natives were sitting on a bench, smoking pipes and whittling sticks, awaiting the one event of Ryson's day—the arrival of the stage. On the edge of the porch sat Tuck Merry, beside his canvas roll of baggage.

At that moment, as Cal was about to get out, he espied three horsemen trotting down the road from the east. He peered at them, and recognised Bloom of the Bar XX outfit, and two of his riders, one of them surely being Hatfield.

"Well, I'll be darned!" ejaculated Cal. "Talk about your hard luck!"

To be made the victim of tricks by his own relatives and friends was bad enough, but to have to endure them in the face of this Bar XX outfit, especially Hatfield, was infinitely worse. Could Wess and his partners have had anything to do with the strange coincidence of the arrival of Bloom and Hatfield?

"Aw, they couldn't be that mean," muttered Cal loyally. The advent of these riders was just an unfortunate coincidence calculated to add to Cal's discomfiture.

He watched them ride past the garage, past Wess and his comrades, who nodded casually to them, and down the road to the hitching-rail under the cottonwood tree near the post office. They dismounted. Bloom and Hatfield approached, while the third rider, a stranger to Cal, began to untie a mail-sack from the back of his saddle. Bloom was a heavy man for a rider, being square-shouldered and stocky, with a considerable girth. His huge bat-wing chaps flapped like sails as he slouched forward. He had a hard face, and though it showed him under forty, it was a record of strenuous life. Hatfield was young, a handsome, stalwart figure. He swaggered as he walked. His garb was picturesque, consisting of a huge beaver sombrero, red scarf, blue flannel shirt, just now covered with dust, and fringed chaps ornamented in silver.

"Howdy, Thurman," greeted Bloom as he came up. "Met your dad this mornin', an' he was tellin' me you'd come to town."

"How do, Bloom," returned Cal rather shortly.

Hatfield did not speak to Cal, though he gave him a sidelong look out of his sharp, bold eyes. Then, as before, it struck Cal why Hatfield had gained the favour of most of the girls of the Tonto. But he was not equally popular with the men. Hatfield had few superiors as a rider and roper, and he was a bad customer in a fight, as Cal remembered to his grief; but though these qualities had entitled him to a certain respect, he had never been a friend of any of the Thurmans. Moreover, he did not come of Texas stock and he belonged to the Bar XX outfit.

These two riders passed Cal, and had mounted the porch before they espied the ludicrous figure of Tuck Merry lounging with his back against a post. Bloom glanced at him, then halted to stare.

"Haw! Haw!" he guffawed, striding on again. "Hat, did you see thet? Reckon it got away from a circus."

Whereupon Hatfield turned to look at Merry. It was not a gaze calculated to flatter or please the recipient, but though Merry evidently saw he was the object of ridicule, he gave no sign. The moment brought Cal both resentment and a thrilling anticipation. Then Bloom and Hatfield, after speaking to the natives on the bench, disappeared in the store.

Cal heard the droning hum of the stage. So did the natives hear it. They woke up and stirred to animation.

"Wal, I'll be doggoned if that ain't the stage comin'," said one.

"Betcha it ain't Jake drivin'," added another.

"Reckon if it is Jake he's been lookin' at licker," snickered a third.

Cal found a grim consolation in the fact that whatever was to be his ordeal, it would soon be under way. He saw Wess and the boys leisurely approaching. Then he caught Tuck Merry's eye and beckoned to him.

"Did you notice the two fellows who just went in the store?" queried Cal.

"I'll say so," replied Merry.

"Ahuh! Well, the fat one was Bloom, head of the Bar XX outfit, an' no friend of the Thurmans. The other was Hatfield, one of his riders. There's bad blood between him an' me. I'll tell you why some day. Of all the—— But never mind. Now look down the road. See those four boys comin'. Well, they belong to the Thurman outfit. Wess, the tallest, is my cousin. They're just the finest fellows. But they're hell on tricks an' fights. They've put up some job on me to-day. Now you just hang around an' watch, until I call you."

"I get you, Steve," returned Merry, with a smile, and then lounged away to his seat on the porch.

Cal remained sitting in the Ford. Wess and his comrades came leisurely on, and lined up on the porch, as calm as deacons. Natives of Ryson appeared on the road, approaching the store and post office. Then the big auto-stage turned into the main road and came on with a roar, leaving a cloud of dust behind. It appeared to be loaded down with bags and boxes, piled on top and tied on the sides. The driver came on with unusual speed, and halted with a bang before the porch steps. When he stepped quickly out, Cal recognised Jake's face and figure, but not his movements. Remarkable and unnatural energy characterised Jake at the moment.

"Hyar we are," he called cheerily, as he opened a side door. Then he proceeded to lift out numerous pieces of hand baggage, grips and bags of a quality and style seldom seen at Ryson. These he deposited upon the steps. Next he helped someone out, speaking too low for Cal to hear what he said.

The first passenger to alight was a very young girl, it seemed to Cal. His view was obstructed by Jake, who appeared to be making a gallant of himself. Everybody on the porch stared. The girl, carrying a hand satchel, tripped up the steps. Cal caught a glimpse of blond curls and the flash of a white face and a rosy cheek. She went into the store. Cal, waiting for the next passenger, made ready to go forward and do his duty. But no one else alighted. Jake lifted out some more baggage, then proceeded to untie sacks from the running-board.

Cal stared. Suddenly he realised that the stage was empty. There were no more passengers. His first sensation was one of unutterable relief. Miss Stockwell's sister had not come. She had missed the stage or had not come at all. Anyway, she was not there. The joke would be on the boys. He glanced away from the stage to the porch. What had happened to that outfit? Wess looked dazed; Pan Handle was in a trance; Tim stared open-mouthed at the wide door of the store; and Arizona seemed suddenly to be recovering from some shock and to be reminded of his radiant personal adornment. He was fussing with his hair, then his scarf. He changed his gloves from one hand to another, and began to walk towards the door in the most hesitating manner.

But he never reached it. He was halted by a vision of youth and beauty that emerged from the doorway. She crossed the threshold, came out on the porch in the light. It seemed to Cal that everyone was struck as he was struck—incapable of movement. But his mind whirled with sensation and thought.

The girl he had imagined a child, now facing him, was certainly a young lady. She had big violet eyes that peered expectantly all around her. Her face was white except for a rosy colour high on her cheeks. Her lips were red as carmine. She wore a tan-coloured dress, stylishly cut and strangely short. It reached only to the turn of her knees. Cal's bewildered glance caught a glimpse of slender, shapely, black-stockinged legs before it flashed back to her face.

"Mr. Driver, you said there was someone to meet me," she spoke up, in a sweet, high-pitched voice.

"Shore thar is, judgin' from appearances," laughed Jake, looking up from his task with the mail-bags. His bronzed face wrinkled with a smile. "An' if thar wasn't, miss, you'd hev no call for worry. Wait till I carry in these mail-bags."

She did not appear in the least embarrassed or concerned in any way, except somewhat curious and interested. Manifestly she expected someone of the group to step forward, and looked from one to another. Arizona began to thaw under the sweet expectation of that look, but the others remained frozen.

Then Hatfield came out of the store, bareheaded, his sombrero in hand, and his handsome, bold face pleasantly alight.

"Miss, I reckon you're the young lady I'm lookin' for," he said easily, as he towered over her.

"I'm Miss Georgiana May Stockwell," she said, with a flashing look, taking him in from heated face to spurred boots.

Cal Thurman's strained attention broke. He fell back against the seat of the car. "By Heaven!" he whispered. "I understand teacher now. She put this job up on me. That—that girl's her sister—the sister I'm to meet." Shocked out of his equilibrium, compelled to face an exigency vastly different from the one he had dreaded, beginning to thrill and tingle with a strange dawning exultation, Cal could only sit there and stare and listen.

Manifestly Miss Georgiana expected Hatfield to introduce himself, and her manner was one of pleased anticipation. She liked the looks of this Arizonian. Hatfield, however, did not seem disposed to tell his name; and his manner, though bold and assured, showed something of awkwardness. Either he was not quick-witted enough for the situation or he had not judged Miss Stockwell correctly. She seemed swift to grasp something strange in his omission or in what might be the brusque way of Westerners, and she lost a little of her self-possession. Her sophistication was not very old or deep.

"Come over to the garage with me an' I'll put you in a car," said Hatfield, and gathering up several of her bags, he started down the porch steps.

"Thank you—I'll wait here," replied the young lady hesitatingly, and she watched him depart. Then Wess Thurman stepped forward to address her.

"Miss Stockwell," he began, with an earnestness that precluded embarrassment, "shore if you go with Bid Hatfield you'll never be welcome at the Thurman ranch."

She stared up at the tall, lean-faced rider, and it was plain now that something seemed wrong to her.

"What am I up against?" she queried tartly. "How do I know who Bid Hatfield is? He appeared to be the only gentleman to notice that I am a stranger and alone. Besides, he said he was looking for me. I took him to be Mr. Cal Thurman."

"Wal, you're shore mistaken, an' Cal won't be flattered," replied the rider. "I'm Wess Thurman, an' we—us heah—thet is I—I come to meet you an' take you to your sister."

Miss Georgiana eyed Wess dubiously, and her thoughts must have been varying and bewildering, until she gathered something of the truth of the situation. Not improbably this contretemps was not new to her, except in its Arizona setting and the individuality of these riders.

"I was told down the road that Mr. Cal Thurman telephoned he would meet me," she said. "Where is he?"

"Wal, miss—you see," floundered Wess, trying to arise to his opportunity, "Cal's only a boy—an' he was takin' a lot on himself. Now I'm a-goin' to take you out to Green Valley Ranch."

"You are very kind," replied Georgiana sweetly. "Did my sister Mary send you to meet me?"

"Wal, I reckon—not jest that—but we—the boys—I mean I said I'd shore see you home safe," replied Wess, swallowing hard.

Miss Georgiana gazed roguishly up at him, and then at Arizona, who was edging closer, and then at Pan Handle and Tim Matthews, now showing signs of animation.

"We fetched the—big car," said Arizona breathlessly. That seemed a signal of encouragement to the other boys. Wess and Pan Handle and Tim crowded round the girl. Arizona refused to be edged aside from his favourable position.

"*We?* Oh, I'm to have several escorts," responded Georgiana demurely, as she gazed up at them.

"Shore we-all came to escort you," put in Tim rather timidly, but with beaming face.

"Lady, you're a-goin' with the right outfit," said Pan Handle.

"Outfit! Oh, then you belong to the Four T's—at the Thurman ranch where my sister lives?" cried Georgiana eagerly.

"Wal, miss, you shore hit it on the haid," drawled Wess, with his engaging smile. He had recovered his balance. Blandly he introduced his comrades. "This heah is Arizona, who ain't got any other name. An' this's Pan Handle Ames, an' heah's Tim Matthews."

Georgiana gave all in turn her hand, and a look that further marked their utter demoralisation.

"And Mr. Cal Thurman—where is he?" she queried.

"Reckon Cal didn't want to bother aboot meetin' you, lady," said Tim blandly. "Last night he beefed a lot. He was heah when the stage come in, an' I guess he beat it."

"Oh, I see," replied the girl. "I'm sorry if my coming has annoyed anyone."

"Wal, it didn't annoy anyone but Cal, I'll swear to thet," answered Tim. His comrades laughed at this.

That was all the by-play Cal heard, for his attention was attracted by sight of Hatfield returning from the garage with a hired car. During the amazing and preposterous stand made by Wess and the boys in their endeavours to work this situation to their pleasure Cal had recovered from his consternation. The boys had been quick to grasp at the trick played upon them by the school-teacher, and meant now to turn the tables on Cal and take Miss Georgiana home. Cal vowed they would never succeed. He drew a deep breath and leaped out of the car. He felt master of this situation, and something stirred in him, deeper and more fiery than the situation seemed to justify.

When Hatfield halted at the porch Cal deliberately looked into the car, and seeing Miss Stockwell's bags, he promptly lifted them out. Hatfield swaggered out of his seat.

"Hey, Thurman, what're you up to?" he demanded.

His loud voice silenced the conversation on the porch, and everybody turned to stare.

"Bid, I'm relievin' you of Miss Stockwell's baggage," said Cal coolly. "I was sent to meet her an' I'm goin' to take her home."

Hatfield's muscular body jerked with a start of angry passion, and for an instant he glared darkly at Cal, with blood slowly leaving his face. There was more here than the mere opposition confronting him. Then he masked his true feelings.

"Well, Cal, you didn't show up an' nobody else in your outfit had any manners, so I offered to escort Miss Stockwell," he said.

"Ahuh!" ejaculated Cal, taken back by the rider's terse reply.

Whereupon Hatfield mounted the porch, and with a gallant bow he faced the girl.

"Miss Stockwell, will you let me take you to your sister or do you prefer to go with Thurman?" he inquired courteously.

The girl had quickened and stirred with the excitement of the moment. Manifestly she was alive to Hatfield's striking appearance and personality. Then she turned her flashing gaze upon Cal.

That was indeed a trying moment for him. Suddenly, it seemed, as he felt her glance take him in, all his assurance and sense of right in the situation oozed away. He wore his old rider's clothes, and never had they seemed so dirty and ragged as now. What a sorry figure he must cut in contrast to this handsome Hatfield, or the boys who had put on their best for the occasion. Cal felt the blood rise to his temples.

"Mr. Bid Hatfield, if it were a matter of choice, I'd much rather go with you," replied the girl sweetly. "But as my sister sent him to get me I can only——"

"Pardon me," interrupted Cal curtly. "I'm glad to get out of takin' you. But I advise you to go with my cousin Wess. For if you go with Hatfield you will not be welcome at Green Valley. I'm tellin' you this for your sister's sake."

Cal turned away, leaving the girl both affronted and troubled. At this juncture someone shouted from the store: "Cal Thurman, you're wanted on the phone."

"Who wants me?" called Cal.

"It's Miss Stockwell, the teacher. She's callin' from the ranger station."

Cal plodded up the steps and into the store, looking neither right nor left. He was aware of footsteps following him in, but he was too miserable to take any further notice of anyone.

"Hello!" he called into the telephone.

"Hello! Is that you, Cal?" was the eager reply.

"Yes, it's me."

"This is Mary Stockwell talking. . . . Cal, has the stage come with my sister?"

"I reckon so," replied Cal grimly.

"Oh—oh—Cal, dear boy, is she all right?"

"I reckon so."

"Oh—hurry, Cal! Fetch her out. I'm wild to see her. And, Cal, you're glad now I made you go, aren't you? You'll forgive me for fooling you—about the picture?"

"I'll never forgive you—never," blurted out Cal hoarsely.

There was no instant response. Then the teacher's voice came again, different in tone. "Why, Cal—you don't mean that! It was only fun. You've played jokes on me. And I thought this would please you. I was so glad you alone of the boys offered to go—to meet what you supposed would be a cross, ugly old maid. It was fine of you, Cal—— Why are you offended—why won't you forgive me?"

"Aw, because I've been made a damn' fool before a crowd," replied Cal. "Wess an' the boys came in to play some low-down trick on me. . . . You see, teacher, I was lookin' for—for the person who'd look like the picture you showed me. An' when a—a pretty kid of a girl hops out of the stage I—I never thought it might be your sister. I was the last to find that out. . . . Then—someone I've no use for went up to her—an' when I woke up an' introduced myself—said you'd sent me to meet her—then—then she insulted me right before him—an' all the crowd."

"Insulted you! Oh, Cal, don't say that," returned Miss Stockwell, in distress. "I'm sorry, Cal. Why, I wanted *you* to be the lucky boy. . . . Tell me, who went up to Georgiana? Was it Bid Hatfield?"

"Yes, it was, an' she told him she'd prefer to go with him. Right before Wess an' the boys an' everybody! That's what's so bad. Why, teacher, you don't know the West. I'll never live that down. It's only fair to say Hatfield was first to show your sister courtesy. But I was locoed, I tell you. . . . Oh, I've made a mess of it. . . . Teacher, I've told her she'd better go home with Wess— that if she goes with Hatfield it might make bad feelin' for you."

"Cal, my sister is coming home with *you*," declared Miss Stockwell, in a voice Cal well remembered. "Call her to the phone."

Thus admonished, Cal turned away, smarting and tingling from the forced expression of his feelings. He almost bumped into Georgiana, who evidently had been standing there. The pertness had gone from her face. She looked perturbed, and her eyes met his rather questioningly.

"Your sister wants to speak to you," said Cal, motioning towards the telephone.

A moment later she returned.

"Mr. Cal," she began, "sister has explained—about my aunt's picture—how your brothers and cousins refused to meet me—that you alone were kind enough—good enough to come. That those boys had framed up some trick to play on you. . . . I apologise for what I said. I'm ashamed. Won't you forgive me—and take me to Mary?"

She had seemed to come closer all the time she was speaking, until her appealing hand touched his arm. She lifted her face that suddenly became beautiful and sweet in Cal's dawning sight. Her violet eyes held him. They were darkening with thought, troubled, sincere, yet audacious. And it seemed that before them, all in a flash, he fell crashing to the first headlong love of his life. After that nothing was clear.

"May I ride in front beside you?" she asked, as if that was what she most wanted to do of all things in the world. She looked it. She spoke sweetly, audibly to the listeners on the porch. But she apparently did not know of their existence. She did not hear the shuffling of their boots as they began to stir forward.

"Sure can," replied Cal, trying to catch his breath. "I'll pack your bags in back."

At this juncture Tuck Merry loomed up, carrying his canvas bag. His cadaverous face did not betray that he and Cal had met, though deep in his eyes gleamed a twinkle of fun and zest over the situation.

"Buddy, would you give a fellow a lift along the road?" he inquired.

"Sure. Pile in with your pack," replied Cal heartily. Right then and there he wanted to hug this lanky new-found friend.

Merry and his pack and the girl's numerous pieces of baggage comfortably filled the after-section of the Ford. Then Cal cranked the engine. It started with a strange sound, entirely foreign to him. Was it only the confusion of his brain? Anyway, it started. Cal climbed in beside the girl, tremendously aware of her presence, of her perfect self-possession and poise, of the smile that enveloped him. His hands shook a little. Then when he tried to drive off he was dumbfounded to see that the car would not budge an inch. The engine had stopped.

CAL sat there at the wheel, suddenly realising that what he had anticipated had begun to happen. He swore under his breath, and for an instant he hated the curious crowd lined up on the porch. This feeling, however, was only a flash. No matter what happened, Georgiana May Stockwell was with him. That would be balm for much more injury he might suffer.

"You stalled the engine," she said brightly.

"Stalled? Well, that's a new one on me," he replied. Then in lower tone he added: "Your sister told you Wess an' his gang had put up a job on me, didn't she?"

"Yes. That's one reason why I was so ashamed."

"I've got a hunch they've fooled with the engine when I left the car at the garage," whispered Cal. "It's sure comin' to me. An' it's hardly fair to ask you to stick by me. But I'm askin' you to. It's started bad for me, but will you stick to me an' be game?"

"Game is my middle name," she whispered back, with a flash of fun and fire in her eyes. "I'll stick if we have to walk. Don't worry about me. This's great. You keep *your* nerve and we'll give them the merry ha-ha."

The look of her as she faced him, young and eager and defiant, the quick whispered words that established her championship of him—these more than compensated Cal for the humiliation he had suffered and completely vanquished the dread that had hung over him. He seemed suddenly to acquire an exalted strength, a something which welled up out of his new-born emotion.

"Reckon I'd better confess I'm no mechanic. I don't know an engine from a fence-post," he said.

Her low laugh was cut short by Wess Thurman drawling out: "Wal, Cal, do you want a team of hosses?"

"Cal, air you drivin'?" queried Arizona, with a grin.

Tim Matthews sauntered down the porch steps with nonchalant confidence.

"Mebbe yo're out of gas," he said, and his whole serene countenance masked the lie of his knowledge.

Wess Thurman strode down off the porch and to the car.

"Cousin," he drawled, "I reckon you want Miss Stockwell to get home for dinner?"

"Sure. An' I'll get her there," returned Cal.

"Wal, not in thet vehicle, you won't," averred Wess. "We've got room in the big car for her an' her packs."

"How about me?" inquired Cal, with sarcasm.

"Wal, there won't be room, Cal," replied Wess, spreading wide his hands. "We've shore got a load as it is. . . . Mebbe Tim or Pan Handle or Arizona might stay in town an' let you go with me."

"I gotta get back to-night," said Tim.

"Cal, your dad gave me one day off an' no more. I cain't afford to lose my job," said Pan Handle.

"Pard, you shore know I'd do a heap for you, but I come in jest on purpose to get medicine for my hoss," said Arizona.

It was the usual response, the apparent innocence. Cal saw how Georgiana was studying them, wonderingly, as if fascinated. She saw through them. She was biting her red lips to hold back her merriment. Then Cal thrilled to see Tuck Merry unlimbering his long length out of the back of the car. Cal had forgotten his other passenger.

"Buddy, let me give this can the once-over," he said. "I used to run a cheese-cutter for the Smith Condensed Milk Company."

His dry, droll manner of speaking apparently jarred on the ears of Wess and his comrades. They hardly knew what to think, and sight of this remarkably tall, thin personage silenced them. They watched him with undisguised amazement. Tuck leisurely went round to the front of the car and threw back the cover of the engine, and craning his long neck he bent his head clear out of sight. He was whistling. Then he straightened up to look over and handle parts of the engine. The crowd took him seriously. But Cal divined that Tuck had more in mind than a possible knowledge of how to start the engine. He rattled things. He turned this and that, with the air of a master mechanic.

"Haw! Haw!" roared the cattleman Bloom from his post on the porch. "Shore this's a side-show."

Merry paid no attention to him, or to the others who laughed at his sally, but went on leisurely examining the engine.

"I don't know what's coming off, but I've a hunch," Cal whispered to the girl.

"Oh, he's just too funny," she whispered back. "Mr. Cal, I believe he's kidding these boobs."

Finally Merry straightened up, and with his hand on the

machine, stood in the posture of an orator about to speak.

"Buddy, this here engine has been monkeyed with by someone who doesn't know the combination," he said blandly. "The carburettor has been detached from the ventriculator and the trolley wire is off. The ignition system has been jammed in the midriff. Then the juice no longer coincides with the perambulator, and as a consequence the spark plug is nix. Outside of that the engine is all right."

"Gee! Isn't there anythin' more out of whack?" asked Cal, almost bursting with glee. Moreover, there was something marvellous happening. His hand had dropped to the seat and the girl, in her excitement, was squeezing it.

"That's all I can see offhand," replied Tuck, "except some parts are missin'. But I can make her run, all right, all right."

That remark appeared to release Wess from whatever it was that had inhibited him.

"Say, stranger, are you tryin' to josh me?" he queried with a note of resentment in his drawl.

"I was addressing myself to the gentleman who offered me a ride," replied Tuck, waving a huge hand at Cal.

"Wal, what'd you mean by thet crack aboot someone monkeyin' with this car?"

"Mister, I meant what I said. Somebody has monkeyed with it."

"Ahuh! Wal, I'm tellin' you thet strangers in these parts better be careful what they say," declared Wess belligerently.

"Why so? Ain't this a free country?" asked Merry meekly.

"Reckon it is, but we're shore particular," growled Wess. "An' we ain't havin' our fun mussed up by any long-legged bean-pole of a scarecrow like you."

"Oh, I see," replied Merry still more meekly, almost abjectly. "I didn't mean any offence—just telling the truth thet way."

"Who'n hell are you, anyhow?" inquired Wess, curious now that he had apparently intimidated the fellow.

"My name's Merry and I'm looking for a job."

"Merry, huh? Wal, thet's shore a good handle, for you're the funniest-lookin' fellar I ever seen. Reckon you'd make some apple-picker, but it ain't a good year for apples."

With that Wess dropped back beside Cal and resumed his genial air and slow drawl. "Wal, kid, I'll relieve you of Miss Stockwell an' get her home for dinner."

Cal regarded his cousin for a long moment. Wess was in deadly earnest about his fun.

"Wess, I'd hate to tell you what I know," said Cal, with mysterious good nature.

"Aw, now would you?" queried the other banteringly. He did not know just how to take Cal's change of aspect and tone. Then his keen eyes saw Cal's hand over Georgiana's and he actually gave a start.

"Wal, takin' all in all, you ain't so slow," he said. "But considerin' thet Miss Stockwell must be got home, I'll have to tag you. Shore it's a cinch you cain't take her in this wagon."

Whereupon he strode off towards the garage. Arizona and Pan Handle hurried after him, but Tim lagged behind long enough to shoot a hard look at Tuck Merry and a languishing glance at Miss Stockwell. Then he, too, strode after them.

"Tuck, hurry an' hook up the engine," said Cal to his comrade. "Let's rustle out of here."

Merry bent over the machinery, dexterously using his big hands, while the bystanders stirred and shuffled on the porch. Some of them laughed and exchanged jesting remarks. The incident, however, did not appear to be closed. Cal caught the eyes of Bloom and Hatfield upon him and the girl.

"Holdin' hands, heh?" queried Bloom coarsely, in his loud voice, that instantly called attention to Cal and Georgiana.

It was Cal who blushed and withdrew the hand that had unconsciously covered hers. Even in the moment of sudden consternation and anger he saw that she showed surprising indifference to the attention thus rudely turned upon her. Merry jerked up quickly from his task over the engine. Bloom must have seen or felt contempt in the girl's utter lack of embarrassment or shame.

"Wal, Bid," he said, just as loudly, turning to Hatfield. "Thet bare-legged chicken is some looker, but you ain't missin' so much. Funny aboot these Eastern females——"

"I'm a stranger out here," said Merry, "I'm from the East and I don't take kindly to the remark you made. Do Arizona men talk that way about Eastern women?"

"They shore do when them wimmen have painted faces an' bare knees like thet girl," declared Bloom.

"But, mister, down East a little artificial colour and a short skirt don't call for insults," averred Merry gravely. "It's the style. I've a kid sister who wears the same."

"Wal, you an' your sister an' all sech as thet chicken had better stay where you belong," said Bloom. "The West won't stand for you. An', stranger, let me give you a hunch. The Tonto Basin is shore West clear through."

"Mister, I've met a lot of men, and with all respect to your Tonto code, I'll say no real man anywhere talks like you."

"Say, you starved-lookin' bag of bones!" roared Bloom furiously. "You pipe-organ, shootin' off your mind thet way! Do you hev any idee who yo're ravin' at?"

"I'm tellin' you, mister," replied Merry, his casual voice so marked in contrast to the strident one. "You're no real Westerner. You're a poor fish. You're a big fat stiff—a blow-hard, a bully. I'll bet you're yellow clear to your gizzard."

Bloom appeared suddenly bereft of reason. Utter frenzied astonishment claimed him. His face turned livid, and he stuttered like a lunatic. Something incredible had happened to him. He appeared to be looking at a monstrosity. With a slow, ponderous motion he swung back his arm.

Then Merry's right hand shot up so swiftly that Cal could not follow it. But he saw the result. Merry's fist stopped at Bloom's nose—not a hard blow, but evidently peculiarly placed. Bloom's head jerked back, and blood squirted from his nose. He let out a hoarse cry of pain. The spasmodic working of his face likewise attested to a sudden excruciating sensation. Then as he steadied himself on his feet Merry's left hand shot out. It hit Bloom in the waist somewhere and sounded like a bass drum. Bloom gave a terrible gasp. His mouth opened wide, and his whole face became a network of strained wrinkles. His hands fluttered to his body and he began to sink down. The breath had been expelled from him. Then as he was sagging Merry knocked him in a heap to the porch floor.

"Where's that swell motion-picture pard of his?" inquired Merry of the bystanders.

"Keep clear of me or I'll throw a gun," declared Hatfield threateningly, moving back into the store.

"Say, you handsome Tonto masher, you wouldn't throw anything but a bluff," retorted Merry, striding across the porch.

One of the men barred his way. "Stranger, let well enough alone. Bid might throw a gun at thet. An' seein' you ain't packin' any, it's wiser to hold in. Don't ever run after any fights in the Tonto. They'll come to you fast enough."

Thus admonished, Merry turned away and went back to the car.

Very curiously then Wess Thurman strode up to Merry, and after him came Arizona and Pan Handle, unquestionably friendly.

But Wess was particularly concerned with this specimen of the *genus homo*. He looked Merry up and down, intently, wonderingly. Manifestly he could not convince himself of certain possibilities.

"Say, what'd you sling at him?" asked Wess, at last.

Merry paid no heed to Wess and went on working over the engine until suddenly it started

"Wal," continued Wess. "Reckon it's no matter what you throwed. But that made you a friend of the Four T's. Savvy? Put her there!"

He shoved out his hand, and Merry grasped it and gave it a single crunch.

"Wow!" yelled Wess, jerking his hand loose. "Man, I was aimin' to be agreeable. Shore I didn't give my hand to a corn-huskin' machine." Dubiously he regarded Merry, smoothing out his hand the while. Then he wagged his head doubtfully.

"Cal, see heah," he said, turning; "you'd better let the little lady go home with me."

"Oh, thank you, Mr. Thurman; you're very kind indeed," interposed Georgiana demurely, "but I'm going with Mr. Cal."

"Wal, you might have to walk," rejoined Wess rather gruffly.

"That would be lovely. I adore walking."

Wess vouchsafed no reply to this, manifestly giving in with poor grace, and with a meaning glance at the rattling Ford he strode back to the touring-car. Arizona, however, had still a thunderbolt to loosen. He bent over the door close to Georgiana, and with great seriousness he said:

"Lady, shore this's the wust season for walkin'."

"Indeed! Why, how strange! The weather seems delightful to me," she replied, smiling at him. Cal gathered the impression that she could not help being prodigal with her smiles, and he was not sure she gave them with perfect sincerity.

"Wal, miss, the weather hasn't nuthin' to do with walkin' in the Tonto," went on Arizona. "Now, my hunch is jest this heah. Shore Cal's old Ford is palpitatin' yet. But it's dyin' an' it'll croak pronto. Thet'll be aboot dark, I reckon, mebbe before. You'll hev to hoof it. An' see heah, lady, do you know about hydrophobia skunks?"

"No, indeed, I don't. What're they?" queried Georgiana.

"Polecats what hev rabies," replied Arizona. "They're loco-crazy. They ain't afeerd of nothin'. They run right at you, an' if you move or yell they'll bite you an' give you hydrophobia. Then you go crazy an' run around tryin' to bite people yoreself. I knowed two fellars what got bit on the nose while they was sleepin' with me. I hed to choke the dinged skunks to make 'em let go. An' both them fellars died horrible!"

"Mr. Cal, is he kidding me?" she asked, turning to Cal, some-what concerned by Arizona's dreadful recital.

"I reckon he is, but all the same there *are* lots of hydrophobia skunks, an' we sure keep clear of them," replied Cal, with a laugh.

"See thet, miss," responded Arizona triumphantly. "Onct in a while Cal shows he's human. So you'd better hedge on thet walk for hours an' hours along the lonely road—in the dark woods—an' come with us. *I'll* see you safe in Green Valley."

"I'll take a chance on Mr. Cal," returned Georgiana archly.

"Aw!" breathed Arizona, in disappointment. "Cal, you ought to be ashamed—draggin' this nice little gurl, with all her pretty clothes, to go trampin' through the dust an' woods."

"Arizona, it takes a long time for anythin' new to penetrate your skull," replied Cal. "Miss Georgiana Stockwell *wants* to go home with me."

"Ahuh! Wal, all right. I was only tellin' her what she's up against."

"Trust me to tell her myself, Arizona," returned Cal heartily. "Jump in, Tuck. I reckon there's no occasion to throw any monkey-wrenches just now. Ha! Ha!"

Merry climbed into the back seat and slammed the door. Cal, with deep and secret misgivings, put on the power, half expecting that the car would refuse to move. But to his delight it started off as if running smoothly was its especial forte.

"Say, Cal," yelled Arizona, "we'll hang along behind an' pick up the pieces."

Cal drove by Wess and Pan Handle and Tim, on past the garage, where the mechanics peeped out in sure betrayal of their part in the plot, and down the dusty road out of the village into the country. The driving, and getting away from Ryson, relieved Cal of the necessity of strain and left him to the mercy of new and strange sensations. Much that he had feared had come to pass, but differ-ently, and it had lost its hatefulness. All the rest seemed mysterious and exalting. Something had happened.

The girl sat quietly for the first mile or so of that journey. Cal saw out of the corner of his eye how still and thoughtful she ap-peared. He noticed when she began to take interest in the ride and in him. Several times she peeped up at him, and each time that sign thrilled him.

Presently she turned to address Merry, whom she evidently had forgotten up to that time.

"Mr. Merry, thanks for—for defending Eastern girls," she said hesitatingly. "That boob was horrid and just what you called him. I never saw anyone hit as you hit him. I'll say you handed him one."

"Don't mention it," replied Tuck gallantly. "I'm a ladies' man. And I've a little sister just like you, only not so pretty."

"Thank you. So you're a flatterer as well as a slugger," she said merrily. "Mr. Cal, what do you think about it?"

"Please don't call me mister," replied Cal. "What do I think about Tuck? Wonderful fellow! Oh, it was grand when he walked up on Bloom and called him all that—and punched his nose—thumped his big paunch—then slammed him hard. Aw, great! If only Enoch could have seen that!"

"Who's Enoch?" asked the girl.

"My older brother. He's the finest fellow. He an' Bloom are set against each other something bad. An' we all side with Enoch. A Thurman sticks to a Thurman, right or wrong. But in this case we're right. Bloom is no good, an' that showy rider of his, Bid Hatfield——"

Cal checked his impulsive speech. Recall of Hatfield was singularly bitter at this incomprehensibly sweet moment. And likewise, Miss Georgiana seemed to feel the silencing effect of the thought of Hatfield. Her pensiveness stormed Cal's heart with an utterly new sensation—the fire of jealousy.

"Did you like Hatfield's looks?"

"Oh, indeed I did! Looked like a swell movie actor to me," she replied naïvely. "I fell for him, I'll tell the world."

Cal's beautiful trance suffered a darkening blight. If he had never before had reason to hate Hatfield, he had it now. Moreover, the way Miss Stockwell talked at times began to disturb Cal and trouble him. He had been most concerned with the vague sweetness of her presence, the tones of her voice. She was wonderful. But the actuality of her began to impress him.

"Well, Eastern girls are no different from Western girls, so far as Bid Hatfield is concerned," said Cal, compelled to a caustic sincerity. "Sure the Tonto girls *fall* for him, as you called it."

"Sort of a man vamp," giggled Georgiana.

Cal had no reply for this. His stirred antagonism shaded into disappointment in her, in himself, and the hour that a moment ago seemed so alluring. By way of forcing himself aloof he began to drive faster, with the result that the Ford performed in a miraculous manner.

"Step on it, bo!" cried the girl gaily. "You can't scare me. I eat speed."

Cal answered to that with reckless abandon until Merry reached forward and, tapping him on the shoulder, said, rather forcefully: "Buddy, cut the speed or you'll spill us. And that big car with your cousin and his pards is right behind us." Thus brought to his senses, Cal slowed down to careful driving.

The sun was about to go down behind the ragged, golden-hazed range of mountains in the west, and the most lovely moment of the day was at hand. Cal was driving slowly up a long, winding road round a foothill and he had opportunity to snatch a glimpse now and then of the country.

To the southward the country fell away into the numberless dark, shadowy lines of ridges and canyons that constituted the Tonto Basin, and at this bewitching moment all was bathed in a strangely beautiful and unreal light, purple and lilac, exquisite and intangible as the shadow cast by a rose.

"You love it all—don't you?" she said, as Cal ended his enthusiastic designation of the country visible to them.

"Yes," he replied, drawing a deep breath of the cool air, now bearing fragrance of pine and cedar.

"Oh, it's nifty, all right," she replied, settling back in her seat, "but too wild and woolly for me. I went to New York City once, and, say, take it from Georgie, there's the place for me."

"Ahuh! I don't doubt it," replied Cal, rather bluntly, in his disappointment. Then, as if to find solace for his hurt he turned to Merry, who had evinced a keen interest in all Cal had pointed out. "Tuck, do you like it?"

"Buddy, here's where I homestead," was the hearty reply. "I've been all over the world. But this Tonto has got 'em all skinned to death. I want to live here a hundred years and bury four wives."

Cal joined with Georgiana in mirth at Merry's facetiousness. Then the hoarse honk of an automobile horn hastened Cal to start on again. Wess was creeping up on him. Cal drove on, down the winding slope of that foothill and up another, towards the dense green wooded country rolling eastward.

"I'm nearly—frozen," said the girl presently.

"That's too bad. I forgot to fetch a robe. Haven't you a coat?"

"Yes, I've a heavy coat, and sweater, too, but I can't unpack them now," she replied. She was indeed shivering. With the setting of the sun and growing altitude the air had become cold, marked by a penetrating quality of the desert land.

For the first time Cal deliberately ran his glance over her from head to foot. Indeed, the light, flimsy dress she wore, low at the neck and startlingly short, was no garment for the Tonto at night. A girl needed to wear wool.

"If you—you suffer from cold—why don't you dress differently?" he queried, in a tone he meant to be casual. But it was not.

"Don't you like this dress?" she asked quickly.

"I should smile I don't," he replied.

"What's wrong with it?" she added, with an irresistible concern. "It's new—stylish. All the boys said it was some swell rag."

"Boys!" retorted Cal. "What kind of boys?"

"Why, all my friends!" she replied, in a dangerous tone that warned him. Then as he did not answer she asked again: "What's wrong with it? I suppose you're the arbiter of style in your wonderful Tonto?"

"I don't know anything about style—or swell rags," said Cal, stung by her sarcasm. "But I've got some sense. This is a mountain country. You're six thousand feet above sea-level right here, and going higher. You'll freeze to death in that—that thing. It's too thin—and too low—and a mile too short."

"How'd I know I was going up into the mountains where it's winter in summer? But if I had known I'd have worn the same, only I'd had my coat out. . . . Mr. Thurman, it may interest you to learn that last winter all the fashionable women wore skirts almost to their knees and open-work lace or silk stockings and slippers. There! Do you get that, Mr. Backwoodsman?"

"Ahuh! I reckon that is interestin'," replied Cal, just as tartly. "Women back East dress that way? . . . In winter-time?"

"Yes, I'll say so."

"When it was cold?" he went on incredulously.

"Yes—cold—slushy—icy—sleety—zero weather," she averred, in triumph.

"Well, they're loco," declared Cal shortly. "Plumb loco—an' that means crazy, Miss New York."

"I think you're horrid," she retorted hotly. "It's strange my sister is so fond of you. . . . I wish I had come with Mr. Bid Hatfield."

Cal felt the blood flame and sting his face. What a little cat she was! He thought he hated her then.

"Ahuh! Thank you. That's two speeches of yours I'm not likely to forget," he flashed back at her. "You've got some Western ways to learn, Miss Stockwell, an' I'm sorry I was fool enough to open my mouth. We don't savvy each other. . . . An' as for what you said about Bid Hatfield—let me tell you out straight—you're bein' driven home now by a gentleman, even if he does live in the back-woods—an' if you had come with Hatfield you'd have learned what *he* thought of your rolled-down stockings."

She turned quite pale and sat perfectly motionless, looking ahead of her. Presently she spoke in a different tone.

"Is that straight talk or just temper?" she asked quietly. "Is it square to Mr. Hatfield?"

"Yes, it's straight an' it's square. I could tell you a lot, but all I'll say is, Hatfield once insulted my sister. . . . Reckon I'll kill him some day."

That gave her a slight start and she turned sharply, with lips parted. "I ought to apologise for—for talkin' familiarly about a lady's way of dressin'," added Cal with finality. "But I'd never have done so if you hadn't said you were freezin'."

What her reply might have been Cal never knew, for as she turned to him the engine emitted a grinding bang from its internals, the wheel turned out of his grasp, and the car ran into a bank with a thud.

The girl was thrown violently against Cal. She did not cry out. There was a sound of breaking glass, and of the baggage shifting in the back of the car.

"Buddy, we struck a hard wave," cheerfully called out Merry.

"That'll be about all," added Georgiana.

5

"MISS GEORGIANA, are you hurt?" queried Cal, suddenly aware of the little head pressing rather heavily against his shoulders.

"I—I don't think—so," she replied somewhat tremulously. "Sort of a—jerk—my neck—like the game crack-the-whip—you know."

"Aw, I'm sorry," said Cal, all his resentment as if it had never been. Her hat was touching his face, her cheek rested upon his shoulder and then slid a little lower. Her hands appeared inert. How slight and frail! Again that ebullition ran riot in his breast, deep, beyond his control, shudderingly. He raised his arm round her, more, he thought, to get it out of her way than anything else. Yet when the slim form seemed to sink a little more, now closer to him, he experienced a comforting sense of strength, of his power to sustain her. Was she going to faint? What should he do?

"Tuck, I'm afraid she's hurt," said Cal fearfully. "What'll we do?"

"Buddy, she can't be hurt bad," replied Tuck as he jumped out of the car and then leaned forward to look at Georgiana. "I guess you're doing about all that's necessary," he continued, with subtle, dry meaning. "Just hold her, Buddy, till she comes to. . . . I hear the other car. It'll be along soon."

At that the girl stirred, sat up, and moved away from Cal. That relieved his anxiety.

"You're a couple of bright guys," she said in an entirely different voice.

Merry let out a hearty laugh at this, but Cal could only stare at her. The gathering twilight under the high bank made her face hard to see in the gloom. It looked pale, sweet, haunting to Cal. Her eyes were dark, deep wells.

"Bright guys?" he echoed, rather dumbfounded. "Why do you say that?"

"I ought to say more. You drove like a soused chauffeur. And your Tuck Merry lets me freeze to death when he's got a bundle of blankets or clothes."

"Right-o," declared Tuck, with alacrity. "Bonehead is the correct allegation for this member of the party." Whereupon he reached for his pack, and swiftly unrolling it he took out a blanket. "Let me tuck this round you."

"Thanks, Tuck. You're well named," said this amazing girl as presently she leaned back wrapped from head to feet in the blanket. "Now where do we go from here?"

Cal sat there silently looking at her, and finally forced his gaze away. He chose to let her think she had fooled him, when as a matter of truth he had suddenly divined that she had leaned so close to him and nestled in his arm just out of a pure feminine deviltry or coquetry.

Just then the big touring-car with Wess and the boys mounted the last bench of the hill behind, and came humming to a stop opposite the Ford.

"Wal, heah you are," called Wess peevishly. "It shore took you a long time to ditch thet Ford."

"Cal, you son-of-a-gun, you run it half-way home," said Pan Handle admiringly. "I'm a-goin' to apolergise fer insinuatin' you couldn't drive. Yo're some driver."

"Aw, fellars, I'm gamblin' thet gent Cal took in is to blame fer spoilin' all our fun," growled Arizona.

"See heah, you long-legged galoot," called Tim Matthews to Merry, who was now examining the engine. "Is she busted—laid out—hamstrung?"

"Mister, do you mean this Ford or the young lady?" calmly queried Tuck.

"I mean thet car, you durn' fool," shouted Tim.

"So you run into thet bank?" added Wess more cheerfully, as he lumberingly got his long length out of the touring-car. "Broke down for good, hey?"

They all got out, leisurely, and swaggered towards the Ford. Twilight had deepened, so their faces could not be clearly seen. Meanwhile Cal had been pondering how best to meet the situation. If only he could turn the tables on them! Suddenly into his mind flashed a daring idea. Impulsively he leaned close to the girl so he could whisper in her ear: "They've been mean and they've got it on me. So won't you please be—be nice an' forget all I said —an' stand by me? I can beat them yet."

"Go to it. I'll play up to your game," she whispered back.

Cal resumed his former position, conscious of an inward tremor. How this girl affected him! Her soft whisper, suggestive of forgiveness and loyalty, seemed to linger in his ears.

"Ahuh!" ejaculated Cal at last. "You feel better now, I reckon.

You've had your joke. You've had one more on the baby of the family. All right. . . . Now listen. It might have been well meant, though I don't trust any of you, but it turned out bad. You know I'm a poor driver, an' when somethin' busted in the engine it scared me—threw me off guard—an' we ran into this bank. Miss Georgiana got a hard jerk an' knock. She fainted twice. I'm afraid she's hurt—maybe bad."

A blank, dead silence ensued. Cal felt elated. He knew these big-hearted boys. If the girl now would only do her part! Then suddenly that silence was pierced by a little low moan of anguish. Georgiana had uttered it, establishing beyond doubt in Cal's mind the proof that she was a consummate actress. He could have whooped aloud. She was a thoroughbred.

"Aw, hell!" gasped Wess, in abject, sincere misery.

"My Gawd! Cal, don't say the little lady's hurt," ejaculated Arizona.

The other two boys were probably beyond expression of their feelings, especially Tim, who had been ring-leader in the plot.

"Don't stand there like a lot of boobs!" shouted Cal. The newly-learned epithet delighted him. "Clear out the back of your car, so I can carry her in there."

"It's done," added Wess sharply, "an' you fellars are to blame. Rustle now." Then he approached the Ford on the girl's side and opened the door. She lay back in the dark blanket, a singularly inert figure. Cal moved over close to Georgiana, and with every show of extreme tenderness he put his arms under her and lifted her. Another little moan escaped her.

"Of all the tough luck!" exclaimed Wess huskily. "Cal, you may beat me half to death. But honest to Gawd I didn't put up the job. It was Tim an' Pan Handle. . . . Let me help you. . . . Easy now."

"There, I can manage," replied Cal as he straightened up free of the car. How light she was! He could have carried her clear to Green Valley. Silently the boys followed him—helped him into the big car, where he sat down to let Georgiana slip off his lap into the corner. But she still leaned against him. Her bonnet fell back. Cal could just see the white glow of her face, and the big eyes, now strangely black.

"Cal, you'd better support her head," said Wess, assuming the authority here. "You know the road's bad in places. Boys, hustle in with them bags. . . . An', say, you elongated stranger, stick your pack on the fender an' ride on the runnin'-board."

In a few moments all appeared to be in readiness for the start. Tim and Pan Handle squeezed into the front seat with Wess, and Arizona got into the back seat beside Cal.

At this critical juncture Georgiana wailed out a most heart-rending cry.

"Oh, Mister—Cal—to think any young men—could be so c-r-u-e-l!" she sobbed out.

"Cal, hadn't we better rustle to Ryson—fer the doctor?" asked Wess hurriedly.

Cal deliberated a moment, during which Georgiana decided that momentous question.

"Take me—to sister," she wailed. "I want to die—in her arms. My neck's—broken—and no doctor could help me now. . . . I need —minister to pray—for my soul—for I'm a very—very wicked girl. Oh—oh—oh-h-h-h!"

The little minx was giving Cal's free hand a sly squeeze at the very moment that she was wailing. She was more than revelling in the way she had helped Cal to turn the tables on these boys.

Never had Wess driven so wonderfully. He had a genius for gliding over the rough places in the road, so as not to jar the little lady who had wailed that her neck was broken. Pan Handle seemed set in a gloomy trance, while Tim Matthews, the instigator of the plot to discomfit Cal, might well have been a criminal on his way to be hanged. Wretchedness was no word to express his state. And as for the fun-loving and easy-going Arizona, always in trouble of others' making, he crouched on the seat beside Cal, and it was evident his heart was broken.

Whenever Wess slowed up at a bump or crossing or wash, Georgiana would utter a faint cry. That it pierced the consciences of these guilty tricksters there could not be the slightest doubt.

The car passed the corral fences, the barns, the sheds, and stopped before the long, rambling ranch-house, from which lighted windows gleamed.

Wess turned to say anxiously: "Cal, how is she?"

"Reckon she's no worse," replied Cal, feeling a strong regurgitation of his former glee.

"Lady—I—I do hope you're recoverin'," faltered Wess in deep-voiced solicitation. Manifestly he was hoping against hope. And Cal felt how the other boys hung on her answer.

"Thank you—I guess—I'm a little better," she said languidly. "The terrible pain—is gone—and I'm easier. I guess my neck's not broken, after all. Please forgive me."

Wess actually writhed and groaned in his self-accusing unhappiness. Her sweetly uttered request to be forgiven was the last straw.

"Wess, go in an' break the news to teacher, but mind you don't scare her," said Cal.

"By Gawd! Cal—I cain't face Miss Mary an' tell her what we've done to her little sister. I cain't," replied Wess distractedly.

Cal felt a sly pinch on his arm, and he knew what to expect.

"Mister Cal—you go in, please—and tell sister," said Georgiana. "Lie to her. Say I'm just tired out—little weak and sick, you know. Then come back after me. I'm afraid I can't walk."

"I'll carry you," interposed Wess, with mounting hopelessness.

"Oh, no, thank you. Mister Cal knows just how to handle me," she replied graciously. "You can carry my baggage."

Cal slipped out, taking with him another lingering, encouraging pressure from that little hand. He ran into the house. The long living-room was bright with two lamps and blazing logs in the huge stone fireplace. Henry Thurman looked up from his paper.

"Wal, heah you be, Cal," he drawled, with a smile smoothing out the net of fine wrinkles in his massive face. He was a large man, grey-haired, beardless, with the stamp of pioneer on every feature. Cal's mother and sister both called in unison from the kitchen that supper was burning.

"Come in here," answered Cal, and when they came in, happily expectant in their hospitality, Enoch and Boyd also entered from the back porch. "Listen, folks, an' don't get scared, now. There's been a little accident. I must tell teacher. Then I'll fetch her sister in. Just wait an' don't be scared."

As Cal hurried out his father drawled: "What air thet boy up to?" Miss Stockwell's room was at the far end of the south porch. Cal knocked on the door and called: "Teacher, are you there?"

"Cal, is that you?" she replied joyously, from within, and then opened the door. She was dressed in white and her comely face seemed happily eager, yet anxious.

"Teacher," whispered Cal almost hilariously, "Georgiana an' I have put it all over Wess an' his outfit."

"You have? Oh, fine! Tell me. Where's Georgie? Is she all right?"

"Listen. I can't tell everythin' now," went on Cal breathlessly. "The boys tampered with the Ford. It broke down as they'd planned. Then we pretended Georgiana was hurt in the accident. But she wasn't, see. Wess, an' the boys are sick. Now your part is to pretend to be terribly angry when Wess comes in. See!"

"Yes, Cal, I see. I'll do my part. But hurry," she replied.

"I'll send Wess an' his gang in first. You be there. You're supposed to think Georgiana is bad hurt an' that they did it. See! Then I'll fetch her in. Oh, say, it'll be great!"

With that Cal wheeled away, and leaping off the porch he ran round the house to the walk, and so out of the gate to the car. All the boys were standing there, dark, gloomy, waiting.

"Grab all the baggage you can carry," said Cal briskly. "An' you, Tuck, go along with them. I'll fetch the girl right in."

When the five young men, heavily laden, had filed through the gate, Cal whispered into the car:

"Come on now. We're sure goin' to have some fun. I fixed it up with your sister. She's on an' she'll do her part."

"I was afraid you'd ball up this part of the play," replied Georgiana. "I didn't want Mary to be frightened."

"Oh, she knows. Don't worry. She's goin' to hop them hard before we get there. . . . We'll hurry."

"I'm all wrapped up," complained the girl, stumbling as she stepped out on the running-board. There she hesitated, looking down on Cal. The gleam from the windows lighted up her face. "I'm supposed to be crippled, am I not? Do I have to walk?"

"Why—why—yes, sure, I—— You can walk to the door. Then I'll carry you." Nonplussed, and uncertain how to take her, Cal just stared upwards into her face. She seemed to be a woman then, infinitely sure of herself, beyond Cal's comprehension.

"Cal, you're a fairly good actor," she said finally, "but when it comes to playing choosies in the dark you are certainly punk."

"Choosies!" ejaculated Cal. "What on earth are they?"

"Your education has been neglected. If I can get up the pep I'll have to take you in hand."

The door of the house opened, sent out a broad flare of light for a moment, and then closed.

"Come on," said Cal, again shot through with eagerness to see the climax of his joke. Georgiana gathered up the folds of the blanket from round her feet, and followed him into the yard and down to the porch.

"Oh, listen," whispered Cal. She grasped his arm in her eagerness and it was certain that she giggled.

" . . . done to my little sister?" sounded the ringing voice of Miss Stockwell, in furious scorn and anger.

"Teacher, it was this heah way," came Wess's humble answer.

"We busted Cal's car. But the durned fool run it into a bank. An' your sister was hurt. But, so help me Gawd . . ."

"You villains!" burst out Miss Stockwell in terrible tones. "You miserable ruffians! It's bad enough of you to torment that noble boy Cal, let alone hurt a poor little sick girl. It's outrageous. You've got to be horse-whipped. And if my sister dies I'll have you hanged!"

Georgiana squeezed Cal's arm. "Deep stuff! Here's where we put it over good. Now, Cal, cover my face with the blanket and carry me in. Be very solemn and awfully grieved. Then—after you've planted the tragedy bluff—set me down on my feet, and leave the rest to me."

Cal folded the end flap of the blanket over her face and took her in his arms. She made her body as limp as an empty sack. One arm hung down and her head fell back.

"Open the door," he called in a hollow voice. It was opened wide by Tuck Merry who, as he faced Cal, wore the most wonderful expression Cal had ever seen. In his loyalty to further the plot he was making exceedingly strenuous demands on his will power. Manifestly he tried to look sad when he wanted to burst with laughter.

In one sweeping glance, as Cal entered, he took in the assembly. His mother and sisters, white-aproned for the occasion, gazed at him and his burden in a perturbation wholly real. His old father cocked his head on one side and peered with infinite curiosity. But his slight smile precluded anxiety. Enoch and Boyd appeared dumbfounded. Miss Stockwell had the centre of the room—she seemed pale in her white dress—with dark, excited eyes, shining wonderfully on Cal. In front of her, lined up as against a wall for execution, stood Wess and Pan Handle and Arizona and Tim, deeply stirred, haggard, and sick, betraying their guilt, honest in their remorse.

Without more ado Cal set Georgiana upon her feet and with one swift motion stripped the blanket from her. She might have been an apparition to most of these onlookers. Bareheaded, with golden curls dishevelled, radiant of face, instinct with palpitating life and joy, she screamed her delight and rushed into her sister's outstretched arms.

"Oh, Mary—Mary—how glad I am!" she cried tremulously

"Georgie, darling!" exclaimed the teacher, with deeper emotion, and she folded the girl close and bent to kiss her again and again.

Cal glanced away to take a look at the four culprits. Then he

tasted revenge sweet and full. How utterly astounded and stulti-
fied! Their wits worked but slowly. They stared with jaws dropping. The significance was only slowly dawning upon them.

Suddenly then Georgiana turned in her sister's arms, and with
the lamplight upon her softened, glowing face, her eyes flashing
purple, and a dimpled smile breaking on her cheek, she seemed
the loveliest creature Cal had ever seen. His great moment had
come, but it was not going to be what he had anticipated. That
tremendous gathering in his breast seemed to await a sentence.

"Mr. Cal, we put it over on them, didn't we?" she cried joyously.

Cal could only stare at her. That moment the something about
her which he hated had vanished, and she appeared only a young
girl, sweet and full of the joy of life and fun, with a wonderful
light upon her face. As he gazed the truth flashed upon him. He
had fallen in love with her.

"*Aw!*" burst from Wess—a huge expulsion of breath indicating
realisation and relief. He was a beaten trickster, but there was
balm in his defeat.

"Miss—Miss—ain't you hurted a-tall?" gasped Arizona, beginning to beam.

Georgiana roguishly eyed these two speakers and then extended
her gaze to the guiltier boys. They were stunned.

"I wasn't hurt," she said sweetly. "We were just fooling you."

Cal ate at the second table that night with the boys and Tuck
Merry, and afterwards he avoided the living-room where his father
and Enoch continued the merriment that had been precipitated. Seldom did they get so good a chance to lord it over Wess and his
contingent. But Cal never reaped all the fun he had anticipated.
That experiment bade fair to cost him dear.

After supper he took Merry to his little bunk-house, and made
him comfortable there.

"Tuck, you can bunk with me until we fix up a place for you."

"Fine and dandy," returned Tuck. "Buddy, I hope you don't
wake me out of this dream. Did you see me stuff myself? Talk
about your luck. I've gotten soft. Cal, I like your folks. Your dad
made a hit with me. And how he did lam it into your cousin
Wess. Funny! You Tonto folks get a lot of kick out of jokes."

"I'm afraid we run it into the ground sometimes," replied Cal
soberly.

"I expect you do. And I suppose you scrap the same way?"

"Scrap! Why, Tuck, fightin' is about as common as ridin'

horses. But at that most of it is fun—among our own outfit."

"And I'm to be one of the Thurman Four's, hey?"

"You bet. Father was plumb glad I'd got you. An' say, Tuck, when he sees you slug some of these fresh riders—whoopee!"

"Buddy, with all respect to your hopes, I'd like to make friends with the boys first."

"Tuck, you'll never make friends until *after* you've licked them. Just you leave it to me. You go about your work and be—like you were in front of Bloom—oh, that tickled me! An' when I give you the wink do the same as you did to him."

"Right-o. And to-morrow let me begin your boxing lessons."

"I should smile," responded Cal, but without his former enthusiasm.

"Buddy, you've lost your pep," went on Merry kindly.

"Reckon I have. It's been a hard day for me."

"But, Buddy, you certainly put it over on those boneheads. That kid Georgiana is a wonder. Don't you think so?"

"Tuck, I don't know what I think," replied Cal, dropping his head.

"Buddy, I saw how you fell for her," continued Tuck earnestly. "So did I. So did Wess and his gang. So'll everything that wears pants, my boy. These modern kids have got the dope. I have a sister like Georgiana. Some kid! I'll tell you about her. But not to-night. I'm kind-a weary myself. Let's fade into our hammocks."

Cal, however, did not want to go to bed just yet. He went out to walk around a bit.

Five, six hours before he had been Cal Thurman, who was now changed. Somewhere during that period he had fallen in love with this Georgiana May Stockwell. Pondering over the strange, undeniable circumstance, he decided he had done so on first sight. When, however, he thought of Georgiana—the newness and strangeness of her—the slim grace and dainty elegance—the pale, sweet face, the golden curls, the dark-blue eyes that could look as no others he had ever seen—when he remembered the alluring proximity of her and how audaciously she had intruded that fact upon him, then his reasoning went into eclipse. His heart was stormed.

Thus Cal paced the pasture, a prey to all that constituted the torment and pain and ecstasy of dawning love in a true heart.

6

MISS STOCKWELL was reflecting that she had come to dread Sundays, where formerly they had been welcome days of rest from her school duties. The cause was Georgiana. Never in her life had a three weeks' period been so filled with love, bewilderment, distress, and fear. And on this quiet Sabbath morning, while Georgiana was making up the hours of sleep she had lost, Miss Stockwell undertook to unravel the chaos of the situation.

The one outstanding and consolable fact about Georgiana's coming was that the love she had borne her older sister years before as a child had never died, and had now re-opened in these few weeks of intimacy to the one and only good, developing influence in her life. That love and that alone had kept Miss Stockwell true to the tremendous responsibility that her parents had thrust upon her.

Judged superficially, Georgiana had appeared to be a very lively and pretty young girl, bringing with her the clothes, habits, and tricks of speech of the East, and she had not been understood. The young men of the Tonto had been drawn to her as bees to honey. To them she was a new species of the female, strange, alluring, irresistible. To the young girls she had been a revelation, a wonderful creature heralding the freedom, independence, and mastery that seemed born in all the women of the modern day. They had already begun to ape her dress, her manner, her slang, even to the bobbing of their hair. The matter bade fair to upset the tranquil Tonto. To the older women Georgiana was a girl beyond their understanding, a menace and an intruder.

To Miss Stockwell this little sister was adorable despite all that could be said against her, and that was an exceeding great deal. As long as Georgiana was loved, petted, and given her own way she was sweet, lovable, absolutely a comfort and a joy. But cross her in the slightest and she was another creature. And it was impossible to keep from crossing her because Georgiana was endlessly thinking of something never before heard of in the Tonto.

Miss Stockwell realised that she now had in her charge, in the person of her seventeen-year-old sister, one of the modern girls forced by the war and the seething renascence of the world into the type which was bewildering teachers, ministers, educators, and horrifying the staid old Americans.

Georgiana was bright, though she hated study. She despised housework, though her mother had seen to it that she could do it. She abhorred any kind of work. There was a hard, sophisticated, material, worldly side of her most difficult to understand. Miss Stockwell had cudgelled her brain, attempting to reach this side of Georgiana. In vain! The girl had come from a world positively new to Miss Stockwell, who had been in the West only six years.

Georgiana was a flirt, roguish, sweet, playful, and apparently innocent of deliberation, but nevertheless a flirt. Her attractiveness and her newness made this propensity to flirt a vastly more serious matter than if she had not brought the Eastern immodesty of dress, freedom of speech, unrestraint of action, and the fatal fascination of a possible attainableness. For Miss Stockwell had come to realise that this sort of thing would not do in the West. The code of these clean, fine, virile young men of the Tonto would not long abide Georgiana. If no one of them grew serious, then perhaps there might not be a catastrophe. But Miss Stockwell believed one of these young men had already prostrated himself at the altar of her charm—Cal Thurman, the finest of the lot. Cal had grown strangely older in these few weeks. What would that lead to if Georgiana persisted in her flirting? It seemed that Georgiana had arrived at Green Valley just a product of her day, a shallow, selfish, thoughtless, mindless, soulless girl, whose only apparent object was to make herself attractive and irresistible to the opposite sex, and to trifle with them. The West with its openness and naturalness, the simplicity of its people, the necessity for development of physical strength, would inevitably remake the girl —unless some catastrophe intervened to send her back East or drag her down.

Miss Stockwell made a decision that day, for herself as well as Georgiana, and it was that the West should claim them both for good. Whereupon she wrote a long letter to her mother, telling much about Georgiana, though omitting the things that would worry and distress, and concluded with mention of the important decision and how it was best for all concerned, and that some day she and Georgiana would make a visit back home.

The children of these mountain people needed education. It was a wild, lonely, sparsely settled region, where only for a few months in spring and summer could the children go to school. She loved the work and knew it to be noble, and, if necessary, she could devote her life to it. But she had vague hope of the fulfilment of her dream.

"Mary, air you aboot heah this mawnin'?" came in Georgiana's languid voice from the little room beyond. This room had been a sort of shed adjoining that end of the house. Georgiana had coaxed Cal to fix it up with Indian blankets on the walls, and deerskins on the floor, and here in very cramped quarters, with the furniture necessary and her belongings, she was happy.

"Yes, I'm here, Georgie. I've been up for hours and have written a long letter to mother."

"For heaven's sake bring me a drink of water," cried Georgiana. "Talk about a dark-brown taste! Good night! The stuff these Tonto jakes call white mule has some kick."

Mary poured out a glass of water from her pitcher, and carrying it in to Georgiana, sat down upon her little bed. The girl half sat up and propped herself on her pillows, and with her sleepy eyes and soft rosy golden tints of complexion, fresh as the morning, and with her slender arms bare on the coverlet, she was indeed distractingly pretty.

Georgiana drank all of the water and then evidently was not satisfied.

"Georgie, did you really drink any of that liquor they call white mule?" queried Mary seriously.

"I'll say I did," replied Georgiana, with a giggle. "But no more for muh! Little Georgie May thought she'd been kicked by worse than a mule."

"Where'd you get the drink?"

"Some of us went into that Ryson restaurant to eat a bite, about midnight. We had to stop dancing at twelve on Saturday night. Well, Bid Hatfield was with us at our table and he had a flask. He dared us girls to take a sip of his white mule. I was curious, but I didn't want it. I hate booze. The girls took a sip, and then I swallowed a mouthful quick, just for a new experience. I got it. Holy Moses! I'll never touch that stuff again, believe me."

"You won't? You promise me?"

"Now see here, Sis. I don't have to make promises about that. I hate promises, anyway. I'll never drink it again because it made me sick."

"Georgie, I don't care much for Bid Hatfield," said Mary thoughtfully. "I'm surprised he'd come up to you when you were with the Thurmans."

"Boyd didn't like it for a cert. . . . I'll tell you, Mary, on the level I haven't any use for Bid Hatfield except to string him along. He's so darned stuck on himself. These Tonto dames have spoiled him, believe me."

"Was Cal there?"

"He rode in on horseback," replied Georgiana, with subtle change of tone. "He got there late. I was teaching some of the boys and girls how to toddle. Cal saw us—and he beat it pronto. What do you know about that?"

"I know a good deal, Georgie dear," replied Mary earnestly. "Suppose we have a long talk, not about Cal particularly, but about everything."

"Oh, Lord! Now you're going to hop me again," cried Georgiana. "Mary, I had enough of that back home. Mother was always after me—raving at me because I couldn't be like she used to be. She couldn't understand. Dad couldn't, either. None of the girls' parents could see that we are different. Times have changed. We won't be bossed. We're going to do what we want to do—and what we want makes all the old folks sick. Good night! That's one reason I was crazy to come out West. Mary, you were just wonderful at first. You seemed to sympathise, and even if you wouldn't stand for something or other you didn't rave about it. But lately you've been getting after me."

Miss Stockwell pondered a moment, while gazing down upon this rebellious little sister. She understood at last that Georgiana could never be driven. Such opposition invited disaster. Some other way must be found to influence her, if that were possible.

"No, dear, I'm not going to get after you again, as you call it," said Mary kindly. "But as we are going to live together and I'm going to take care of you till you are well and strong—isn't it fair that we have talks—understand each other's point of view?"

"Sure it is. I'll try. But I'm only a kid, and—and I'm going to raise—to have a good time or die. I'll be young only once. Can you understand that?"

"I think so," replied Mary, weighing her words, "It's youth. I had a feeling something like it when I was seventeen, enough for me to realise what you mean. But your attitude towards life is an exaggeration of that feeling. But you're not a fool, Georgie."

"No, it's because I'm wise that the old bunk doesn't go with me," replied the girl.

"By bunk do you mean religion, education, refinement, love and marriage, as they used to be?"

"No, I mean it always has been a man's world until *now*," declared Georgiana with spirit. "Why don't you get down to brass tacks? Your disapproval of me sifts down to just one thing—how I dress, talk, and act before men! That's all. There isn't any more. . . . Well, we kids have got it figured. We're wise. We see how our sisters and mothers and grandmothers have been buncoed by the lords of creation. By men! And we're not going to stand for it, see? We're going to do as we damn' please, and if they don't like us they can lump us. But good night—the proof is they like us *better*, if they don't know it."

Miss Stockwell strove to hide her consternation and to apply all her wits to the following of this twentieth-century maiden. It was useless to be shocked. Emotion certainly could not help this perplexing situation. If intelligence and logic and persuasive common sense could not reach Georgiana, what could? The child was bitter. Bitter at men! It was astounding. Yet Mary had to confess the justice of some of her convictions. There was a very wide range between her philosophy and Georgiana's. No doubt, however, was there that her sister had evolved a decided attitude towards life, and it bore the hard mark of materialism.

"Georgie, you were active in Sunday school when I left home," said Mary, taking another tack. "Have you kept it up?"

"Do you think I'm a dead one?" flashed Georgiana. "I quit church when I was fourteen, and that was a year longer than I wanted to go. The churches are back numbers, Mary. Nobody goes any more."

"Perhaps that accounts for a great deal," mused Mary. "Dawn of a godless age! . . . You are not to blame, perhaps, for losing interest in church work."

Mary bent her grave gaze upon this petulant, passionate little sister, and pondered silently for a moment for some inspiration. None seemed forthcoming. She was baffled. Yet if she talked naked truth, could she not approach this girl?

"Very well, let's get down to brass tacks, Georgie dear," she said brightly.

"Go to it," replied Georgie, with doubt in her big eyes.

"Do you love me?"

"Why, Mary—what a question!" burst out Georgiana in surprise. "Of course I love you."

"Would you stay out West of your own free will?"

"You bet. At least a long, long time—and maybe always if I

could cop out some nice rich rancher like Enoch. But you've your eagle eye on him."

"Georgie!" protested Miss Stockwell, blushing furiously. "How dare you?"

"Oh, come off, sis. Didn't you say something about brass tacks? You've fallen for Enoch, and if you had any sense he'd be eating out of your hand—pronto. Mary, he's a backward, slow sort of chap. He's afraid of you—thinks you're way above him. But he loves you and if you want him there's nothing to it but wedding bells."

Mary covered her hot face with her hands and strove for self-control.

"You're a dreadful, terrible little girl," she cried.

"Cut out the little, unless you mean size, sister dear," went on Georgiana. "Take it from me. I've seen Enoch watching you when you didn't see him. That's that. Now go on."

"Where was I? Oh, yes—you acknowledged you loved me and you said you would stay out West of your own accord. Well, so far so good," resumed Mary, gradually recovering from the break in her thought. "That means you stay indefinitely. Now, Georgie, do you realise you're a flirt?"

"That's getting too personal and I won't admit it!" replied the girl loftily.

"No matter, you are, whether you realise it or not. Coming back to your way of dressing, acting, talking—do you think it safe with a man like Bid Hatfield?"

"Safe! Good night, I should say it wasn't," retorted Georgiana, with startling candour. "He's a cave man. . . . But that's why I get such a kick out of it. Then he's a swelled-up mutt—thinks he's a lady-killer. It makes him so easy."

"You just denied you were a flirt," continued Mary.

"Certainly I denied it. I can know a thing without being that, can't I?"

"Well, if you're so wise, as you call it, and see that Hatfield is really a dangerous young man for a girl to trifle with—*and* if you love your sister well enough to spare her shame and unhappiness, how do you propose to trifle and spare—at once?"

"Simple as ABC, sister darling," responded Georgiana, with a dazzling smile. "I'm far too wise to be alone with Hatfield, away from company. Not on a bet! At that, I'm not afraid of the brute. I saw Tuck Merry make him crawl, and I'll bet I could, too. But for your sake, Mary, I'll not take any chances."

"Georgie, you're bewilderingly considerate," responded Mary, trying to hide her wonder and anger at this incredible young person. At the same time she wanted to laugh. How Georgiana disposed of risks! She certainly was no fool, whatever were her weaknesses.

"There are other men like Hatfield," went on Mary. "Because the Thurmans hate him he's in the limelight. But there are others like him. You'll meet them." .

"Yes. I *have* met a couple, and sized them up quick, believe me," replied Georgiana complacently.

"These boys do not *understand* you, Georgie dear. They're tremendously attracted. You're a new species. They're eager for your flirting. They can't see the line you draw between flirting—and worse. They wouldn't see it if you flashed it in their faces, which you'll certainly have to do. I *know* what most of them believe, and I can see trouble ahead. It's going to come when one of these wild Tonto boys falls genuinely in love with you. That will come, if it hasn't already."

"It has come, sister," replied the girl sullenly. "Your favourite Cal Thurman has gone off his head. He begged me—only three days ago—to *marry* him."

"Oh, Georgie, that is terrible," returned Mary, greatly troubled. "It is what I feared."

"Bah! It will do him good," flashed Georgiana. "He needs to be taken down a peg. . . . Cal was dandy at first. I liked him fine until he began to get serious, sort of bossy, and jealous. Then good night."

"Georgiana, I marvel at your vanity and stupidity. There's one boy you can't make a fool of. When he asked you to marry him he proved how fine and earnest he is. I'm ashamed of you."

"Why, for tripe's sake? I don't love him."

"But didn't you trifle with him, the same as with the others?" continued Mary scathingly. "Oh, I saw you flirt with him—outrageously."

Georgiana was unable to meet her sister's scornful and indignant gaze. She dropped her eyes a moment.

"Mary, we clashed right off the bat," she admitted. "Honest to God I liked him best—I do yet, to be on the level—but he made me sick."

"How?" queried Mary sharply.

"Why, about the other boys—and my clothes—and especially my roll-downs. The last time he hopped me about them I just stuck my foot up on the fence and rolled my stockings down *farther* right under his eyes."

"Oh, mercy, you little devil! . . . Then what did Cal do?"

"He beat it, mad as the devil," replied Georgiana, evidently thrilling at the remembrance. And he hasn't been near me since. But he was going to honey around last night, only that toddle stunt of mine made him sore again. I'll give him about another day. Then he'll crawl."

"Georgiana, this boy is fine, sweet, manly. He's much too good for you. You can't see his bigness. You're too set in your attitude—your silly, sentimental, vain obsession to get the best of men. Think over what I have said," concluded Mary, rising. "I shall not nag you. I love you dearly and am thinking only of your happiness. You *cannot* go on with this—this provocativeness. Not out here in this wild Tonto. It will land you on the rocks. These boys are uncouth, primitive, fun-loving and fight-loving, and as such they seem immensely interesting to you. But you don't understand their reserve force. I tell you they have a savageness in them, a strength born of this wilderness, a heritage from fierce, ruthless, natural men. And they have a code of honour that no woman can risk breaking."

Miss Stockwell loyally endeavoured to rise above her doubts of the good she might have accomplished by this blunt talk with Georgiana. On her own account, however, she felt easier in mind, for she had done what seemed her duty. The only sure result of it, apparently, was to make this strange materialistic girl not only more than ever set in her modern way, but it also piqued her vanity. Alas for poor Cal Thurman! Miss Stockwell had a foreboding of calamity.

Sunday was company day for the Thurmans; they had all gone away to visit relatives, leaving the teacher and her sister to get their own dinner. On former occasions this duty had devolved solely upon Mary. To-day, however, Georgiana answered to one of her caprices and insisted on getting the dinner herself. Forthwith she donned a dainty white apron, trimmed with lace, and sallied out to the kitchen.

"Sis, it's always wise for a girl to doll up, in a strange place like this," she exclaimed. "Somebody might run in. That's the dope and I'm giving you a hunch."

"Georgie, are you wearing the apron because you're going to do housework, or doing the housework because you want to exhibit the apron?" inquired Mary blandly.

"There you are with your hammer again," replied Georgiana good-humouredly. "It's a lead pipe you have me figured, Mary. You ought to be tickled if anything made me work."

Half an hour later Mary felt compelled to acknowledge that her sister's course in domestic science had not been wholly in vain.

"Georgie, you *might* make some man a good wife, after all," mused Mary.

"Sister, old dear, get this," retorted Georgiana. "I'll make a darn' sight better wife than the crocheting, old-fashioned, two-faced, mealy-mouthed tabby-cat you'd have me."

"Oh, so you have really condescended to imagine you might marry some day," laughed Mary, always amused at a different phase of Georgiana.

"I don't see how a girl can have a home and babies without a husband," complained Georgiana.

Just then a sharp clip-clop of trotting hoofs sounded outside on the hard road.

"That's Cal," spoke up Georgiana quickly. "Wonder what brings him home so early."

"You, probably," replied Mary dryly.

"Me? Nix. We're on the outs. Gee! if he comes in here he'll see our spiffy spread and I'll have to invite him to eat. Sis, you ask him."

"Of course I will. But how do you know it's Cal?" queried Mary, going to the window.

"I know his horse's gait."

Miss Stockwell looked out along the front of the house and then down the road to the corral. She saw a horseman leaning over to open the corral gate. When he straightened up she recognised Cal. His face was bloody. And there was yellow dirt on his blue jumper.

"Oh dear!" she cried, startled.

Georgiana jumped up, and running to the window peered out. She could not, however, see what Mary had seen, because Cal's back was turned and the high corral fence obstructed the view.

"What's the matter?" she queried.

"Cal's face was all bloody," replied the teacher in dismay.

"Was *that* all?" returned Georgiana, apparently without any particular interest. And returning to the table she began to pick at things. But her former appetite and pleasure appeared wanting. A little frown puckered her smooth brow, and her eyes shadowed thoughtfully. Mary divined that Georgiana was more interested than she cared to admit.

"Wonder if he'll come in," she mused presently.

"He certainly will not," declared Mary. "Don't you know the boy better than that?"

"Know Cal Thurman? I know him frontward and backward," answered Georgiana scornfully.

Miss Stockwell then began her own lunch without comment, yet she kept a covert eye upon her sister. Georgiana seemed to be silent, so as to listen the better. What she expected, however, failed to materialise. Presently she rose to go to the back door, which was open, and she looked out.

"Cal," she called instantly. No answer. "*Cal* . . . Oh, I see you. What's happened?"

"Aw, nothin' much," came the surly answer from the yard.

"You're all bloody," cried Georgiana.

"Nope. You can't see straight. This's only wet Tonto mud."

"Say, bo, you can't kid me," called the girl derisively. "What's happened?"

"I just ran into somethin'."

"Tell me!" ordered Georgiana impatiently. Then as he did not answer, she stepped out upon the porch. "Cal, please come here."

"What you want?" he growled.

"If you don't come here I'll come out there," she threatened.

Here Mary stepped to the doorway herself, and espied the young man now coming up to the porch. He held a blood-stained scarf to his cheek.

"You're a pretty-looking sight, I don't think," went on Georgiana as he mounted the steps. "Cal Thurman, you've been fighting again!"

"Is that all you wanted to say?" he inquired sarcastically, as he confronted her with troubled face and eyes of fire.

"I'll say a mouthful presently," she replied as she reached up to pull his hand and scarf away from his cheek. The action disclosed a rather ugly cut from which blood was oozing. "Oh, that's dreadful, Cal. So close to your eye! Let me bathe and bandage it for you."

She flew into the house with more of excited concern than Mary had ever seen in her before.

"Cal, have you been fighting again?" queried Mary gravely.

"You ought to see the other fellow," laughed Cal grimly.

"Who?"

"Never mind, teacher. But I didn't get licked."

Before Mary could question Cal further, Georgiana returned with her hands full of things, most noticeably a basin of water and a towel. Carefully they then bathed Cal's wound, which turned out to be a painful but superficial one, and endeavoured to bandage it. But Cal objected to being half blindfolded, so they managed to dress it with cotton and adhesive tape. Whereupon Georgiana drew back and surveyed him with proprietary interest.

"Cal, did you lick him?" she asked very curiously.

"Reckon it was fifty-fifty this time," returned Cal grimly.

"Who?"

"What's that to you, Georgiana?" asked Cal.

"I know. I can read your mind, Cal Thurman."

"Well, if you can, you sure look surprisin' cheerful an' sweet," he said with sarcasm.

That reply, or something Mary was not able to guess, rather took the pertness out of Miss Georgiana. She seemed at a loss for words. Then suddenly she had one of her bewildering changes and this time she became appealing.

"Cal, come in and see the wonderful lunch I got—all by myself. There's plenty for you, too. Won't you—just to please me? See how I really *can* do some useful work ! . . . Oh, wash those bloody, dirty hands—and let me brush you off. Looks as if you rolled in the road."

Presently she got him indoors and to the table, where Mary joined them. Georgiana did the serving, but she had grown quiet. Mary felt the need of easing this situation and she talked. Cal lost his sullenness and the air of grim satisfaction he had worn and slowly responded to Georgiana's charm. Mary imagined it a sort of burned-child-dreading-the-fire process Cal was going through. And indeed he kept dignity enough to make Mary certain that he was not a fool, however great his subjugation. It was her opinion that Georgiana did not make the progress of which she had boasted, and presently she divined that Georgiana saw she knew it. This apparently was gall and wormwood to the young lady. The arrival of some of the Thurmans broke up an amusing and rather embarrassing situation for Mary.

Later Cal, manifestly having watched for an opportunity, approached the teacher when she was walking alone in the yard.

"Come out with me a little—away from everybody," he begged.

"Why, surely, Cal—but won't Georgie be jealous?"

"Don't, for God's sake, tease me now. You're the only friend I have, except Tuck, an' I can't tell him everythin'. Teacher, are you on my side?"

"You mean in your—your trouble with Georgie?"

"Yes. I never spoke out to you before," he went on, breathing hard. "I wanted to wait. I thought I would get over it. . . . But I grew worse. An' to-day I fought a fellow who—who said somethin' about Georgie."

"Yes?" queried Miss Stockwell quietly, turning to look at Cal. He was pale, earnest, sombre.

"I—I can't tell you what he said," hurriedly went on Cal. "That doesn't matter. Only it—I couldn't stand it."

"Cal, aren't you taking Georgie too seriously?"

"Reckon I am. But I can't help that. I don't know what's happened to me, but it has happened. . . . Will you be on my side, teacher?"

"Indeed I will, Cal," she replied feelingly, with a hand going to his shoulder.

"Thanks. That'll help a lot," he said huskily.

"What do you want of me?"

"Lord! I don't know. Reckon just to feel you understand—so I can talk to you. I'm afraid to have you tell Georgie that—that the way she does—with the boys—is goin' to raise hell here in the Tonto. I'm afraid. She's so darn' clever. She'll know I've been talkin' to you."

"Cal, I gave her that very talk to-day," returned Miss Stockwell earnestly. "And I told her straight out that she could not go on with her flirting."

"Flirting. . . . You said that word once before. . . An' what did she say?"

"She laughed in my face, made light of my accusation, and simply could not see anything dangerous in you Tonto boys."

"She calls us boobs," he rejoined. "She said if there were hay in the Tonto we'd be hayseeds."

"Oh, Cal, I'm just as helpless as you are," cried the teacher. "I'm worse off. I have to take care of her. I have to stand it. I have to go on praying and hoping. She's—she's a little devil. But she's my sister, and, Cal, I love her. . . . You can turn your back on her any day. I'd not blame you if you did."

"Can I, though? I've done it, but no use. That's the wrong way. . . . Tell me, teacher, tell me the *right* way with Georgie."

"Cal, I don't know—unless you go back on her. That's what fetches most girls."

"Reckon it'd never fetch Georgiana May. Besides, I can't go back on her. I can bluff it, but she knows. It doesn't work. Then that makes her worse. . . . Honest, teacher, these three weeks have been three years to me."

"Cal, have you made up your mind that you *must* go on trying to make Georgie like you?"

"Teacher, she *does* like me," he replied quickly. "I know. That's the hell of it. I feel somethin' I can't explain."

"Well, must you go on trying to make her like you more?"

"Reckon that's just about where I am now."

"Well, then, you've made a decision," responded the teacher. "Live up to it. Do your best. I fear Georgie isn't worth it. I'm afraid you're in for bitter disappointment. But if you must go on, why, do it with all your heart. You're in earnest, Cal, which is more than any of these other fellows are. Don't be ashamed of that. Don't mind their tormenting—the tricks and jokes. Faint heart never won fair lady."

"My mind was workin' it out a little that way," he said. "To-day I persuaded father to let me homestead the Rock Spring Mesa."

"Cal—you don't mean it!"

"Reckon I do. An' to-morrow, maybe to-night—if these boobs give me a chance—I'll tell Georgiana. Wonder what she will say."

"She will laugh, of course, and make all kinds of fun of you. But I shouldn't let it bother me."

"Teacher, nothin' is goin' to bother me after this but the one thing I'm afraid of."

"And what's that?" demanded Miss Stockwell suddenly tense.

He lowered his dark head, and crushed a twig in a sudden powerful clasp.

"If Georgie keeps up her—her flirtin'—as you called it—there's goin' to be hell. *We* don't savvy that. There are girls here who make eyes an' hold hands an' kiss—that sort of fun, you know. It's natural, I reckon, an' it often leads to courtin'. But that's not what Georgie does. She called that 'kindergarten stuff.' "

Miss Stockwell had no reply for this. She was striving to be ready for anything.

"Teacher, I looked in the dictionary to see what flirtin' meant," went on Cal, deadly earnest. "It said 'triflin' at love'. . . . That says a lot an' it comes somewhere near Georgie's way. But it doesn't hit it square. Reckon it's beyond me yet. But I know this sure—if she keeps it up there'll be blood spilled."

"Oh, Cal—dear wild boy—what are you saying?" implored Miss Stockwell. It was sorrow rather than shock that actuated her. In fact she was not shocked.

"I'm sayin' a lot, I know," he concluded, "an' I feel better for it. If I only dared tell Enoch! . . . Let's go back now, teacher. I'm thankin' you for your promise to be on my side."

Cal took the lecture from Tuck Merry with meekness. He realised he had been too ambitious and had relied too soon upon the dearly earned experience Tuck was daily giving him.

"Buddy, you would have licked that guy all to pieces if you hadn't lost your temper and forgot," Merry said. "Soon as he poked you one on the beak and hurt you, why, you blew up. At that, you gave him as good as he gave you. But I was not satisfied. You forgot the hooks I've been trying to teach you. It doesn't make any difference how hard anyone hits you or where—you just take it and smile."

"Aw, Tuck, that's impossible," burst out Cal. "How can you smile when you're hurt awful? Why, whenever you give me what you call the 'nose jab' or the 'tooth rattler' or the 'belly zam' I'm ready to scream an' commit murder."

"Buddy, I don't care how it hurts—you've got to hide it," went on Tuck. "Whenever a guy sees or thinks he can't hurt you then he's licked. But you're doing fair and I'll back you presently against any of these boys. You've got some punch, believe me, and soon as you learn to place it where you want, and get your footwork better, you'll lick the stuffings out of Tim or Wess."

"Tuck, it'll only be fun to lick them," said Cal, with a grim laugh. "But I might as well tell you I'm layin' for Bid Hatfield."

"Buddy, I had you figured," returned Tuck seriously. "That guy has twenty pounds of weight on you, which is too much handicap when the other fellow can scrap. He's older, too. Hatfield strikes me as being a bad customer in a rough and tumble. You see, he'd never stand up and fight. And I'm doubtful about your holding him off. Better let me spoil his handsome mug."

"Tuck, I'm goin' to try, just the moment you let me," returned Cal.

"*I'm* a-rarin' to go, as Wess says," replied Tuck. "Here I've been for over three weeks with a million chances to take a smack at one of these Arizona riders. My natural good disposition is apt to sour presently if you don't tip me the wink."

They had been out at their secret covert in the brush where

they kept the boxing-gloves and sand-bag and where they repaired every day or so for Cal's instructions. From the very first Tuck had been pleased with the way Cal could thump the swinging heavy sack of sand. But his pupil took rather slowly to the feints and dodges and tricks of boxing. Cal wanted to wade right in and swing wildly, and when he did this, Tuck would halt him with some swift and painful blows.

They parted at the gate of the orchard, Tuck wending his way down the lane towards the sawmill, while Cal thoughtfully proceeded on to the pasture to get one of his horses. All the horses except his had been driven to the corrals, and it so happened that the first one he could catch was his pinto Blazes. Of late he had taken more of a liking to this rather wild little bronco, for the reason, no doubt, that Georgiana May Stockwell had preferred Blazes to any other of the Thurman stock. Blazes was really too spirited and dangerous for any girl new to the ranges. This fact, however, had made Georgiana all the more determined to ride him. She had tried twice. The first time she had succeeded so well that she was elated, but the second time Blazes had bucked her off. Cal had vowed he would not let her try again, and, strangely, this was not so much because he feared she would be hurt, as because he got an amazing degree of satisfaction out of the fact that she had taken to coaxing him. More than that, Blazes had suddenly leaped into peculiar favour with the boys. Before Georgiana's advent he could not have sold Blazes or traded him for the meanest mustang on the ranch. As it was now, Cal was always receiving flattering offers for Blazes.

Upon approaching the high coral fence, he was amazed and somewhat disconcerted to espy Georgiana astride the topmost pole. She wore her riding-suit and an old sombrero and a red scarf around her neck. One glance at her made him aware that she was waylaying him. His heart quickened, and then it sank. For three days, ever since he had come home with the cut on his face and she had bathed it, she had been bewilderingly nice and friendly and sweet. This demeanour had roused him to meet her with apparent indifference and aloofness, but he was not true to his real feelings, and he was afraid she would discover it.

"Howdy, Cal," she drawled. "I reckon you shore read my mind this mawnin'."

"That so? Well, I did it without thinkin'," he replied, and he halted before her.

"Cal, you're a peach to fetch Blazes for me to ride," she said with a dazzling smile.

"But I haven't done anythin' of the kind," he rejoined bluntly.

"Aren't you going to Tonto Canyon?" she asked.

"Who told you?"

"Your dad. He told me he was sending you to see if there were any cattle ranging the ridges on this side. He knew I was crazy to see the Tonto and he said I could go."

"Oh, he did! Well, I reckon that doesn't make any difference to me," replied Cal, eyeing her coolly. The prospect of taking her on the long, hard ride to the Tonto was indeed an alluring one.

"Cal, please take me," she begged.

"No, I won't," he replied, turning away from those blue eyes.

"Oh, Cal, why not?"

"It's a long, hard ride, an' not for a tenderfoot."

"But I'll *always* be a tenderfoot if *you* don't roughen me up," she protested.

Cal was not deaf to the subtle content of this speech, and he had a miserable consciousness that, whether it was true or not, it possessed some strange power to hold him.

"Georgiana, can't you be on the level?" he asked plaintively.

"Why, Cal, I am on the level."

"You only want to ride Blazes. If it weren't for that, you'd have some of the other boys take you to the Tonto—an' make a rider out of you."

"Cal, I'd rather ride with you or go anywhere if—if you'd only——"

"What?" he interrupted swiftly, turning to look at her again.

"Well, be on the level, as you asked—if you'd just be a good pal and cut the mush."

"You mean—stop makin' love to you?" he queried stiffly.

She nodded, and her manner struck Cal as being wistful. But she had as many moods as the winds.

"I have stopped," he declared.

"Yes—you've stopped that and everything. You don't see I'm on earth. It's all or nothing with you, Cal Thurman."

"Aw! I guess you hit it then," sighed Cal, with deep breath.

"Cal, give me a chance to learn to *like* you, can't you?" she retorted with swift change. "Why, I've never been rushed that way before! You're too deadly in earnest. . . . I want to have some fun."

This was one of the frequent instances when Georgiana bewildered him with what seemed a natural and sweet wholesomeness.

She was practical, and, after all, she was only a child.

"If you don't like me now you never will," returned Cal, with resignation. "An' I guess you never will."

"I *do*. I just said 'like' because I didn't want to use the—the other word."

Cal realised he was lost, yet he had the impulse to pretend one moment more. Without another word or look he started again to lead Blazes into the corral.

"Do you want me to hate you?" she shot at him hotly.

"Yes—if you can't do the other," he retorted.

When he got inside the corral gate there she was confronting him, and it seemed that the brown of her comely face had slightly paled.

"Cal, you know Tim will be crazy to take me," she said.

"Sure I know that."

"Well, I'll *ask* him unless you take me. And I've never deliberately asked anything of him or the boys—except you. I'd *rather* go with you."

"Georgie!" he exclaimed helplessly. "If I could only believe you!"

"I'll prove it. Ride Blazes yourself, and give me the scraggiest cayuse in the outfit."

Cal could hold out no longer. That last speech, coupled with the fact that Tim was sauntering over, leading a saddled mustang, proved his undoing.

"You win, Georgie, an' I'll let you ride Blazes," he said, throwing the halter to her, and he made off towards the shed to fetch a saddle.

"Mawnin', Cal. Looks like you got first prize at a rodeo," drawled Tim maliciously.

"Howdy, Tim," was Cal's short reply. Then he heard Tim address the girl:

"Mawnin', Miss Georgie. Shore am tickled thet you're ridin' with me to-day."

"Guess again, Tim," was Georgiana's arch reply.

Wind was all Cal could hear, but when he got to the saddle-rack and turned to look, he saw Tim leaning close to Georgiana, evidently unable to see when he was refused.

Cal picked out his lighter saddle and, carrying it back to Blazes, he swung it in place and tightened the cinches.

"Wal, I'm shore glad I'm ridin' down Tonto way this mawnin'," Tim was saying.

"You're ridin' Mescal Ridge," spoke up Cal. "That's where father said you were to go. An' if you come belly-achin' along with me, I'll tell him."

Tim swung round sharply. "See heah, boy, do you want the other side of yore face mussed up? Thet there word you used is offensive to me."

"Ahuh!" ejaculated Cal tartly.

Tim looked belligerent then, and there might have been trouble had not Georgiana come laughingly between them. "You fellows make me tired. Some day I'll call your bluffs and make you fight."

"Wal, Miss Georgie, when you do there'll be only two blows struck—one when I slam Cal an' the other when he hits the ground. . . . Shore I hope you have a nice ride, but I'm gamblin' Blazes will spill you to-day. He looks mean an' he shore hates the brush." With that parting shot and an elaborate doffing of his sombrero, Tim turned away.

"Cal, was Tim just kidding me?" queried Georgiana dubiously.

"Reckon he was. Blazes seems in fine temper to-day. Now you coax him an' feed him some sugar, an' lead him out into the grass before you mount. Then if he bucks you off you'll light soft. I'll go get my horse."

Before Cal caught his other horse, Georgiana came loping down on Blazes and helped corner the bay. She was radiant with joy. The pinto appeared unusually amenable and pranced around with her. Georgiana looked well on a horse and she was learning to ride.

"Georgie, run the edge off him," said Cal. "Lope up to the end of the pasture, then cut loose an' make him run back."

"Oh, Cal! Really? You *mean* it?" she flashed.

"Sure I mean it. But remember all I told you an' hang on."

As she wheeled with a little cry of excitement and delight to urge the willing pinto to a lope, Cal watched her critically. Indeed she was improving. She kept her seat in the saddle very well. Upon reaching the fence, she turned back and let Blazes go. Cal was now unable to watch her critically. He could only gaze with a strange pleasure the sight of her gave him. Blazes could run, and at this gait was easy to ride. Georgiana's golden curls shone bright in the wind. As she neared Cal he saw her face as never before, and something warm and splendid swept over him. He had found a way to make her happy. Blazes came tearing down on a dead-level run, and Cal saw it was the fence more than the girl that stopped him.

"Oh—that was—grand," trilled Georgiana, glowing and dishevelled. "Why didn't you—ever let me—race him before?"

"You're learnin' to ride, Georgie," he replied, stirred by her gladness. "You've improved a lot since you rode with me last."

"Am I? Gee! I hope you mean it. I've tried hard enough, good-ness knows. But none of the boys have horses like Blazes. I feel easier on him."

"Blazes sure has an easy gait," replied Cal. "It'll be a tough day on you, Georgie, an' you'll need to take some lunch."

"I put some up—myself—enough for both of us," she said.

"Ahuh! You did? Made sure you were goin'?" he queried.

"Of course I knew you'd take me. You've never refused me any-thing, even when I was meanest."

"Don't bank too much on that," he said soberly. "Well, you ride down to the lower pasture gate, an' I'll catch up with you. Give Blazes a drink—— An' say, where'd you leave that lunch?"

"It's hanging on the corral gate," she replied. "Don't forget it."

Cal located the khaki bag containing the lunch, and as he lifted it off the fence he smiled to feel its weight. What a sly little minx she was! She knew from past experience what a wonderful treat it was for a rider to have a share of such lunch out in the open. Saddling up, he mounted and rode by Wess and Arizona with only a casual nod.

"Hey! Think you're some punkins, don't you?" called Arizona jealously.

"Cal, kiss her for me," added Wess in good-natured maliciousness.

It was such remarks as this last that Cal found hard to endure. His cousins and comrade riders did not mean anything vicious, and any one of them would have been quick to resent an insult to Georgiana. But the implication somehow roused Cal's sensitive jealousy. It somehow cast a slur upon the girl—gave her a shallow and light character that hurt him.

Cal bit his tongue to hold back a reply to Wess, and riding out of the corral into the pasture, he took to the trail along the fence and soon reached the lower gate where Georgiana was wait-ing for him.

"Let's go," she cried gaily.

"Can you trust the lunch with me?" he inquired as he bent to open the gate.

"Cal, I'd trust you with anything," she said.

"Even yourself?"

"Well, that's a hard one," she replied. "Sometimes you are a cross, jealous, mean boy—and dangerous, too. Not that I'm afraid of you! . . . But I guess if I ever wanted to trust myself to any-body I'd pick you."

"Ahuh! I've a hunch that's more of a slam than a compliment."

"Calvin Thurman, you don't have any idea what a great compliment that is—coming from *me*."

"I'm growin' wise, Georgiana. . . . Well, it's ride some now. This is a bad trail. Follow me, but not too close, an' do what I do. If Blazes slips on the rocks, jerk your feet out of the stirrups quick. An' if he falls, throw yourself off away from him."

"Oh, is that all?" queried Georgiana, with a laugh utterly devoid of concern.

Cal had seen Western girls used to horses ride down this rocky ravine and do it with a full appreciation of the bad places. He hoped Georgiana would have good fortune, but he was somewhat worried. There was no telling what a horse might do in unexpected situations. There was hardly any sense in spoiling the girl's pleasure by suggesting things that might not happen. Blazes was a sure-footed pony, not easily frightened or given to shying, and considering that he was carrying a light rider and one who would not spur or hurt him, he was to be trusted. Then Cal had another argument in his resignation—a feeling he tried to discountenance, and it was that if Georgiana was destined to have an accident, which seemed inevitable, he wanted it to happen while she was with him.

Once Cal turned to Georgiana, intending to ask her if she did not like this place. But the question would have been superfluous. To the girl's excitement had been added something of intense and dreamy appreciation. Cal had longed to have her love his country, and now there seemed some hope of it. He did not break the spell until he espied a flock of wild turkeys crossing the ridge ahead.

"What! Wild turkeys? Why, they're tame," she cried.

"Sure they're tame, but they're wild, all right," he laughed.

"Like we had for dinner that Sunday?"

"Ahuh. An' I noticed you ate some."

"Um-m-m! I sure fell for wild turkey, Cal. . . . Oh, there's a gobbler! How perfectly enormous!"

"He's not a big one. Wait till I show you some of the whoppers up on the Rim."

"Cal, I'm a-waitin' very patiently for you to do a lot of things you promised. You're making good to-day, but *when* do I go turkey-hunting with you?"

"After the fall round-up. We'll be ridin' a lot until then. You see, it's rough country an' takes hard work to find the cattle."

"You promise to take me?" she persisted.

"Yes—if you promise not to go huntin' with any of the other boys," he replied hesitatingly.

"Cal, I don't need to promise that."

He pondered over this reply. Like many of her speeches, it was open to question, yet he could not help taking this one personally. Georgiana had a trick of making him feel that he was the exceptional one. This was a sweet balm to his wounded feelings. But it held a bitter drop. Others of the Tonto boys had remarked about this peculiar trait of Georgiana's in their own interest. Suddenly Cal turned to ask:

"Georgie, have you ever ridden off the road with any of the boys?"

"No. Mary laid down the law and said I could not go with any boy but you. Aren't you flattered?"

"Would you disobey her?" asked Cal bluntly.

"Not in that. I hate to be bossed, Cal, but I know where to draw the line."

Cal did not voice another query that stirred him just then. This girl seemed most contradictory and amazing. To-day she seemed to be wholly good to Cal. Presently the trail took a sharp turn between two sycamores so close together that a rider had to be quick and skilful to save his knees. Georgiana slipped her left knee back out of danger, but she was not quick enough with her right and struck it hard. Cal heard the thump.

"Oh—damn!" cried Georgiana. "Oh-h! I hit my knee!"

Cal did not need to be told, nor did he need to see the sudden wrinkling of her smooth, happy face, or the starting tears. That sound of her knee in contact with the tree had been enough. Any rider knew that sound. Like any other rider, too, he had to laugh.

"Georgie, I told you to look out when you had to go between trees."

"You're laughing!" she exclaimed in surprise. "Cal Thurman, you're a brute sometimes, I just feel it. . . . To laugh! I tell you that hurt like—like——"

"You bet it hurt," interrupted Cal. "That's why I laughed. Besides, it sort of tickled me to find out you are human."

"Thanks, Cal. That'll help some," she replied.

Below the sycamore grove the trail split, the right branch continuing down the gully and the left sheering up into the brush-covered foothills above which towered the vast green cliff-dotted slope.

Cal had ridden this cattle trail since he was a mere boy just able to climb astride a horse. He knew every foot of it, and many a time he had descended it in the pitchy darkness of night. Like all the trails and one other distinctive feature of his boyhood home, it was something that now seemed strangely dear to him. It had been a part of his life. Riding the ranges was his chief occupation. And he was sorely puzzled now at the realisation of how strangely and deeply he wanted this Eastern girl to share something of his feeling for this wild, steep trail.

"Good night! Do you expect me to climb that?" queried Georgiana aghast.

"Sure. Why, this's nothin' much, Georgie—compared to the Rim or Diamond Butte."

"If I make good here, will you take me to climb those places?" she asked, with eyes dark and flashing on his.

"Ahuh," replied Cal, and his short affirmative in no way attested to his thrills.

"I'll do it or die."

So Cal led on with these last words ringing in his ears. This girl had feeling. She would come to love the Tonto. He felt what he could not analyse. From the Bench the trail slanted up into the brush and disappeared. Cal's horse crashed into the thick scrub oak and broke through, while Cal bent low over the saddle. Looking back, he could not see Georgiana, but he heard her horse. When he reached the turn where the trail took its first zigzag, he saw her emerge from the thicket, sombrero awry, her blouse covered with leaves and bits of brush, and her face rosily radiant. Her eyes met his glance, and he saw she was now unconscious of herself. She was revelling in this new experience. He rode on then, and never before had the dry fragrance of the brush been so sweet or the dust of the trail so endurable, or the stings of the thorns somehow pleasurable. At every zigzag turn he halted his horse to let him catch his breath, and Georgiana would ride up the slant below him to do the same. She was out of breath, too. Her bosom heaved. And when she removed her sombrero he could see her hair damp on her brow. Then Cal reached a steeper ascent where the trail led up over rough granite. Here were many sharp, white marks made by the iron-shod hoofs of horses. Cal bade her dismount and walk here, as he did. But once beyond this place, he mounted again, intending to ride the whole of the remaining ascent. There were places where he thrilled even in his fear for Georgiana, and dared not look back. He should not have let her ride up such treacherous steps and turns. But somehow he was stern and dogged about it. She never uttered a single cry, and there were times when she appeared to be in difficulties. Cal noticed that she had sense enough to let Blazes choose the way, and she confined herself to holding on, a matter not at all easy for a tenderfoot.

Long as was that slope, it seemed only too short to Cal. The last ascent was a lengthy one, and Cal's horse, having warmed to the climb, surmounted it far in advance of Georgiana's. When he turned to look down from the top, she was just emerging from a wall of green to enter upon that last straight piece of trail. She waved her gauntleted hand to him, and her call pealed upwards. He watched her closely while she climbed the remaining distance, conscious that something tremendous was being decided for him. The moment seemed full, and the great slope of grey and green held only the bright moving figure of the girl.

At last she reached his level.

"Somewhat frazzled—but still in the—ring!" she panted out joyously.

There were black brush-marks on her face and a bloody scratch on her chin. She had jammed the sombrero on backwards, and from under its rim straggled locks of tangled golden hair. The top button of her blouse had been torn off, exposing the brown and white of her neck. The sleeves likewise had suffered sundry tears. Altogether, she appeared a considerably dishevelled young lady. Then Cal looked again into her face—looked keenly this time. He saw a light there—or was it in her eyes? And quickly he averted his gaze.

"You—sure did—well," he said awkwardly, in the grip of his feeling. "I'll tell you now—that's no trail for a tenderfoot girl."

"Then I've graduated?" she queried.

"Well, hardly that, but you've advanced a grade. . . . Georgie, did you like that long, hard ride?"

"Cal, you'll never believe me," she replied, with impulsive earnestness, "but I'll say that's my idea of a great time."

Then, with a strange prophetic knocking at his heart, he bade her look down at the beautiful Green Valley Ranch, shining in the morning sunlight, at the blue smoke curling from the log-house, at the apple orchards red with fruit, at the white, winding road that led on past the old sawmill to disappear in the heavy timber beyond. He showed her the brown speck that was the school-house where her sister was teaching, and the glistening ribbon of water that was Tonto Creek, and lastly the billowy slopes of timber that led up to the noble Rim, standing up gold-barred and black-fringed, to face the sun.

Two hours of riding, much of it down rock-strewn trails, brought Cal and his riding comrade to the divide. Here began the long-sloping bare ridges and the shallow heads of canyons that, inclining endlessly down, grew more rugged and deeper and rockier, to break off suddenly into the black chasm of the Tonto.

"Oh, how barren and wild!" exclaimed Georgiana. "I expected it all green, because you said it was cattle country. There's no grass —nothing level—all seems so terribly rough. Surely we can't ride down there. Can we?"

"You bet we can. Yes, it's hard goin', but cattle live in those canyons an' there's where we chase them, rope them, brand them."

"No!"

"Sure is. I'll tell you, Georgie, it's really rougher than it looks, but it's also better for cattle than it looks. There's water in the canyons an' those grey, bare spots are grass. Look. See that old white-faced bull standin' down there lookin' up at us. An' there's three steers lower down in the brush. Georgie, that's what I'm ridin' this ridge for—to get a line on where the cattle are. They're stragglin' all over an' it takes a lot of lookin' to locate them. An' when it comes to roundin' them up—well, it's what you call 'good night!' "

Georgiana gazed everywhere but the right place, and had to have the cattle pointed out to her. It pleased Cal to see she was interested.

"What do you know about that!" she exclaimed. "A few white dots—faces of cattle—in all that awful up-and-down country. It's so different from what I imagined. I thought a cattle ranch a wonderful level green plain, dotted with cows and calves—and the rest of the cattle folks—and water and shady trees. Gee! it takes some guy to be a rider, doesn't it?"

"Ahuh! If you mean a fellow not afraid of long hours, hard ridin', bad cows an' steers——"

"Bad cows? Are there really such?"

"Georgie, the wild old cows with calves are sure bad. They will chase a rider off the map. I've seen many a spill, an' some gored horses, sorry to say."

The girl became thoughtful, and swept her gaze from the first shallow depths of the canyon, where the cattle were grazing, to the far-distant, dark depths of the Tonto, and beyond to the great domed, black mass of Diamond Butte, and to the wonderful lines of ridges sloping endlessly away from it down out of sight into the basin.

"If I were a man, I'd love such a life," mused Georgiana.

That remark was so compelling that Cal had to fight to hold back the news of his intention to give the pinto Blazes to her.

"Well, Georgiana, I have work to do," said Cal finally. "The three canyons to look over, an' that'll take ridin'. But when I leave the trail to ride off a little ways here an' there you can stop to rest."

"Let me ride everywhere with you," she said.

"Nope. You'll get enough before the day's over. Besides, there'll be places where you can't follow me. Come on now."

"Say, Cal—don't forget that swell lunch I put up," she returned.

"Ahuh! I thought you'd remind me of that. But it's hours before we can eat."

"Hours? . . . Look here, boy, I can't live on scenery."

"Georgie, the longer we save that lunch, the better we'll enjoy it."

"I suppose you think I can live on love," she pouted.

"No, Georgiana. I've had wild dreams about you, but never any as wild as that," he replied, with a steady look at her.

"Ahuh!" she retorted, imitating him again. "All the same, my wise friend, I *could* live on it if *I wanted to*."

Cal rode on, certain that the day would be lost, and perhaps something of its charm, if he continued to bandy words with Georgiana. So calling for her to follow, he trotted his horse down the trail. At a point below, where the depression of the ridge formed what riders called a saddle, he turned off to the left and surveyed the ocean, dusty patches of ground until he found a well-defined cattle trail leading down over the ridge into the next canyon. Cattle tracks showed pointing in each direction, and the fresher ones were headed away from him. To his keen eyes this was an indication that cattle from the canyon to his left were watering in the canyon on his right. That was all he needed to learn about this immediate locality. He rode on then with eyes searching the slopes for the white and red of the Thurman cattle. These were few and far between, and after a mile of riding he knew the scarcity of cattle sign meant that grass was scant this season on these mescal ridges. The blades of the soap-weed had been nipped, and likewise the low scrubby oak brush. His cattle browsed on leaves when they could not find grass.

Riding to and fro across this slowly-descending, league-long ridge, he used up all of the rest of the morning hours and some besides, and frequently he had to leave Georgiana alone for longer than he liked. But he did not shirk the task given him.

"Believe me, Cal, you're the first fellow who ever took me out and left me to entertain myself," complained the girl.

"Georgie, you came with me," he protested. "I've got to do my work."

"Oh, it doesn't matter—only I imagined you were crazy about me," she said indifferently.

Cal could only stare, not uncertain how to take her, but far from knowing what to do. As often before, his silence worked better than any words.

He led on then, down a steep slope littered with loose rocks where the horses found hard going, down through mescal and oak, and over patches of bleached grass, to the wall of the Tonto.

"If I ever want to jump over the top into no man's land, lead me here!" ejaculated Georgiana. And that was all the tribute she paid the Tonto.

Cal's observant eye noted that she did not dismount without a little sign of lameness. He tied the horses and then, possessing himself of the lunch-bag, he led Georgiana to a flat rock, where a low piñon made shade, and the drop was sheer.

That half-hour, during which they dispatched the lunch to the last morsel, was the pleasantest and happiest he had ever spent with Georgiana. She was just nice—not teasing, not provocative, not lofty or strange or haughty, not coquettish, not anything but a hungry, wholesome girl, unconsciously glad to be alive, to be there in this wonderful place.

"Cal, you're growing thoughtful," observed Georgiana.

"Ahuh! Would you like to know my thoughts?"

She gave him a comprehensive little glance, and then shook her head dubiously.

"I reckon not—if they are the same as your looks."

"Georgie, I'm goin' to homestead the Rock Spring Mesa," he declared bluntly, without regard for her wishes.

"You told me that once before," she said. "But you didn't explain what it meant. . . . Homestead. The word's a new one on me, but it sounds nice."

"Listen," he began earnestly. "In unsettled parts of the West the government encourages homesteaders. Now a homesteader picks out one hundred and sixty acres of likely ground that he can clear an' cultivate. The better soil an' water, of course, the better his chances to develop a good ranch. He builds a log-cabin an' a corral. The government requires him to do so much work on this place—so much improvement a year for three years. Then if he proves up, as they call it, he is granted a patent for the land an' owns it. That entitles him to certain range rights. He can run so many cattle on an' near his ranch. . . . An' that's what I'm goin' to do."

"You'll be a regular pioneer," replied Georgiana dreamily. "I read something once—some book about a pioneer girl. Believe me, she sure had it coming to her."

"What? Work, loneliness, struggle?"

"I'll say so. . . . Cal, when you stay on your 'homestead' will you be by yourself?"

"I should smile. I'll have to cook my own meals, do the washin', chop wood, milk the cow, plough an' sow an' cut an' haul."

"Good night!" She regarded him with a new curious thoughtfulness, as if she were seeing another phase of him.

"Cal, don't be offended, but you're no country jake, no boob, as I call them. You're a smart fellow and you could do well in the city. Why don't you do that?"

"Long ago, Georgie, I had my temptations," he replied dreamily. "Many boys go to the cities, an' none I ever knew did well. I love the open country—the lonely places. My people were all pioneers. It's in me. An' let me tell you, Georgie, the pioneer, the rancher, the farmer are in my eyes the real Americans. There would never have been any cities, or any business men, if the pioneers had not blazed the trails an' opened up the wild country."

"Cal, I'm what they call the twentieth-century girl, the modern flapper," responded Georgiana, with sudden bitterness. "We're a queer type, so I read. We won't be bossed. We're bound to have our own way. We defy all conventions. We're going to do as men have always done. We're going to be free."

Pondering that for a long moment, Cal finally replied: "Georgie, I don't understand what you mean, an' I don't want to argue with you about it. But I'll say this. I *know* the things you mentioned are not the *big* things of life. If the girls of your kind are all thinkin' that way, it'll be bad for the future. Women are to make homes."

"Listen to him!" exclaimed Georgiana. "Make homes? Yes—for the lords of creation—for men. Cal, that's the same old talk, the same old bunk."

"Bunk?" echoed Cal, suddenly stirred. "It's nothin' of the kind. Everybody has to have a home or—or else . . . Georgie, all the wild animals have dens, burrows, caves—homes. An' they have mates. That's all they live for. Now if you women—you *new* women—don't intend to make homes for men, what's to become of us?"

"You can search me, Cal," she replied, with a gay laugh. "They'll all have to 'homestead,' like you're going to."

Cal gazed silently down into the depths of the canyon. Her words jarred on him. They seemed flippant. They were somehow false. She did not know what she was talking about. He could not reason out the explanation for his convictions, but he felt their truth. How long had Tonto Canyon yawned there under the blue sky of day and the dark mantle of night? How many races of men had come and gone since this gorge had been made? Times changed, the peoples changed with them, but the fundamental relation of man and woman would never change.

"I'm sorry if I hurt your feelings," resumed Georgiana presently. "Cal, maybe I'm not so rotten as I seem."

"I think you're all right," replied Cal soberly. "Well, if we want to get back to the ranch by sundown, we'd better be rustlin'."

"Oh, it's so nice here. Will you fetch me again?"

"Sure. Next week we round up the cattle here an' drive them to the big pasture. That'll be worth seein'. But you've got to be sensible an' careful now, an' do as you're told. Some of these wild cattle are bad."

"I promise. And will you let me ride Blazes again?"

"Well—after to-day, I reckon you'll not have to ask me that," he said with an air of mystery.

"Cal! Do you mean I'm no longer a tenderfoot?" she flashed eagerly.

"No, I wasn't thinkin' of that."

"What then? You're so—so queer."

"Reckon Blazes won't be mine after to-day."

"Oh, Cal—you wouldn't sell Blazes or trade him to *anybody!* When I love him so!"

"I sure wouldn't."

"Say, boy, you're talking riddles," she protested, and she sat up and got to her knees and confronted him with earnest, shining, doubtful eyes.

The moment was pregnant with both joy and pang for Cal. Something had been decided for him. And never had the Tonto so filled him with its peace and promise, or seemed so sad and lonely, and strong with its sense of ages.

"Georgie, after to-day Blazes will not belong to me," he said, with eyes steady on hers.

"Why?" she queried, quick as a flash.

"Because—this mornin' I gave him to you."

Georgiana gazed at him blankly. It took a second for that wholly unexpected fact to penetrate. Her eyes opened very wide, her lips parted.

"Gave—him—to—me?" she echoed breathlessly.

"I sure did. Blazes—with saddle, blanket, bridle—is yours."

"Oh, Cal! *Mine?*"—she cried rapturously.

"Sure is," replied Cal, beginning to shake. Her face had changed as if by magic. If he had expected to see it joyous, his imagination had failed him. Smile, flash, light—these were ecstatic, and as he gazed spellbound by her loveliness, the golden rosy radiance paled to a singular degree.

"You darling!" she cried, and she bent swiftly to kiss him full on the lips.

Cal sustained a shock. For an instant all around him seemed to reel and his heart laboured high in his breast. Presently the green canopy of the friendly piñon became as formerly, and the Tonto yawned beneath him, deep, lonely, wild, with its murmuring waters. And the everlasting rocks seemed to share something of life and eternity with him. Georgiana had flown to where the horses were tied, and Cal could now hear her laughing and crying out her joy of her precious possession. Then he heard her quick, light footsteps returning. He got up and turned to face her.

"Cal, I'll say you're a regular fellow," she said, with hand outstretched, and she came right up to him where he now leaned against the big branch of the piñon.

Cal took her in his arms. She did not draw back, rather leaned to him, with glad face uplifted and the little gloved hand going to his shoulder.

"Georgie—you shouldn't—have kissed me," he said huskily.

"Why not? You sure deserved it. And I *wanted* to. . . . I'll do it again if you think it wasn't enough."

"I didn't want thanks," he replied unsteadily. "I just wanted to make you happy."

"You succeeded, boy, and I'll never forget this day."

"But, Georgie—I—I love you," he burst out.

"Well—all the more reason I should kiss you," she declared.

"No. No . . . unless you love me."

"Of course I love you, Cal—that is—I think——"

Cal clasped her tight, lifting her slender form, and bent to her upturned, glowing face. A bewilderment of sudden joy overwhelmed him and his restraint went to the winds. He kissed her hair, her cheeks, and then her mouth. And realisation of her response suddenly made him blind—strong—rough in the expression of his love. But he knew when she cried out in laughing protest and forcibly drew back from him. Still, she did not wholly slip out of his arms.

"Cal! You don't want a homestead. You want a cave. You're some little caveman, I'll tell the world."

"Georgie—forgive me—if I was——"

"Cal, where did you ever learn to kiss like that?" she interrupted, with mock or arch jealousy. Her face was rosy, her sombrero had fallen off, her hair was dishevelled. It took all Cal's will power to refrain from enveloping her again. Probably he would have yielded to it but for her strange question.

"Why, Georgie . . . I didn't learn—it's only because I love you," he protested.

"Now don't you try to kid me, Cal Thurman," she replied, shaking a finger in his face. "I've half a mind to think you a regular lady-killer of the Tonto. No fellow could come across with kisses like yours unless——"

"Georgie, I swear to Heaven I never kissed but two girls—an' that was long ago—when I was a mere boy."

"I'm the only girl you ever loved?" she demanded, half in earnest and yet half mockingly.

"Why, of course," he said simply.

"All right, I believe you," she rejoined, after a long look into his eyes. "But it was a close shave. . . . Now I think we had better start home before you get gay on my hands again."

"Wait, Georgie," he returned, detaining her, "I—I haven't said all—what I must ask. . . . Georgie, will you marry me?"

"Now you're going to spoil it," protested Georgiana plaintively. "Couldn't you be satisfied with all I've said and done?"

"Satisfied, yes. Wonderfully happy an' grateful. But that only made it right an' necessary for me to ask you again. . . . Georgie, I'm crazy about you an' dead in earnest. Won't you be engaged to me?"

"No, I won't," she replied frankly. "Not now; maybe sometime. . . . Cal, I'm not sure of myself. To-day I love you a little—and I did want to kiss you—I *did* like your kisses; but to-morrow I might feel differently."

"You'll break my heart," he said desperately.

"Hearts don't break so easily."

"Mine would," he returned, eyeing her darkly.

"Cal, why won't you cut the marriage stuff and just be my good pal? Let me have my way. You'll have to, anyhow. But I do like you best. We can have such spiffy times."

"Georgie, you want to hang on to me, an' still have what you call spiffy times with the other boys, don't you?"

Again her gay frank laughter trilled out. "Caught with the goods! Cal, you're a wiz. That's just what I want."

"Georgie, you'll not have any trouble hangin' on to me," he said bluntly. "But you'll have a hell of a lot of trouble if your spiffy times with the other boys get as—as far—as what you did to me."

"Oh, is that so?" she replied haughtily. "If that isn't just like a man! . . . Cal, when anyone tries to boss me I always do the thing I'm forbidden."

"Georgie, let's not say any more," he said resignedly. "I didn't mean I would give trouble. You don't savvy these Tonto fellows. . . . Let's be rustlin' back home. It's nine miles, an' uphill most of the way."

When they reached the ranch, twilight had mantled the valley. The bright lights from the windows of the house were cheering. The air was cold with breath of frost in it. Somewhere a coyote was yelping wildly. There was no one in the corral. In the gloom Georgiana looked down upon Cal as he stepped to the side of her horse.

"The end of a perfect day," she said, with a deep sigh. "Lift me off."

Wearily, and with a low moan, she essayed to move out of her saddle, and almost sank a dead weight in his arms.

"Poor kid! I was afraid it'd be too much for you," said Cal solicitously, as he placed her on her feet. "I told you, Georgie. That was too much of a ride for a girl. But you made it, an' I'm handin' you a compliment even Tonto girls don't often get."

"Oh-h-h-h! I'm all broken bones and blisters," she said ruefully. "I'll be a dead one to-morrow. But I wouldn't have missed that ride for anything. . . . Cal, I owe you for the very happiest day of my whole life. If you just hadn't——"

Without completing what she had intended to say, she turned away and slowly limped towards the house. Cal watched the slight form merge into the gloom. There was a pang in his breast. Yet the day had been for him what she had confessed it had been for her. Standing there with a hand on the hot flank of the horse he had given to Georgiana, he received a strange strengthening intimation of faith to go on and stand by his love and his hope.

8

SEPTEMBER gave way to October, and all the uplands of the Tonto augmented their autumn colours.

Down in the foothills the bright golds and reds were limited to isolated bits set like gems in the dark green of the brushland. Here and there a grove of walnut trees still held enough leaves to make a contrast; and down in the winding ravines, between the foothills where water ran, there were clumps of sycamores still holding their foliage, growing more colourful and beautiful as the October frosts advanced. On sunny southern slopes there were little patches of sumac, growing red, and some of the ledges of rock showed crimson and bronze vines. But in the low hills the prevailing huè of the season was the dark grey-green of mingled oak, juniper, cedar, and manzanita.

Towards the Rim, however, the long slopes ended in a glory of brilliance. The yellow crags and the zigzag path of the red belt of rock that characterised the long, irregular face of the Great Mesa were subdued and dulled by the more vivid colours of the foliage. The leagues of pine forests that sloped up to the Rim were invariably dark rich green until they reached the foot of this huge mountain wall. Here they ended, except in dark clefts of gorges and canyons that cut into the rock. Most compelling to the gaze were the clumps of maple trees under the ledges at the apex of canyons. Here was a riot of colour. Magenta and cerise and blood-scarlet vied with an exquisite purple for dominance of beauty. Lone trees of maple, full-foliaged, seemed more like live fire than coloured leaves. Farther up the great slopes, where the notches of canyons were black with pine and spruce, began the gleam of gold of the aspens. They were as gold as the pure golden lightening the west after sunset. Above this stood out the broken battlements of the Rim, crowned by the fringe of pine forest.

One evening at Green Valley when the cattle count was over, and the round-up not far off, Henry Thurman called his riders together.

"Boys, thet 'air sorghum share ought to be cut," he said. "It'll only take a few days. Gard is sendin' his boys down to-morrow.

So you pack an outfit up to Boyd's homestead an' rustle thet job."

"Suits us," replied Wess. "Reckon it'll take all of three days. An', Uncle Henry, after the round-up who's drivin' the cattle to Winslow?"

"Wal, reckon you'd better see Enoch aboot thet. You cain't nary all go. Cal's daid set on homesteadin' Rock Spring, an' some of us will hev to cut an' haul logs."

"Say, boy, what you-all rarin' aboot?" drawled Wess, turning to Cal.

"I wasn't in a hurry until I got a hunch Hatfield has an eye on Rock Spring Mesa."

"Oho! He has. Who told you?"

"Father got it straight from Uncle Gard."

The old pioneer nodded confirmation of this and told the boys how Hatfield had long known of Cal's interest in Rock Spring, and that it would never do to let the Bar XX outfit get a wedge into their upland cattle range. Then in the serious discussion which followed, the fact came to light that there was evidence of the Thurmans losing cattle. Rustling on a large scale was a thing of the past, but the loss of unbranded calves had grown to be more than the mere mistakes natural to cattlemen of a wild range. Someone was deliberately driving Thurman calves from the cows, before they should have been separated, and was branding them.

"Serge Thurman marked some calves last month," said the rancher, "an' he done it so slick no one but him could tell. Wal, Serge has missed a couple of them calves, an' he's shore lookin' fer them."

"Humph! What good will it do if he finds the Bar XX put their iron on them? We can't prove anyone knowed our unbranded stock from theirs," replied Wess.

"Wal, I reckon not," admitted Henry.

"Shore it'll only make wuss blood between Enoch an' Bloom. Reckon thet's bad enough right now."

"All I can say, boys, is fer you to keep your mouths shut an' yore eyes open. I'll lay off at the mill an' fetch Tuck Merry up to Boyd's to help you fellers cut the sorghum. An' I'm willin' to bet you all thet he'll cut more an' carry more than any of you."

"Thet limber-legged galoot beat me at rustlin' sorghum!" ejaculated Wess, in high dudgeon at the suggestion. Wess had long enjoyed the pre-eminence at this Tonto game of sorghum-harvesting, and he was extremely tenacious of his record.

"Wess, nary you or any of the boys figger my sawmill hand

correct," drawled Henry with his dry chuckle. "Shore I've told you how he beat you-all holler in the sawmill. Best hand I ever hed."

Wess was disgruntled. His supremacy had been questioned, and that by a tenderfoot from outside. Naturally, the other boys made it worse by backing up Henry and offering to make bets on their own opinions. Cal capped the climax by offering to wager a horse against one of Wess's that Tuck Merry could beat him.

"Aw, ain't you gamblin' a little free with yore hosses?" queried Wess sarcastically. "You bet yore best hoss you'd lick Tim inside of a year. An', Cal, time's a-flyin'. Then you give Miss Georgie yore pinto—which it ain't hard to calkilate how you was gamblin' there an' how you'll lose. Now you've gall enough to bet me yore last good hoss. I hate to take advantage, Cal, considerin' yore failin' intelleck, but yo're on."

Cal surveyed his cousin with considerable disfavour.

"Say, Wess," he said loftily, "you're so darn' smart. I'll give you odds I win all *three* bets."

"What'll you bet?" snapped Wess, and he slapped his knee with a broad hand.

Cal began with a deliberate enumeration of the last two of his horses, his Winchester, and his lasso, also his silver-mounted spurs, which Wess had always coveted, and his only saddle, and he was about to add fifty dollars to the list when his father interrupted.

"Cal, shore thar must be some truth in Wess's hunch aboot yore bein' plumb loco," he drawled. "You jest cut out any more bets. If you homestead Rock Spring you'll shore need airy darn' hoss an' sich you own."

Next morning, when the first grey light in the east heralded the coming of the dawn, Enoch Thurman stalked out of the house and yelled in stentorian voice that penetrated to the very sleepiest brain there:

"The day's busted!"

Enoch was the chief of the Thurman clan, and his call was a signal for all to rouse. By daylight breakfast was steaming on the long kitchen table, and by sunrise saddles and packs were being strapped, and soon after the riders were on their way to the sorghum ranch.

It was a flat piece of land about three miles from Green Valley, towards the Rim, and suffered greatly by contrast with the lower fertile ranch. Boyd Thurman had founded his homestead here, and eighty of the one hundred and sixty acres were under cultivation.

These eighty acres comprised one great level field of sorghum, a yellowing plain somewhat resembling corn or cane, though not so high. Weeds and wild flowers grew quite as thickly as the stalks. Little cultivation had been given this field since the planting of the sorghum.

A stream-bed ran along the western border of the field, as did also the dusty road leading to the school-house up in the woods, and the cabins and ranches of the other Thurmans farther up towards the Rim. This stream was surface water only, and was now dry except for a few pools in rocky places. At the lower end of the clearing stood a couple of cabins and a barn, all weathered and in bad state of repair. Since proving up on his homestead, Boyd Thurman had lived mostly at his father's. And this immense field of sorghum was the property of all the Thurmans. Jointly they had planted it, and jointly they would harvest and divide it.

While the boys from Green Valley were unsaddling and unpacking their outfit, and pitching camp under the trees near the cabins, the other contingent of Thurmans hove in sight, nine riders strong, with more than that number of pack-horses. They whistled and they sang, between cigarettes, as they worked with the dexterity of long practice, and innumerable were the jests and banterings they flung at one another. At nine o'clock they were sitting or standing round the pine tree which marked Enoch's camp, and all were sharpening their knives on the little whetstones each carried with him. In all they numbered seventeen workers, not including Henry Thurman. Despite his years, he could work along with most of the boys, when it pleased him to do so.

"Wal, fellars," spoke up Enoch, as he tested his knife-blade with a broad thumb, "one man to a row an' pack all he can."

"Enoch, I got a bet on heah an' I'm rarin'," growled Wess.

"Ahuh! An' what're you bettin, an' who?" replied Enoch with great interest.

Wess told his version of the matter forced upon him, and his tone was at once grieved and flamboyant; and then Cal poured oil upon the fire by his boastful confidence in Tuck Merry; and lastly Cal's father added the last straw to Wess's burden.

"Wal, is airy one of you fellars achin' to bet me? I'm shore a-backin' my sawmill hand."

Whereupon an animated discussion, rather heated on Wess's part, took place, and various and incredible bets were placed. Finally the gamblers had apparently exhausted resources, and the conditions were put up to Enoch.

"Wal, dog-gone me!" he ejaculated. "Shore it ain't a square deal. Wess was cuttin' sorghum when he was knee-high to a grasshopper, an' I reckon our long-legged pard Merry never seen a sorghum field till he hit the Tonto."

"Right-o," declared Tuck. "I'll do my darndest to win for you who're backing me, but don't fail to notice I'm not betting any myself."

"Be a sport, Tuck," spoke up Cal, and he winked at his friend. "I'm goin' to win another bet to-day beside this one on you. So let's plunge."

"Oh, if that's the dope, I'll kick in," responded Tuck, with a meaning twinkle in his eye as he returned Cal's look. "Wess, I'll lay you ten I'll beat you cuttin' this junk and another ten that I can carry more of it."

"Ten what?" demanded Wess belligerently.

"Ten bucks—ten good old U.S. simolens—ten cartwheels," replied Tuck, jingling silver in his pocket.

"Wess, you big dumbhead, he means ten dollars," explained Cal.

"Aw, I'll take double thet," responded Wess grandly.

"That's my limit, Wess, and I'm making you a present of it," said Tuck.

"Shore he is," interposed Enoch. "Wal, now listen, all you buckaroos. I'll work along with Tuck this mawnin'. It's only fair to break him in. Then after the noon-hour rest we'll have the race. Cuttin' up the field once, one row, an' back heah again one row. An' I'll be jedge. Is that satisfactory, Wess?"

"Reckon it's fair," replied Wess.

"Wal, then, let's go to work," said Enoch, getting up. "Tuck, you come alongside me an' do what I do."

Thereupon they advanced to the western side of the field, and each taking a row of sorghum to himself, they bent their long bodies to the labours of harvesting.

The method of procedure was simple. The sorghum stalks grew about a foot apart. They were slender but tough. A knife had to be sharp and the hand strong. When the stalk was cut it was shifted into the hollow of the left arm, or laid on the ground, according to the cutter's particular way of working. The field was nearly a mile long, and the rows of sorghum ran the whole length.

At once the line of advance grew irregular. Wess took the lead, without any apparent effort, and he just stalked and stooped along as if he were picking up apples. He forged ahead, and the other

boys advanced according to their capacity and inclination. Enoch
did not lose much time or get far behind, even though he was
instructing Tuck. Some of the boys kept even with each other,
and some gradually straggled out behind. Of these Cal Thurman
and Tim Matthews were two, for the reason that Cal never had
shown any great ability as a sorghum-harvester, and Tim, who was
a rider, hated the work. Cal, however, kept quite far in advance
of Tim.

Wess reached the starting-point ahead of all his followers, and
the time was one hour and a quarter for the round trip. His
blue shirt was as wet with sweat as if it had been soaked in water.
His hands were grimy. His face was black with dust and streaked
with lines where the sweat ran down. He started on a new row
before his comrades got back to the starting-point. As soon as they
arrived they moved over, as had Wess, and started again.

Serge Thurman had left off after the first trip, and by the time
the others straggled back he had a noonday meal almost ready.
One by one they trooped in after Wess, to drink copiously and wash
their dirty hands, and then fall down gratefully in the shade. But
their spirits soon revived.

Cal beat Tim in by a dozen rods or more, and he made way for
his covert design by casting reflections upon Tim's lax ambitions
as a harvester. Even the least word from Cal could stir Tim's
temper, especially since Tim had fallen in to the black looks of
Miss Georgiana Stockwell, and Cal had apparently gained favour.

But Cal made no more sallies. He sat to the meal with a sense
of exciting anticipation. The event he had longed for was primed
for consummation. He saw it in Tuck Merry's slight superior smile
of knowledge of mirth held in abeyance.

"Wal," drawled Enoch, when he had eaten the last morsel on
his tin plate, "which one of these heah two entertainin' stunts are
we goin' to see first?"

"Two?" asked his father. "What airy one besides the cuttin' race
between Wess an' my man?"

"Didn't you heah Cal say to Tim: 'Wait till after grub-time'?"

"Reckon I did. An' what was Cal meanin' by thet?"

"Wal, Cal's got to lick Tim sometime this year or lose his best
hoss," observed Enoch.

"Son, you shore make fool bets," replied Henry.

"Dad, this one is not so foolish as you think," said Cal with open
cheerfulness.

"Cal Thurman," spoke up Tim with asperity, "I'm regardin' thet hoss of yorn as my property."

"Boys, you cain't spend all day like a lot of bettin' Indians," put in Henry. "Reckon I don't mind if you do the work."

"We won't lose any time on Wess an' Merry," said Enoch. "We'll march right along with them, an' after we're through Tim an' Cal can beat each other up."

Whereupon they returned to the harvest-work as before, only Enoch started Wess and Merry ahead of them. And it was noticeable that every time a harvester would straighten up he would take a moment of keen interest in the rivals, working so furiously ahead. Wess forged to the front and gradually drew away from Merry. They made the dust fly, and scattered the crows. The lusty calls of the workers in the rear pealed out in the hot, still air. The burros brayed in raucous stentorian hee-haws, as if they too were much interested in the race. Wess's dog ran alongside him, barking encouragement. Almost all of the workers' cheers were for the benefit of Merry.

"Stay with him, boy," called one.

"He's a-rarin', Tuck, but he won't last," yelled another.

Indeed, this appeared to be true. The lengthy tenderfoot had begun to close the gap between him and the seasoned harvester. Wess had been pushing himself too hard or was slowing up to gain breath for the finish. But he made the end of the field in record time, and was several rods on the return trip when Merry reached the turn. Here Enoch left off working and went back with the rivals. His men, however, were not long in getting their faces towards the home stretch. Wess kept his lead, and finished far enough ahead of Merry to prove his very considerable superiority. The others trooped back in due time to begin an animated discussion over gains and losses.

"Reckon it ain't decided yet," declared Enoch. "Wess wins the cuttin'. Now let's see who can pack the most sorghum?"

Thereupon Wess began to walk along a row of cut sorghum, raking portions of it into a pile. When he had arranged a number to his liking, he took a bundle of stalks in his arms and then went on to the next, until he had collected an enormous quantity. He was completely hidden under a huge shock of sorghum. While he held it Enoch measured its girth with a string. Then Wess set the immense bundle on the ground with the stalks upright, and it stood there like a shock of corn.

"Wal, Tuck, it's your turn," said Enoch. "An' between you an' me, I think you can beat him."

Thus encouraged, Tuck Merry began to rake the cut sorghum into piles, somewhat after the manner of Wess, though not so neatly. Measured by lengths of rows he piled up much more than Wess.

The lanky tenderfoot began to pick up the piles he had collected, and it soon became evident that he could have saved himself much strenuous labour if he had made larger and fewer portions. For when he got a great bundle in his arms he had difficulty picking up another portion. He had to feel for it with his feet, then drop his burden on it, and absorb it with wider stretch of arms. He grew to be a walking stack of sorghum, a most interesting and amusing sight to the watchers. Wess's dirty face began to express his astonishment.

"Son-of-a-gun has me licked now!" he ejaculated in admiration.

But Tuck Merry went on picking up portions until he had lifted the enormous amount he had piled. From somewhere under the burden sounded a smothered voice.

"I—can—pack—more," he called hoarsely.

"T'aint necessary," replied Henry. "You win by a heap, I reckon."

"Wal, let's see," added Enoch as he threw his cord over the great bundle, and then sprawled on the ground to find the end. Rising then, he circled the pack and got the measurement.

"I'm a son-of-a-gun," he exclaimed with a grin. "He's beat Wess by a whole foot."

"Aw, I'm beat, but not thet bad," declared Wess.

"There you are, Wess. Measure it yourself," replied Enoch.

"Nope. I guess you're right. Let go, Merry—an' shake hands."

Tuck dropped the rustling shock of sorghum, or rather emerged from under it, a dust-encumbered, ludicrous figure. Wess met his outstretched hand and shook it as a man who had respect for his better.

"You win thet heat," he said. "Now let's measure arms. I'm sorta curious how you done what nobody else ever done."

The two tall harvesters stood facing each other with right arms extended, and the remarkable fact became plain to all that Merry's arm was six inches longer than Wess's.

"Wal, thet tells the story," concluded Enoch. "All bets off, boys. It shore was a draw. . . . An' now let's go back to work."

When the harvest was over for that day, one-third of the great sorghum field had been cut—a showing which Henry Thurman viewed with simple delight.

"By golly! thet's a fine day's work," he exclaimed. "You all done well, 'cept Tim, who hates work, an' Cal, who'll never be no sorghum-rastler."

"Wal, I reckon them two was savin' up," drawled Enoch. "They shore was slow."

"Now I forgot all aboot thet," returned Henry. "I'll shore enjoy seein' Tim lick Cal again. Say, Tim, air you a-goin' to do it before supper or after?"

"Seein' you tax me, I'll say I'd like what little exercise it'd take before I clean up fer supper," retorted Tim.

Thus the issue came up squarely on the moment when Serge was busy at the camp fire and the others were grouped around in restful postures.

It found Cal more than ready. His keen eye had caught sight of Georgiana and her sister Mary out on the road. They were returning from school, where Georgiana had spent the day, and on the moment were approaching the gate under the walnut trees a little distance from the camp. No one, save Cal, apparently had observed them.

"Ahuh!" exclaimed Cal, with a cheerfulness wholly reflected in Tuck Merry's cadaverous image. He leaped to his feet. "I forgot all about that. . . . Come on, Tim—you bow-legged little hop-a-long bronco-buster. I'm hungry an' I want to get this over before supper."

The crowd greeted Cal's speech with both amaze and delight. But Tim shared only the former. Slowly he got to his feet, his red face, from which he had wiped the dust, showing a dubious contempt. He squinted at Cal. He was not so sure that there existed perfect justification for his contempt.

"Come an' take it," cried Cal banteringly. "Come out here. I don't want to pile you up on Serge's supper. Tim, you've had the fun of lickin' me four times, an' you ought to be sport enough to take your medicine like I took mine."

"You make me mad, Cal Thurman," growled Tim. "You're too fresh. An' I'm gonna lick you fer the fifth time—which'll be all you'll ever want."

He slouched out on to the grassy plot away from the group under the tree, and certainly in plain sight from the road. This was what Cal wanted. He had not the slightest doubt of the outcome. Tuck

Merry had assured him that Tim could not last three minutes.

Suddenly Cal extended his hands, still wearing his old gloves, and he began to dance around Tim with the quickness of footwork that had been a part of the painful education imparted by Tuck Merry. Tim, rough-and-tumble fighter that he was, crouched close in on Cal, but could not find an opening. Cal increased his dancing steps, and began to feint with his fists, and saw instantly how Tim was bewildered by such tactics.

"Boys, don't miss this," called Cal piercingly. "You all know how Tim hates to have anyone hit his big ugly nose. Now watch."

Manifestly the watchers were intensely absorbed and thrillingly expectant. Dancing round, Cal kept shooting out his left at Tim, just to bewilder him and make him dodge and swing until the favourable instant came. Then with his right Cal flashed a hard, cutting blow to Tim's nose. No doubt about the effect!

"Tim, that's a nose-jab," called out Cal gleefully, as he avoided Tim's heavy rush, and danced round; and then, quicker than before, he shot his left to the same sensitive spot. This time the blood started.

"I'll nose-jab you!" shouted Tim, hoarse with pain, as wildly he swung. But it was only to encounter a still stiffer blow.

"Aw!" bawled Tim.

"Holler, you boob!" returned Cal, with the fun of the thing giving way to the heat of action and sight of blood and thought of just revenge. Tim had hurt him many a time and had crowed over it. This was retribution and there was Georgiana Stockwell sitting on top of the high gate.

But Tim did not cry out any more. He was too much in earnest now, too furious. All the yelling came from the onlookers.

Then, just as suddenly, Cal changed his footwork so that instead of dancing around Tim he jumped towards him and then away. Tim did not do any backing. He followed, and always appeared at a disadvantage, too slow to reach Cal. All at once, Cal beat down Tim's waving fists, and pushed his left into Tim's face, not hard, but once, twice, three times; and then as Tim lost something of his poise, Cal swung a right powerfully into the pit of Tim's stomach. It made a deep sound. And then Tim gasped out his propelled breath.

"That's the belly-wham!" called Cal. "Look out now—here comes the tooth-rattler!"

Tim, with terribly distorted face, eyes starting, mouth agape, jaw falling, seemed to be standing motionless, helpless, silent except for a singular gasping sound. Precisely as Tuck Merry had done to Bloom, so Cal had done to Tim. How ridiculously easy! Tim's breath had been expelled and he could not get any back. Then Cal ended the matter with a hard swing to the jaw. Tim went down in a heap and stayed down.

In the silence of astonishment that ensued, Cal stood over Tim, scarcely panting from his exertions, and looked down at his fallen adversary.

"Get up, Tim—before I cool off," he called.

But poor Tim had just begun to be able to draw a little air into his lungs. He could not get up. He could not lift his dizzy head. Whereupon the other boys suddenly recovered from their astonishment and began to give vent to wild and whirling mirth. They howled and rolled and roared, and not for several moments could Cal distinguish a word they said.

"Wal, I'm a locoed rustler if Cal didn't knock Tim out!" ejaculated Enoch in absolute astonishment.

They were all amazed, and some were sceptical at Cal's queer dancing around, and several were incredulous, especially old Henry.

"Wot'd—he hev—in them gloves?" huskily demanded Tim as Enoch helped him sit up.

"Just my fists," replied Cal, taking off the gloves and throwing them at Tim.

The vanquished rider pathetically pawed over the gloves.

"Aw—he had—rocks in them," wailed Tim.

"No, Tim, he hadn't nothin'," said Enoch kindly, as with his scarf he began to wipe the blood from Tim's face. "He just licked you damn' quick an' good."

Cal dropped to one knee beside Tim and held out his hand.

"Do you want to shake on it?" he asked.

Tim sat up and gazed wonderingly at his assailant. He could not believe his eyes, but he had been convinced of what had happened. It was a hard moment for him. Slowly he held out a shaking hand.

"Cal, you shore—licked me," he replied, with a gulp, "an' I'm sayin' I got what was comin' to me. . . . . But how'd you do it? A hoss-kick is bad enough, but aw!—when you hit me, it was orful."

SATURDAY, the last day of the October round-up, was the date of the principal dance of the season. Whereupon Mary Stockwell observed that late in the afternoon two processions were noticeable—one of the riders trooping wearily back to the ranch, and the other of a stream of vehicles on the road towards the school-house, where the big dance was to be held. This main social event of the season called families from all over that section of the country. They would start out early in the morning, so as to be at the school-house in time to get dinner before the dancing began.

When Mary went out to watch the October sunset, she saw Pan Handle Ames and Arizona, with clean-shaven, shiny faces, and dressed in their best, sitting on the porch. They appeared to be overcome by mirth.

"What's so funny, boys?" asked Mary.

"Aw—we just seen Lock Thurman comin' back leadin' the hoss he thought his gurl was goin' to ride," replied Pan Handle.

"She's gone to the dance with another fellar," added Arizona in positive joy.

"An' Lock's face was as long as a mescal pole," continued Pan Handle. "Lock's orful sweet on Milly. An' she'd promised to go to this dance with him."

"Why then did she not?" inquired the teacher curiously.

"Wal, all Lock knowed was that he was too slow gettin' there, an' she went with Bid Hatfield."

"No!"

"She shore did, an' if thet doesn't cause a real fight, I'll swallow my spurs," replied Arizona.

"But—what's so funny?" asked Mary. "I think Milly's treating Lock that way is too bad. And prospects of a fight are not fun."

"Aw, now, Miss Mary," expostulated Arizona. "Lock is orful stuck on himself an' he said he had Milly eatin' out of his hand. An' shore prospects of a fight *is* fun. It's more'n fun, considerin' that Hatfield fellar. 'Cause somebody has got to lick him powerful good. Besides, it wouldn't be a regular dance if some gurl didn't jilt some fellar an' if there wasn't a fight."

"Huh! Strikes me there's a-goin' to be two fights," interposed Pan Handle. "Tuck Merry has asked Ollie Thurman, an' she's a-goin' with him. Lord! but Abe Turner will be a-rarin' to-night. Looks like Ollie's on the fence now between Abe an' Tuck."

"I ain't got no gurl to take, but I wouldn't miss this heah dance fer a million dollars," observed Arizona complacently.

"You're mischievous boys," said Mary Stockwell.

"Wal, teacher," drawled Arizona, with a mysterious gleam of fun in his eyes, "there's some round heah who's sweet on you."

"Oh—indeed!" replied Mary, somewhat surprised into confusion. She felt herself blushing, and turned away rather quickly to walk out into the yard. When she got out to the fence she was quite conscious of a heightened pulse.

"These boys!" she soliloquised. "How full of deviltry! Yet I like them."

This magnificent sunset might have been made for Mary's particular benefit. October had brought more vivid colours to the hills and more beautiful cloud effects in the skies. A dusky purple veil lay low in the notches between the high, rounded knolls, and above them the golden light of sunset spread vast and wide behind the clouds of rose. Sunsets here seemed different from those she remembered in other places. It was Arizona land—quite different from any other. She had come to love it. And the Tonto Basin was the wildest of Arizona lands. She tried to put into thought just what that meant. Wide spaces of unsettled country, standing on end, deep-fissured and pointing its mesa ruins into the clouds, bare, grey, grassy ridges and hills of soft bright green and the great slopes of dark pine, the rugged bronze canyons and the rushing streams, the ledges of red rock standing out and the yellow crags against the foliage of spruce, wild birds and wild animals everywhere, seen on the way to school and back, the slashes in the forests these pioneer people called ranches, and lastly the stalwart, sturdy boys, simple and kindly yet rugged and hard as the wilderness that had developed them—all these in Mary Stockwell's thoughts could not wholly explain the fullness of her appreciation.

That night, Georgiana was in one of her dangerous moods. Judging from the expression of Cal's face at the supper table, he and Georgiana had quarrelled about something. As a result, Georgiana was aggravatingly slow in dressing for the dance, and held up the party that was going in Enoch's car. Mary was amused at the impatience of the boys to be off, but she was a little concerned over Georgiana. The girl was no longer in fun. She had been hurt, or she had grown tired of dissimulation, or she had begun to change for the worse. Mary feared the last.

Presently, Georgiana emerged from her little room, gorgeously and scantily arrayed, with more powder and paint on her face than Mary had ever seen yet. But for this false acceleration of colour she would have looked beautiful. Her eyes, however, did not need counterfeit. They were dark and flashing and full of the devil.

"Well, dear, if you want to create a sensation at this dance, you'll have your wish," said Mary soberly. "But I'm afraid it'll not be the kind of sensation you like."

"Bunk!" exclaimed Georgiana. "Men are all alike—at home in New York, or in darkest Africa—or the Tonto Basin."

"Georgiana, you think men *want* to see a girl look—as you do?" inquired Mary incredulously.

"I don't think. I know. . . . My sweet sister, there are some things you'll never learn. Believe me——"

She was interrupted by a knock on the door. Mary opened it to disclose Cal standing there.

"Hello, Cal! Come in," she said.

"No, thanks," he replied as he stood on the threshold. The light shone on his face. It was pale and troubled, almost stern. Mary thought he looked singularly handsome. He wore a dark suit that lent a marked contrast to his usual rough rider's garb.

His keen gaze swept over Georgiana from head to foot, and to Mary it held a singular expression.

"Then—I'm not goin' to take—you?" he declared bluntly.

"Not to this dance, or any dance, or *any* place," she replied cuttingly.

"Who's goin' to take you to-night?" he queried stiffly.

"That's none of your business, but if you're aching to know—I'm going with Tim," she replied.

"Tim!" ejaculated Cal.

"Yes—Tim!" she retorted, stung by his surprise or something not clear to Mary. Georgiana had never gone anywhere with Tim Matthews.

"You sure are hard up," rejoined Cal with sarcasm. "But I'm sayin'—if Tim kicks on that dress—you might get Bid Hatfield to take you."

"*Tim* is a gentleman," retorted Georgiana. "And Bid Hatfield

knows how to act like one, which is more than I can say for some
people."

"Reckon—you'll dance with Hatfield?" queried Cal, as if compelled to voice a question he hated.

"Will I?" Her counter-query was a tantalising defiant assurance.

It brought the blood to Cal's pale face.

"Georgie," he began in an earnestness that excluded jealousy,
"I know you despise me an' you have no use for any of us Thurmans, but you love your sister—an' for her sake don't dance with
Hatfield—an' don't try those new dances you've been teachin' some
of the boys an' girls."

"Come and watch me," said Georgiana deliberately. There was
a red spot in each of her cheeks that was not all paint.

"I'll not be there," returned Cal, and turning on his heel he
strode off the porch into the darkness.

Mary closed the door. "Georgie, I thought you and Cal had been
such good friends lately."

"We were. That's what makes me so sore. I thought I had
him canned."

"Poor Cal! What has he done now?"

"Done? He jumped me to-day because I was teaching some
new dance steps. And just after dinner he told me if I wore this
white dress he wouldn't take me to the dance. Of all the nerve!
Why, the fool is getting bossy! . . . So I asked Tim."

"Well, Cal is young and hot-tempered and jealous, I know. But,
Georgie, he certainly has been thoughtful of our interests. We're
strangers to this country. You've done some silly things. Perhaps
Cal has kept you from some real break."

"Oh, Mary, to give the devil his due—Cal has been nice. I *did*
like him. I'm not a liar. But I can't stand this ownership stuff,
and believe me I'll show him to-night."

"He'll not be there," replied Mary.

"You know a lot about men, sis, I don't think. Cal couldn't be
kept away from this dance."

"There! Enoch is honking his horn again. Let us hurry! You
must bundle up warm. These nights are cold. I—almost wish this
dance was over."

"Mary, it's a great life if you don't weaken," returned
Georgiana.

Outside the yard in the road the big car was full of merry Thurmans, all of whom, except Enoch, were crowded into the back seats.

Enoch manifestly meant to make up for lost time. Along the level bottom-land of the valley he drove so fast that Mary was thrilled and frightened at once. The bright lights sent round rays ahead along the yellow, winding road, with its fences of upright poles and borders of brush. Coyotes and skunks and rabbits crossed the bright flare. The foliage of the trees took on a rich green hue, the juniper berries shone like diamonds, and the smooth branches of manzanita burned red in the light. The night air was now penetratingly cold and the dark-blue sky wonderful with its myriads of stars. The time came when Enoch had to drive slowly and carefully over rocky washes and round steep bends. The ten occupants of the back seats kept up a continual merriment.

"Mary, tell me what ailed Cal," asked Enoch in a low voice. "I never saw him like he was to-night."

She told him briefly and did not spare Georgiana.

"I'm worried about him," went on Enoch. "Shore this will never do. You understand, don't you, Mary?"

"I think so," replied Mary.

"Wal, I always felt you understood us. An' you've been a world of good. Cal's the best of all the Thurmans. An' I reckon your teachin' him two years had a lot to do with that. Father an' mother feel as I do—we owe you a lot, Mary."

"Oh, no! You owe me nothing," murmured Mary, surprised and quickened at the singular warmth of his low voice.

"Wal, we won't argue. But we ain't blind to your influence on your school. We never had anyone like you. Our poor kids, comin' from all over this rough country, took school as a hard dose. But they like you an' they learn fast. It's a good work you're doin', Mary Stockwell."

"Thank you, Enoch. . . . I—I can only say I'm glad you think so—and that it's a work I love."

"Wal, do you intend goin' on teachin' our kids?"

"Surely. Just as long as you will have me."

"An' you're not gettin' homesick for the East—an' all you had there?"

"No, indeed."

"You reckon you want to stay on in Arizona?"

"Yes. I love it."

"Wal, that's fine," he went on, and for once his Texas drawl held a note of eagerness. "If you feel that way, Mary, an' want to go on teachin' our children, you must like us Tonto folks."

"Indeed—I do," returned Mary.

"We're just plain pioneer folk an' pretty rough," he said.

"Well, if that is so, I guess I must have some pioneer blood in me," returned Mary rather nervously. Enoch's tone stirred her. There was something back of his kindly, earnest statements. She felt him leading up to it. And her heart began to beat quickly. Was this ride to explain the strange glamour that had haunted her during the sunset hour? Something was going to happen. She stole a side look at Enoch. It was impossible to see him distinctly, but he appeared as calm and steady as usual, and he drove the car over bad places very carefully.

"Mary," he began, after a long silence, "I reckon I've been in love with you since you first came heah. But I never had no hope till lately. An' now I'm bold enough to ask if you'll marry me."

He did not ask her if she realised what a rancher's wife must be in that hard country. Somehow the omission, and the simplicity of his proposal, seemed a compliment to Mary. Was she as big as he believed? However that might be, she knew she was happier than she had ever been in her life.

"Yes, Enoch, I—I will marry you," she said softly.

His right hand dropped off the wheel and groped for hers. Mary met it half-way. Through her glove she felt the ruggedness and strength and hardness of it as he clasped hers close.

"Wal, shore I reckoned this heah dance was goin' to be a happy one for me," he said.

So Mary found herself trying to realise the sudden change of the direction of her life. Her pulses were thobbing and her nerves tingling. Something warm and full and hopeful swelled her heart. After all, her little romance had not been a dream. Her secret love for this stalwart scion of a pioneer people had no longer to be held as something of which she dare not think. She was grateful for the wonderful opportunity to be a woman and a helper. She had found her place.

Enoch held her hand tightly and managed the wheel with the other. Behind them, the merry crowd grew merrier as time passed. Henry Thurman hummed one of his fiddling tunes. Everybody, except Georgiana, seemed gay. Mary, in that moment of happiness, did not forget the wayward and wilful little sister; and somehow she felt that as Enoch's betrothed she might have a stronger influence.

Deeper into the dark forest the car penetrated, climbed a long hill, and hummed along a winding level, at last to plunge down into what appeared a bottomless canyon. Enoch was not exactly reckless, but he was not exactly careful, either.

Ahead, the blackness gave way to a yellow flare, and soon a huge camp fire shone brightly. It stood at the edge of the school-house clearing. A crowd of young people and children were grouped around it, and every one of them was eating ice-cream. A stalwart youth, wearing a red scarf, was ladling it out from the first of a row of freezers. Manifestly the directors of this social event meant to furnish enough refreshment.

The advent of the Thurman car created an uproar. The crowd yelled its delight at the arrival of the chief factor in the evening's entertainment—the old fiddler. Young people poured out of the school-house. A number of horses were hitched along the edge of the clearing, and the noise frightened some of them. One began to buck. Half a dozen boys ran to hold him down. But he broke his halter and bolted down the road.

The merry young people hustled Henry Thurman into the school-house. Mary found she was being led by Enoch, who at the same time was trying to protect the basket of pies. Mary lost sight of Georgiana.

The inside of the school-house was familiar enough to Mary, yet to-night it seemed to have meaning and picturesque significance. The whitewashed walls had in places been covered with coloured prints from newspapers and magazines. The light, furnished by a small lamp at each end of the room, was so dim that Mary found it difficult to recognise anyone. All the desks had been removed. A line of benches and chairs and boxes ran along the walls round the room. In one corner was a stove, behind which sat a group of women with babies in their arms. Children ran everywhere, squealing, laughing, crying out their particular pleasure in this annual event.

"Unlimber thet thar fiddle," called out a lusty-lunged rider to Henry; and his call was seconded by many.

Henry Thurman's grey old face beamed. He was the keynote of this dance and showed his pride in his importance. What his reply was Mary could not distinguish. He sat down on a box, and bending over his fiddle, he began to saw on it. Lock Thurman sat close to him, bending forward, and with two slender pine sticks he beat time upon the strings of Henry's fiddle.

This was a signal for the dancers and the children. Forty couples and half as many youngsters began to cavort round the room. The young people danced their modification of the two-step, and the children played tag. Mary found herself swept away on Enoch's strong arm. Then all Mary could see was the throng of dancers. From time to time she felt the children running by or dragging at her skirts, and she could hear their merry shrieks, but she could not see them. For a rough rider who had worn heavy boots all his life, Enoch certainly acquitted himself creditably. Like others of those long-legged Arizonians, he did not dance badly. The embarrassing thing for Mary was that he did not tire and the fiddler kept on interminably. Nevertheless, Mary enjoyed the dance and felt herself now a part of this simple pioneer life.

When finally Henry and Lock ceased their united efforts, the young people rushed outside to eat ice-cream. Most of the girls forgot to put on coats, and one of these was Georgiana. In the bright glare of the fire she presented a sight calculated to be etched indelibly on the memories of the young people who saw her. The boys stared in undisguised obsession; the girls marvelled at the audacity and beauty of that white gown; the older folk looked at Georgiana with distrust and scorn.

It did not take Mary more than a moment to see that Georgiana was enjoying the sensation she created, particularly among the boys who flocked round her. Here in the bright light Mary had a good look at Hatfield. He appeared a tall, powerfully-built fellow, handsome in a bold way, and he certainly wore picturesque garb. Like many of the young men present, he danced without coat or vest. He wore a blue blouse, red scarf, a silver-buttoned belt, and tight-fitting dark trousers that showed the round hips and supple legs of a rider. The pearl handle of a gun protruded from his right hip pocket. This surprised Mary, and she called Enoch's attention to it.

"Wal," he drawled, "I reckon Bid ain't the only one packin' hardware heah."

His tone and his look made Mary's pulse leap. Underneath the gaiety and simplicity of this dance lay the sterner instincts that had been inherited from a wilder day.

Mary resolutely put away all untoward thoughts. This might mean much to her, and she wished to enjoy it while she could. She had a feeling that trouble would come soon enough. Wherefore, she paid no more attention to Georgiana and gave herself up to the enjoyment of the moment.

She danced four consecutive two-steps with Enoch, all long dances with innumerable encores, and then she was claimed by Wess for a dance called "tag."

Several of the boys entered this dance without partners, and they had the privilege of tagging dancers who had partners. It was a dance they all particularly enjoyed, where they began to warm up, and Mary and Georgiana had a continual procession of changing partners. Georgiana, in fact, scarcely could get started with one dancer when another dancer tagged him. Bid Hadfield was having his trouble trying to find a moment with her. At last he got hold of Mary and she found him the best dancer there. Then Enoch, for the first time during this long tag dance, forced himself upon her partner. He whispered in her ear: "Reckon I don't care for Hatfield dancin' with my girl. An' I'm goin' to tell this outfit you're engaged to me."

"Oh—not yet," she whispered back. But Enoch smilingly shook his head.

The end of this dance found Mary warm, breathless, and exhausted for the moment. She was glad to rest. The children, all of them pupils of hers, gravitated towards her and seemed to have discovered a new interest. Pale-faced and big-eyed, they showed the effects of unusual excitement and were about ready to fall asleep. Mrs. Gard Thurman and another woman were putting the babies to bed in a corner. Ten babies in all soon lay fast asleep side by side, on beds of rugs and blankets evidently brought for that purpose.

When the dancers filed in again, old Henry Thurman rose, fiddle in hand, and twanged a few sharp notes to attract attention.

"Folks," he drawled, "as a member of the school board it fell on me to-night to extend a vote of thanks to our good teacher, Miss Stockwell. We shore do appreciate her. An' it was to be my pleasant duty to ask her to stay long heah with us. But thar won't be airy need of askin' now. Miss Mary has elected to make her home heah in the Tonto . . . an' the darn' lucky man is my son Enoch."

It was then, in the few crowded ensuing moments, that Mary found how she was regarded by the children and their folk. Her happiness would have been complete if only she could have been sure of Georgiana. She wondered why Georgiana did not come to her, as had so many. But it turned out that Georgiana had not been present when the announcement was made. In the middle of the next dance, while Mary was resting and talking to Mrs. Thurman, Georgiana came hurriedly to her, followed by Hatfield, who evidently was her partner.

"Mary—he said your engagement to Enoch was announced," she burst out, with strong feeling.

"Who said so?" asked Mary smiling.

"My partner—Mr. Hatfield," replied Georgiana. "I thought he was kidding me, but he swears not. . . . Mary, you look——"

"My dear, I'm very happy to say it's the truth."

"Oh! You're going to marry Enoch—to live here in the Tonto?" queried the girl, with something incredulous in her voice. Her eyes were dark, dilated with quickening thought.

"Yes, Georgie," replied Mary.

"My God! What will become of me?" muttered the girl under her breath.

Just then, before Mary could reply, Hatfield stepped forward. He was quite gallant and made a favourable impression.

"Miss Stockwell, I congratulate you," he said. "Enoch Thurman——"

He was interrupted by the arrival of Cal, who came rushing up to Mary, eager and pale, and he bent to kiss her.

"Never was so—glad about anythin' in my life," he said breathlessly. "You'll be Enoch's wife an' my sister. I'll say we're lucky."

"Why, Cal—you—you embarrass me," replied Mary laughing. "I had no idea I was so popular."

Then Cal took notice of Georgiana and Hatfield. She gave him a curt little bow and her escort spoke. Cal eyed them steadily, with cool intent, then without word or nod he turned his back on them. Georgiana flushed scarlet under her paint and powder. What semblance of dignity she had was lost in her over-sentimental turning to Hatfield.

"Come on, Bid. You sure dance divinely," she said, leaning to him and looking up into his eyes.

Hatfield was not slow or timid in his response to that invitation. But, according to Mary, if Georgiana had expected to crush Cal by this means, she had reckoned falsely. Cal apparently neither saw nor heard her.

"Dance with me, please," he asked of Mary.

"Wait for the next, Cal," she replied. "They danced me down last time, surely."

"What! The night of your engagement? Why, teacher!" returned Cal teasingly.

"Oh, I'm not down and out, as Tuck Merry calls it, but I need a little rest."

"Where's Tuck? He was in for it to-night."

"Come to think—I haven't seen Tuck dancing. But of course he's here. He came in the same car with us. . . . Cal, did you ride up horseback?"

"Yep. An' after I made up my mind I came a-flyin'," replied Cal with a frank laugh.

"You said you were not coming. What brought you?" inquired Mary, in kindly curiosity.

"Well, it wasn't to have a good time. I got a hunch somethin' was comin' off an' I might be needed."

"Cal, do you mean a fight?"

"No, I reckon I wouldn't have come to get into a fight or keep anyone out."

"Then why?" went on Mary, more interested. Cal was labouring under strong suppressed excitement. He seemed more manly, full of reserve force, and the touch of sadness became him. He was evasive, however, and laughed off Mary's queries. She watched him keenly as he sat there making himself agreeable, and she noted how his dark eyes roved over and among the dancing couples to single out Georgiana. When, however, during the whirl of the dancing circle, she drew near to where he sat, he gave no indication that he had seen her at all. Mary noted, to her dismay, that Georgiana's dancing became wilder.

"Cal, you said you didn't come to have a good time," spoke up Mary. "You don't mean that. You must dance and enjoy yourself."

"Teacher, my heart is broken," he replied, with sudden sombre change of face and tone.

"Oh, Cal!" she exclaimed in distress.

Abruptly he left her, and did not return until the music started up for the next dance. Then he seemed more like his old self. Still Mary was not reassured. Something rankled deep within Cal. She felt it, and a sense of fear grew upon her. During the whole of that dance she revolved in mind some things she meant to say to him.

"Boy, you didn't dance so well as usual to-night," she said.

"Reckon not, teacher. My mind wouldn't stick to the steps."

"Cal, what's on your mind?"

Before he could reply Enoch loomed over them and drew them out of the crowd.

"Cal, I'm askin' you to stay in heah till I come back," said Enoch earnestly.

"Ahuh," replied Cal. It was a promise as well as an expression of his conviction. He had guessed why his brother had asked him to stay indoors.

"Come, Mary, I want you out heah," went on Enoch, and led her out into the dark, cold night. The stars were bright above the black pines. Gay chatter and song and laughter sounded from the yellow flare of bonfire. Couples appeared to be strolling into and out of the gloom.

"Mary, when I was comin' in someone tagged me an' told me Georgie was carryin' on sort—sort of wild with Bid Hatfield," whispered Enoch, bending close to her. "Now with Tim drinkin' an' Cal heah this will never do. Someone is goin' to tell them an' then there will be hell."

"What can we do?" asked Mary.

"I reckon all we can do is to get Georgie inside an' keep her there."

"I'm sure I can guarantee that," responded Mary.

"Wal, mebbe. Reckon you don't savvy Georgie. Anyway, she's out there in my car with Hatfield. An' I'm tellin' you strong we've got to break that up or somebody is goin' to——"

"Wait here, I'll go," interrupted Mary.

WITH mingled emotions of shame and anger Mary hurried out into the darkness to find Georgiana. She did not intend to mince matters. It was not quite clear to her just what catastrophe impended, but she felt that here was one. Cal had seemed too cool, too intense, too pleasant to be safe, and the significance of Enoch's words had not been lost upon her. Georgiana was an outsider, and it began to look serious for her.

There were lovers strolling to and fro under the pines, and here and there low voices coming from the darkness. Mary had some difficulty in finding Enoch's car, and it was Georgiana's well-known voice that guided her.

"Cut it out, will you! I don't want my dress mussed any worse," Georgiana was saying.

Hatfield's reply sounded rather deep and pleasant. "Say, kid, there isn't much of it to muss."

Mary hurried up to the car. In the gloom she could see Georgiana's white form. She appeared to be in Hatfield's arms. On the moment he bent to kiss her. Georgiana then endeavoured to free herself, but her action was not by any means desperate.

"Georgiana, get out of that car and come back into the school-house," demanded Mary in a voice she had never used before.

Hatfield released Georgiana and stepped out of the car. Mary could just see the pale gleam of her sister's face. Georgiana sat there a moment in silence.

"Am I a child to be ordered about?" she asked.

"Your conduct is disgraceful," replied Mary coldly. "If you have no respect for yourself, I insist that you have some for me."

"Mary!" cried out Georgiana.

Then without another word she flounced out and hurried towards the school-house. Mary started to follow her, but was intercepted by Hatfield.

"Miss Stockwell, I reckon it's only square for me to take the blame," he said. "Georgie didn't want to come out."

"No apologies are necessary, Mr. Hatfield," replied Mary. "I do not blame you in the least. But if you are in need of advice, I would say that you are courting trouble."

"Thanks. Sure I know what I'm up against. But I can't see where I'm called to show yellow. Your sister must like me or she wouldn't stand for—for me. An' if that's so I'll fight the whole Thurman outfit."

"I agree with you," returned Mary. "But the worst of this is—Georgiana doesn't care in the least for you. I—I honestly wish she did, so that I would not be ashamed of her."

"Look here, Miss Stockwell," he rejoined bluntly, "I'm thinkin' you're on the level. Reckon I'm in love with Georgie, an' she could make a decent fellow out of me. No girl could kiss—an'—an' talk like Georgie unless she cared. Sure she's a wild little filly—an' wants the boys crazy over her. But she couldn't go so—so far unless she cared."

"I think Georgie could," replied Mary. "I don't know, for certain, but you're welcome to what I believe. Georgie seems to be devoid of shame, of conscience—not to say more. She's just playing with you."

Hatfield started as if he had been struck. He bent to peer closely into Mary's face.

"You say that—her sister?" he queried, with a catch in his breath.

"Yes. I believe it. I don't want to be unkind to you or unjust to her. But the situation is bad, you must admit."

"I reckon it is. Mebbe worse than you think," he muttered.

"I've no more to say, Mr. Hatfield," added Mary, moving away.

"You've said a heap. You've showed me a hoss of another colour. I'm thankin' you an' I'm sorry she's your sister. If you'll take a hunch from me, you'll send her back where she belongs. The Tonto won't stand for little hussies like her."

Mary bowed her acknowledgements and hurriedly returned towards the school-house. Hatfield did not appear to be such a bad sort, and probably a really good girl might have done wonders for him. He struck Mary as having the same crude manliness characteristic of all these riders of the Tonto. His last words, and especially his suggestion as to Georgiana, troubled her exceedingly. Indeed, the girl did not fit here among these primitive people.

Then Enoch loomed over Mary and his hard hand, seeking hers, seemed something to cling to.

"Wal, you shore fetched her," he drawled. "She came a-rarin', an' when I tried to stop her—what do you think she said?"

"Goodness knows," replied Mary helplessly.

"Wal, it was funny. I seen her comin', an' I said: "Wal,

Georgie, as I'll soon be a sort of dad to you, reckon you'd better come an' make up with me.' "

"Enoch, you didn't?"

"I shore did. An' the little wildcat glared at me an' says, sassier than I ever heard her: 'How'd you like to go where it's hot?' "

Enoch's mellow laugh rang out and he slapped his leg with a broad hand. But Mary could not laugh. She was on the verge of tears.

They entered the school-house to find the dance at last in full swing. The children were all asleep in the two corners reserved for them. The old folk were looking on and chatting. Henry Thurman had warmed up to his fiddling job. And the young people were settling down to real dancing, as Enoch put it. Mary found the only difference to be a more crowded floor, a swifter step, and a mounting significance of more than pleasure and excitement. She gathered now that this was a serious matter, this endless swaying to the old fiddler's rhythm, and was in fact the courting-time of the young people of the Tonto.

Everybody seemed to act and talk with perfect naturalness, so that Mary could not help doubting fights were imminent. Cal sat with his Uncle Gard and appeared to be ignoring the feminine contingent. Hatfield had a window seat where he reclined between very attentive young ladies, strangers to Mary. Georgiana sat under the lamplight, which fact Mary believed was no accident, and she was not lacking attendants. Tuck Merry appeared to be most happily engaged, with no rivals near the lady he favoured. If he had been in fights, he assuredly did not show it. Tim Matthews had a very red face and a very loose tongue. Apparently, however, he was still good-natured. He was with some boys near the door, all standing, and when he started to leave them, someone dragged him back. Enoch said there was a bottle in that crowd and if Tim touched it a few more times he would be ready to be thrown out. Mary had no difficulty discerning that most of these kindly boys were hanging on to Tim to keep him out of mischief. Not improbably Tim was the only person at the dance who had not remarked Hatfield's attention to Georgiana.

It was altogether a homely scene of backwoods life, yet it appealed strongly to Mary. Simplicity and virility had faded out of many walks of American life. But they abided here. Almost every one of these boys had seen service during the war, and some of them had been in France. What a record Boyd Thurman had brought back! Still, no one would have guessed it. Even the stress of a great war could not change these Arizonians. Their lives had been too free, too rough, too hard for war training to make any material change in them.

Mary remembered well what Serge Thurman had said in reply to her query as to what he had gotten out of the war: "Wal, I reckon all I got was the 'flu an' a knock on the haid."

Henry Thurman brought the intermission to an end with a twang of his fiddle.

"Rustle yore pardners now," he called. "I'm a fiddlin' fool an' I'm lookin' to see some of these heah long-legged riders danced down."

A shout greeted Henry's speech. Evidently it was a challenge put forward by the girls and accepted by the boys. The music started and the dancers took to the floor with a rush.

Enoch came striding up to Mary. "Wal, I've been lookin' everywhere for you. Reckon it's my dance."

"This is that tag affair. I'll be torn to pieces. Couldn't you hang on to me, Enoch, instead of parcelling me off to every Tom, Dick, and Harry here?"

"Reckon I can stave off some of the boys."

But Enoch reckoned without due consideration for the accelerating warmth and spirit of the dance. Mary was more than ever a mark of approval. She was taken away from him at once and every time that he succeeded in getting her back, he did not have time to make one step before he got tagged again. Finally he gave up in disgust. Mary had a hectic time of it during this dance. It was a romp to music, and these riders, manifestly put on their mettle by the challenge of the girls to dance them down, were gay, persistent, and absolutely tireless. Mary danced until her head grew dizzy and her feet dead. Yet the fun of it was contagious.

From that hour Mary became a spectator. The dance went on and grew in every sense from the fiddling of old Henry to the action and endurance of the participants. Gradually, however, the married couples withdrew, leaving the floor to the young folk. All during the evening Mary had heard the occasional monotonous sing-song voice of the old fiddler as he called out something she could not distinguish. But now she had opportunity to listen, and she grew much interested and amused.

> "Cinch 'em tight
> An' swing all night—
> Tee dell de tee dell de."

Every few moments Henry would break out with one of his improvisations. Manifestly they were eagerly awaited and happily received.

> *"Serge's mad an' I can see*
> *Trouble ahead 'twixt him an' Lee."*

This brought forth shouts of approval and inspired Henry to greater heights.

> *"Edd's shore a-walkin' on air*
> *An' all the while trompin' on Clair."*

Edd Thurman was the giant of the assembly and danced like a lumbering rhinoceros. A huge laugh went up at his expense. Henry was quiet for a long time, his grizzled head bent over his fiddle, and he had a manner of profound meditation.

> *"Them riders air weakenin', girls, as I can see*
> *Their feet air draggin', 'twixt you an' me."*

Henry must have imagined the content of this last rhyme. There was no justification for it that Mary could see. As the hours wore towards dawn, these lengthy riders appeared to grow fresher. If any lagging showed at all, it was on the part of the girls.

> *"Mere an' Merth are pretty little twins.*
> *Go to it boys an' see who wins."*

That seemed to exhaust the old fiddler for a long spell. When at length he raised his head to call out again, it was in stronger voice:

> *"I'm the fiddlenest fool*
> *Full of White Mule."*

Then after a full pause, as if for effect, he roared out:

> *"Listen, boys, an' heah this verse.*
> *Some of you go out an' fetch a hearse.*
> *Tuck Merry's slammed three of our best;*
> *It'll never do till he meets the rest."*

At this hour, which was about three o'clock in the morning, the enjoyment and excitement of the dance appeared to be at its height. The dancing had become almost continuous. It grew to be a contest. The riders who had just finished the fall round-up, the hardest week of the year, refused to be danced down by the ambitious girls. So it looked as if there would be a deadlock, with physical exhaustion for both sides as the outcome.

Mary, happening to remember the untoward fears of the early evening, remarked to Enoch that apparently she had exaggerated the possibilities of trouble.

"Wal, it's only the shank of the evenin' yet," he replied enigmatically.

"What do you mean?"

"Shore I cain't say. But I've a hunch somethin' is goin' to come off. The longer it waits the worse it'll be. . . . An' now that you make me thoughtful, I want to tell you that none of us older folks like your sister's dancin'."

"Oh!" cried Mary in dismay. "I was—worried. But Georgiana has been dancing very—very decorously for her."

"Reckon she has up to this heah dance. Take a look at her."

Mary was not long in picking out her sister's lithe, supple, wriggling form. Her partner was Dick Thurman, the youngest of the family, and he was one, Mary remembered, that Georgiana had coached in the new Eastern dances. How sadly out of place was the jazz dancing here in this backwoods' school-house! Mary was fascinated as well as repelled. Georgiana was indeed a striking little figure. She bent, she swayed, she gyrated, and seemed to inspire her partner to be oblivious of all save her.

"Wal, that wouldn't be so damn' bad if Georgie was dressed different," muttered Enoch, as if correcting his own judgment.

Mary endeavoured to catch Georgiana's eye. This appeared to be impossible. Georgiana apparently had no eyes for anybody except her partner. Yet of course she must have been aware of the sensation she was creating.

"Wal, I'll be dog-goned!" burst out Enoch. "She's got some of the kids doin' it. Mary, it's all plain as print. Georgie has taught that dance to some of our crazy youngsters, an' now they're aboot to spring it on us. The nervy little devil!"

When Mary verified the truth of Enoch's observation her dismay increased. Three young couples had begun to dance in a way calculated to excite mirth and disgust. Their intentions were plain, but their execution was ridiculous. Georgiana's dancing had grace, rhythm, and beauty despite the quality that was objectionable. Many couples left off dancing the better to watch this new and bewildering style. Gradually Georgiana and her pupils drew the attention of old and young alike. There was no mistaking the undisguised disapproval of the mothers and fathers present, nor any doubt about the young people being fascinated.

That dance ended, to Mary's infinite relief. Then she asked Enoch if it would not be wise for her to seek Georgiana, though not to compel attention, and advise against further dancing of that kind.

There was the usual short intermission, in the middle of which Bid Hatfield swaggered across the empty floor and went straight to Georgiana, manifestly to claim her for the next dance.

"Wal, I reckon Bid ain't to be blamed much, but it's sort of hard luck for him," spoke up Enoch.

"Why—hard luck?" faltered Mary. When had she ever seen Enoch's eyes flash like grey lightning or his lean jaw bulge and set hard as flint?

"Mary, you know we Thurmans fight among ourselves—at a toss-up—just for the fun of it. But we're shore slow to fight with outsiders. Hatfield has gotten away with a lot of stunts—slapped right in our faces. Reckon we all think Cal's no better than anybody else, but it looks like Georgie has given him a dirty deal. So has Hatfield. . . . Wal, to come to the point. Georgie an' Hatfield has got pretty thick an' it's offensive to us Thurmans. If they have the nerve to dance that—that nigger stuff together, it'll break up——"

The loud discordant twang of old Henry's fiddle interrupted the conclusion of Enoch's statement. Mary did not need to hear it. She was distressed, yet somehow she was resentfully and thrillingly awaiting the issue. This time, for some strange reason, the couples were slow to get into the dance. Couple by couple they started out as if impelled to dance because the music had begun. But plain it was that they would rather have watched. This tardiness gave Georgiana and Hatfield an opportunity they were not slow to grasp. They started off in a close embrace and with swaying motion Mary knew had never before been seen on that floor. Critically she watched them. Either Hatfield had been more carefully instructed or had taken to this style of dancing more skilfully than the others who had essayed it. For he presented an admirable partner for Georgiana. They both did very well indeed what never should have been done at all. Hatfield was not cool, but he was defiant. No doubt, he realised infinitely more than Georgiana the sensation they were creating. As for Georgiana, her face was hot and her eyes were wicked. Youth, pride, vanity, and mistaken sense of conquest had brought her to a risk she did not realise.

Mary looked up at Enoch and was relieved to find him smiling as he watched. He was as broadminded and kindly as he was forceful. Then Mary glanced from Enoch to the older Thurmans near at hand. She could not discern any difference in their demeanour. But presently, the stalwart Gard Thurman, the uncle of Cal, got up

C.W.—6

and strode along between the dancers and the wall until he reached old Henry.

Suddenly the fiddling stopped so shortly that everybody seemed startled into an expectant pause. Gard Thurman stood up on a box, high above the dancers. His square shoulders appeared aggressively wide. He had a strong, dark visage, weather-beaten and rugged, with deep-set, fiery eyes and grizzled locks.

"Folks an' friends," he began in a sonorous drawl, "before we go any farther with this heah dance, I've got a word to say. . . . We've had good times heah in this old school-house, an' many an' many a dance. They've shore been aboot all the fun us Tonto folks can look to. . . . Wal, I reckon these dances hevn't been much to brag aboot, but they've always been decent an' they're always goin' to be decent. An' I'm statin' flat thet no outsider can come in heah an' make our dances indecent. . . . Thet's all. I'm sayin' this as a gentleman an' allowin' fer the foolishness of young folks. But there won't no more be said."

A blank silence followed the conclusion of Gard Thurman's speech. He stood there a moment, a powerful figure, menacing yet with all friendliness, his deep gaze fixed upon the guilty dancers. Then he stepped down and his brother Henry began to fiddle valiantly, as if to make up for lost time and an embarrassing moment. Again the dancers fell into their shuffling, rhythmic movements.

But Georgiana and her partner did not dance again. Mary's keen eye followed them out of the throng to the comparative seclusion of a far corner, where they evidently talked with their backs to the dancers. Soon Georgiana wheeled about and came hurriedly down the room, to the corner where the coats and wraps had been left. Hatfield followed her. Mary saw him spread wide his hands as if expostulating or appealing. Georgiana apparently paid no attention to him. She was in a hurry.

Mary left her own seat, and in going round the room she lost sight of Georgiana for the time being. Meanwhile Enoch had disappeared. When Mary reached the far end of the long room, near the door, she found Enoch there, talking earnestly to Cal. As soon as he saw Mary he discontinued whatever he was saying. Cal was as white as a sheet. There were others near, some of them women, but Mary had no interest to note who they were.

Georgiana appeared in the act of dismissing Hatfield. He looked angry. She did not deign him so much as a glance, and she turned towards the door. She had put on her heavy coat, and she was tying a white fleecy shawl over her head. She came straight for the group in front of the door. At sight of her face Mary's anger softened.

"Georgie, where are you going?" she asked hurriedly.

But Georgiana might not have heard her, for all the sign she gave. She did not see Mary's outstretched hands. Just then the music ceased. Georgiana walked straight to Cal and looked up at him. Mary, though watching her so closely, still saw the intent, curious faces of others in the group.

"Cal, will you take me home?" she asked in a low but distinct voice. "Tim is drunk. I'm afraid of Hatfield. There isn't anyone else I'd ask—except you. . . . Will you take me?"

Then Mary found it in her heart to both pity and admire this little sister. Georgiana had experienced a sudden violent shock. She seemed under an intense strain, about ready to collapse, yet upheld by spirit. She was brave. She made no apology or excuse. But pride, defiance, deviltry had gone out of her face. The fire and force of her had faded.

Then Mary bent a most eager gaze upon Cal Thurman. He too was intensely curious, and Mary knew in him Georgiana had a friend, despite her faults.

Of all the young men present, who had seen her humiliated, she had chosen to ask the one least calculated to stand by her in the moment of her shame. That would have been the verdict of the crowd. But did her intuition guide her rightly in this trying ordeal? The fact was that when the catastrophe had fallen she had appealed to Cal. Mary realised, from the dark, hard gleam in Georgiana's eyes, from the strained white resoluteness of her, that if Cal repudiated her, gave her scorn for scorn, she would go home alone, she would walk every step of that long, lonely road through the forest. Would he give in to the natural human weakness to hurt her as she had hurt him? But Mary divined that if Cal was ever to win the love of Georgiana, this was the time to do it. There was no telling all that revolved in that girl's mind.

"Why sure I'll take you home," replied Cal, with dark, steady eyes on hers. He was as self-possessed as Enoch. "I came to take you home."

Then in the quick break of Georgiana's composure was a proof that she had not in the least been sure of his chivalry. But, womanlike, in the hour of stress she had put him to the test. She drooped her head. Perhaps only his loyalty could have shamed her.

Cal took her arm and led her through the opening crowd before the door, and out into the dark.

"Hey, Cal," called Enoch, after him, "fetch the car back for us."

It was the noon-hour up at Rock Spring Mesa, and the December sun shone so pleasantly that the men ate in their shirt-sleeves.

There was a white line of snow up on the Rim, and patches of white down the timber-protected slopes. But snow seldom lay long on the south slopes. Wild turkey and deer wintered down on the warm sunny benches.

According to the men, Cal Thurman had chosen the finest site in the Tonto for his homestead. It appeared high above the rolling black-timbered land of the basin, yet it lay far below the lofty level Rim. In reality it was not a mesa, for it had only three sides. The fourth was a level extension meeting the cedared slope. Promontory would have been a more felicitous name. It was a wide, flat-topped bench, covered with cedar, juniper, and some pine, that extended out over the basin farther and higher than other benches which ran down from the Rim. A yellow rocky bluff stood out blunt and ragged at the end of the level, where mesa met the slope, and here under the cliff bubbled the famed spring that gave the place its name. For years the Thurmans had felt they owned this perennial water, but in reality they never had until the day Cal arrived there to build his homestead.

During November they had cleared fifty acres of it, fine red soil mostly free of rock. This square piece comprised the front end of the mesa, except for a fringe of timber left on the west and south.

"Shore the wind's going to blow logs right out of yore cabin," said Gard Thurman.

"I reckon it's got to be darn' strong an' heavy," was old Henry's reply to this.

"Wal," drawled Wess, in the tone he always adopted when he meant to be funny, "we can snake big logs down heah an' we can heave them into a cabin no north wind'll bother, but Cal himself has shore got to find an' keep what goes along with homesteadin'."

"Ahuh! You mean Cal's got to find himself a woman," replied Henry thoughtfully. "Wal, I never seen before thet gettin' a woman was powerful hard for a Thurman."

"Time enough for that," broke in Cal gruffly. "But if you men eat an' gab all day long we'll never get the cabin run up."

"My son, learn to be patient," replied old Henry, kindly. "Shore there's no hurry. You've got the land, an' now you've all the time there is."

Cal strode away from the camp, out along the edge of the cleared land, through the odorous green-and-brown belt of timber to the edge of the mesa. Here had been a favourite outlook of his as long as he could remember. When he was ten years old he had played there and pretended to build his cabin.

Cal had not been down to Green Valley for a month. He longed to see Georgiana, but pride kept him from going. Not since the October dance, from which he had taken her home, disgraced in her own sight, had he been with her. That night he had risen above his resentment. But he had waited for Georgiana to make amends for the wrong done him. All the way home on that memorable ride through the forest she had scarcely spoken a word. Upon arriving at Green Valley she had left the car at the gate, saying: "You need not go in. . . . I thank you, Cal Thurman. I'll say I've misjudged you. But for you I'd never have come back here at all. . . . I'm not worth your respect—nor anything else. Good night."

"Aw, Georgie, don't talk like that. Wait!" he had implored. But she had fled. And he had not set eyes upon her for a week afterwards. Then she seemed changed. When he did make opportunity for her to speak, to right the wrong she had done him, she talked only of casual things, and soon found excuse to leave him. Cal's lips had been locked. And in the succeeding weeks they had drifted farther apart.

Cal had not suffered grievously under this estrangement. It hurt him more that Georgiana could never forget the insult dealt her at the dance, could never understand, could never believe that she had really not disgraced her sister. But when the weeks passed and gradually Georgiana had come back to friendly acceptance of attention from the boys, though colder, it seemed to him, then Cal could no longer endure the situation. He won his father to instant execution of the homestead plan, and now he had been away a month. Enoch and his riders had returned from the Winslow cattle-drive, and were now helping hew the logs for his cabin. In another day the logs would be notched and flattened, ready to be raised into the finest cabin ever built under the Rim.

Nevertheless, Cal was bitterly unhappy. He could not stand it much longer. Almost desperate, he sat there on the rocky edge, under the juniper tree that seemed an old friend, and at last he cried out, inarticulately: "Oh, what shall I do?"

What a relief to voice his agony, his longing, his impotence. It was as if he had denied it and had proudly refused to ask for help or light. Pride was about to fall. He was alone, with no eye but that of all-seeing Nature and God upon him in his abasement. Sound of his voice was the final step in his surrender. From that moment began a subtle change and uplift in him. Here was the place and now was the time. All that he lacked was Georgiana Stockwell. In a kind of dream or trance then, as he closed his eyes, it came to him—what must be done to save himself. He must have her. That was all. It did not matter what she had done or what she was or what she wanted. That was his only chance. She had liked him once, enough for him to feel like a man in pressing his suit. Could she have changed all in a day? No! If anything, she must think more of him than ever. Only, she would die before she would confess it!

Cal found himself, found understanding and decision, there in the favourite place of his boyhood. The cold, fragrant December wind bore something down from the Rim; the chequered juniper tree, sturdy and gnarled, old and grey, bent over him with the lesson of its struggle; the loneliness spoke to him; the black depths of the canyon jungle called him in the name of primitive men; the noble brow of Promontory seemed to shine with a golden light; the dim purple Mazatzals gave of their mystery and strength—and all about him breathed the insidious whisper—go claim his mate.

"But how—but how?" burst out Cal, aghast, yet almost happy in his revelation. There was no answer to that. The elements did not conspire with him. They merely spoke passionlessly, bidding him listen to the nature that was in him.

Sixteen men, all of them Thurmans, heaved the notched logs for Cal's cabin. It was a distinction seldom given a log-raising. Cal heaved with them, with all his might. He wanted his strength, too, in the upbuilding of this homestead.

It was to be a cabin like Gard Thurman's, in fact, two cabins with one roof. The rooms were fifteen feet in width, twenty feet in length, and the space between them was to serve as a covered porch. No wheel of wagon or car had ever gotten within five miles of Gard Thurman's home, and this of Cal's was farther up the rugged slopes. Burros had for days been packing lumber from Henry's sawmill—boards for floors and doors and casements and closets. The four windows had come from Globe, and had been entrusted to old Jinny, the safest packer of the burros. Slender poles of pine had been cut to point the gable roof, that was to extend clear across both rooms and the intervening space. A fine-grained pine tree had yielded the shingles—"shakes," they were called—and these were piled neatly near by, ready for the shinglers. Cheerily, lustily the men laboured. This was pioneer work, and they were blazing the path for civilisation.

One Saturday noon, close to Christmas, old Henry wiped the sweat from his wrinkled brow and called to the few Thurmans he had kept to finish the job. "Done, you sons-of-guns, an' shore she's a daisy!"

Such a double cabin had no counterpart in all the Tonto. The wide shelving eaves sheltered a porch all along the front. There was a ladder leading to the loft above the space between the cabins —ample room for storage or for sleeping-quarters. An open fire-place of stone on the west side was Henry's especial pride. It would hold as large a fire-log as a man would care to lift. Home-made furniture, rude but serviceable, such as tables, chairs, bed-steads, had been made.

"Boy, yore homestead is ready," said Henry to his son. "Come down to Green Valley for Christmas. Then we'll pack up yore outfit, an' a stove for the kitchen, an' a lot of grub. I'll give you some hosses an' cattle—an', wal, I reckon thet's aboot all I can do for you."

"Cal, when you fetch yourself a woman we'll shore storm this heah cabin," remarked Edd. Somehow the idea of cabin and homestead was not complete without a woman.

12

THE men packed their tools and effects kept there during the building, and rode away, leaving Cal with his friend.

Tuck had to see everything and his interest was stimulating. They went all over the cabin, up into the lofts, and then out into the cleared field, where the stumps were still burning. Tuck had to have a drink of the spring, and he was loud in his praise of everything.

"Is there any more to see?" he asked finally.

"Guess you given it the once over, as you say, except my lookout point. It's as high as the fire ranger's station on the Diamond," replied Cal.

"Lead me to it," said Tuck with enthusiasm.

Whereupon Cal led him across the field of red soil, into the timber and out to the promontory. The day was unusually fine and clear.

"You can't often see the Sierra Ancas in winter," said Cal, pointing to the most distant range, far to the south.

Tuck gazed from far to near and from near to far, and then all around. How comforting was his delight; Cal began to find something of his old joy. After all, he had to live there and work out his destiny there. Perhaps in time . . .

"Buddy, for a city man that is beyond words. Just grand! You won't be bothered by gasoline smell here or rattle of the elevated or second-story burglars—or bill collectors, or anything! To make it perfect you need only——"

"What?" queried Cal, as his friend hesitated.

"Georgiana Stockwell," replied Tuck deliberately.

At that Cal suddenly sat down on the flat stone under the juniper. Tuck's reply was like a blow in an unguarded moment. A rush of emotion almost overcame Cal.

"Pard," he said, with lowered head, "you're hittin' below the belt."

"Not on your life!" exclaimed Tuck, with his long arm going round Cal's shoulder. "I came up to-day on purpose to tell you that, and I expected to see you duck. But don't feel bad. Cal. It's tough, especially as you're a Thurman who won't *try* to win the one woman."

"Try! Why, Tuck, you're crazy," declared Cal. "I've crawled on my knees."

"Sure. But, Buddy, you didn't crawl at the right time, nor far enough. And you're too proud. You expected Georgie to crawl, just because she *ought* to. Boy, you don't know women. That kid crawl! Never in this wide world! But she could be scared into 'most anything."

"Scare Georgie!" echoed Cal. "That couldn't be done. She has more nerve than anyone I ever knew. Besides, what use to scare her?"

"We'll come to that presently. Now what I want to get straight is this. I haven't seen you for several weeks, and during that time I figured you'd brace, take the count, and get back into the ring again. But you haven't. You've quit. And I'm fearing it's worse with you than I'd guessed. Tell me, Buddy. You'll never know what a friend you were to me when I was down and out. What seems to be wrong between you and Georgie?"

"I guess she doesn't care, that's all," replied Cal dejectedly.

"But she did—as much as her kind ever cares for any fellow. They got to be handed a couple, her kind, before they are gentle. She'll never care any more unless you make her. And I think this absent treatment of yours has made her care less. If you don't do something quick you're going to lose her."

"What on earth can I do?" blurted Cal, goaded to desperation.

"It's a case of rough-house," replied Tuck with a grin.

"I'd do anything that wasn't dishonourable," replied Cal.

"Buddy, makin' this wild kid marry you wouldn't be crooked, believe me. I want to state that it'd be her salvation and a genuine blessing to Mary Stockwell."

"Ahuh! If you can prove that, talk quick," said Cal sharply.

"Listen, then, and don't butt in till I get this off my chest," went on Tuck. "I've kept close tab on Georgiana and all that concerned her these last four weeks. You know she came here for her health and improved wonderfully at first. Well, now she's going back. She doesn't ride and run around in the open as before. She moped in her room until her sister made such a rumpus that she had to come out. But her pep is gone. This sort of thing can't last. She'll run off, or do some fool stunt. Miss Mary has lost patience with her, which is no wonder. And of course since the dance scandal the Thurmans are a little chilly. The situation is bad for Georgie. Everybody misunderstands your attitude. Thinks you, too, have thrown her down. Such gossip gets to her ears. I dare say Georgie imagines she hates you now. I know when I mention you she blazes like fire. But maybe that's a good sign. It wouldn't do, though, for you to go honeying around her. . . . Well, lately, the last week, I've seen things that bothered me. For one, Bid Hatfield called at your house to see Georgie."

"You don't say!" ejaculated Cal in dark amaze.

"Yes, I do say. He didn't get to see Georgie, but he left a note, which was given her. That wasn't so bad. But twice this week I've seen Hatfield ride down that hill trail below the sawmill. Twice, in the middle of the afternoon. Well, by inquiring casual-like of Miss Mary, I found out that Georgie has been taking walks, when the afternoons are sunny, and——"

"Tuck! Has she been meeting Bid Hatfield?" queried Cal tensely.

"I don't believe she has—yet. I've no call to say so, except I think the kid is really on the level. If she's met Hatfield, it's been by accident. If she hasn't, it's a cinch she soon will meet him."

"Tuck, if that happens, an' my folks hear of it, Georgie won't be welcome at my home any longer."

"Right-o. I had that figured. The worst of it is, if Georgie knew that, she'd be more inclined to meet Hatfield. Queer, girls are! She's in a state of mind and health when she's liable to ruin her life. Now let's change all that for her."

"All right. But how?" queried Cal eagerly.

"I've figured it all out, Buddy," continued Tuck just as eagerly. "The Sunday after Christmas I'll ride down to get Parson Meeker. I've met him a few times, and think he likes me. Anyway, I can handle him. I'll make up some story that will get his sympathy. In the Tonto, you know, anybody can get married quick if he fetches the lady. That'll be your job, and if I'm not mistaken it'll be *some* job. Now I'll fetch Parson Meeker by trail, round the Diamond to Boyd Thurman's cabin. No one living there, and if it's cold we can make a fire. We'll be there about noon Monday, and wait for you. Wal, I reckon that's about all, as Enoch says."

"All! Good Heavens, man, it's nothin' to my part in this—this wonderful plan," cried Cal excitedly. "What have I got to do?"

"Grab the little lady and tote her up there—and we'll do the rest," declared Tuck loquaciously.

"Wha-at?" stammered Cal. Indeed the idea had dazzled him.

" All you've got to do is to catch Georgie out of the house or drag her out of the house. Have a horse handy, hidden in the brush. Carry her if you have to. You want to act mad, quick, and rough. Don't talk much. If you talk she'll get the best of it. Scare her into the middle of next week."

"It's easy to talk of scarin' Georgie, but how can it be done?" asked Cal wildly.

"You're afraid of her. Well, make her afraid of you. What does that kid know of rough men? Act like some of the Tonto outlaws she's heard about. Make her think she has driven you to it. She's only a child. All that nerve of hers is just modern bluff. Scare it out of her. Then make her swear not to tell Parson Meeker you carried her off."

"Ahuh! An' then, supposin' all this—this dream comes off, an' I do get her married—what then?" asked Cal, as one whose brain was whirling.

"Pack her up here to your new cabin. You can have all ship-shape by that time."

"An' then—after I pack her up here—what'll I say?" asked Cal feebly. His heart was swelling and rising to his throat.

"Let me see," replied this arbiter of wisdom, reflectively. "I think I'd make a grand finale of it. I'd *carry* her in and drop her down and say, in a big loud voice: 'Now, Mrs. Cal Thurman, I want my dinner. I'm not in a mood to sing for it or whistle for it, but I *want* it!' . . . Then go out, and let her come to."

Cal shook his head sadly at what he considered the mental aberration of his friend. Yet the insidious voice of temptation was irresistible. His last and only chance! It was doomed to failure, in any event. If he did succeed in forcing Georgiana to marry him, there was no possibility of keeping her a prisoner.

"Buddy, don't overlook this fact," put in Tuck, as if he read Cal's thoughts. "Once you marry Georgie, she'll not find it so easy to get out of as you think now, and as she'll think. Nobody is going to believe you kidnapped her, and if she runs off from you, she'll disgrace her sister sure this time."

That idea struck home to Cal's grasping hope. It would be a serious situation for Georgiana. But however she reacted to it, the most alluring prospect was the fact that if he succeeded in marrying her, there could be no further danger of her flirting, no more risk for her in trifling with men. The code of the Tonto was a rigid thing, and even men like Bid Hatfield respected it. Married, she would be saved from herself, so far as the Tonto was concerned, no matter what she did.

"Next Monday! Five more days! . . . My God!" ejaculated Cal, in defeat that had its exquisite torture of joy.

"Buddy, so help me Heaven, it'll work out fine," responded Tuck, with great relief and satisfaction. "By springtime you and I will sit right here under this old juniper, and you'll be telling Tuck Merry he's square with you."

Cal rode back to Green Valley that afternoon late, a very much obsessed young man, pondering the part he had to play. His morbid depression had vanished. It was going to be difficult, when the crisis came, to pretend a dark, sombre, brooding, and dangerous trend of mind before Georgiana.

The cold winter twilight had fallen by the time Boyd Thurman's deserted ranch had been reached. Sight of the old log-cabin where he had planned to marry Georgiana brought realities to his mind. He thrilled despite the utter wildness of Tuck Merry's plan.

It was dark when he and Tuck reached Green Valley. All the riders were in, judging from the saddles on the rack. He heard the horses and cows munching hay in their stalls. The familiar odours of the barns were sweet to his nostrils. Before presenting himself indoors, he went with Tuck to their tent quarters, and there, by the light of a candle, he shaved and changed his clothes.

Supper had been held for his arrival, and the boys greeted him with a yell and a rush to the table. His mother remarked that he "shore looked sort of pasty," and his sister asked him if he thought it was Sunday, "All cleaned up an' shiny-faced."

Mary Stockwell and Georgiana came in to take their seats at the far end of the long table. When they saw Cal they added their greeting, Georgiana called: "Howdy, Cal! You shore don't look like you been a-rollin' logs."

Cal bent over his plate. How the sweet, high voice shook his heart! For a moment his eyes were dim. Just to hear her worked havoc in him again. And in the moment the thought came that all which sustained him was remembrance of the deep-laid plot. He blessed Tuck Merry for evolving it. He did not glance at Georgiana again during that merry supper-time, and when they repaired to the living-room she did not stay. Mary came to shake hands with him.

"How are you, Cal?" was her kind query, and her eyes searched his face anxiously.

"Fair to middlin', teacher," he replied gaily. 'An' when's the great day for you an' Enoch? I have my mind on a weddin' present."

"I'll tell you when it's decided," she replied.

"How's Georgie?" he went on, trying to be casual.

"Did you look at her?"

"Not particularly. Why?"

"I think you would have seen a change."

"Ahuh! Is she sick?"

"Georgie seems well enough, but she grows thinner and paler. I am worried, Cal. She—— But I'll not tell you now. Sometime soon when we have a good chance."

"All right, teacher. Anythin' I can do—you know me," he said soberly. Her tone, her look, acted upon his heart like a weight of lead.

"Just a word now," she went on in a lower voice, as she drew him a little aside. She hesitated, almost faltered, and there was something wistful in her clear eyes. "Cal, you've changed. You're older—more of a man. I like your face better. You've suffered. . . . Now tell me. Are you over it?"

"Over what?" he asked.

"Your—your infatuation for my sister," she whispered.

"Can I trust you?"

"Oh, Cal—yes, indeed you can," she replied. "I can't tell you how I hope you still care for her."

"Listen, then," he said, bending close to her ear. "I love Georgie—more than ever."

He had his reward in the flash of gladness that crossed her worn face. It struck him then that she too appeared somewhat paler and thinner. He was indeed not the only one to whom Georgiana had brought trouble.

The next day Cal borrowed Tuck's services at the sawmill, and the two of them drove to Ryson and filled a car full of supplies and utensils needed at the Rock Spring homestead and also Cristmas presents. It was the lack of capacity of the car and not Tuck's consternation that compelled Cal to leave off buying. They returned to Green Valley, and spent the remaining hour of that day stowing away these purchases.

The following morning Cal and Tuck, with the help of some of the boys, packed nineteen burros and horses. By noon that day they unpacked in front of the porch of Cal's new home. They had a good deal of excitement in spreading the outfit and finding where every bit of it should be placed. Mid-afternoon overtook them before this pleasant labour was ended; and then followed the task of finding the strayed pack animals and driving them home. They arrived at Green Valley just before dark, tired out but happy, and ready for their great adventure.

Christmas Eve found twenty-odd Thurmans at the Green Valley Ranch. And what with Mary Stockwell and Georgiana, added to the several riders who likewise were no kin of the Thurmans, there was a large household.

Cal sprang a little surprise at them. That day at Ryson, in the excitement of purchasing and the thrill of possible events he had bought presents for everybody. The best the Ryson stores could show was not too good for Cal. He had saved his wages for years. This Christmas signalled the one great event in his life, for weal or woe, and he was celebrating it.

Enoch toyed with the gun he had long ago seen in Ryson and had coveted. "Wal, Cal, shore it's damn' good of you."

Tim Matthews had a wonderful beaver sombrero thrust into his hands, with the words: "Merry Christmas, Tim." Now Tim had never completely become reconciled to Cal since the fight at Boyd Thurman's sorghum field.

"Wh-a-a-t?" he stammered. "This heah forty-dollar beaver for me? . . . Aw! Cal Thurman, if you ain't some sport, I'll eat this hat. Put her thar! I hope to wear it at your weddin'."

A great deal of hilarity attended the presentation of these gifts. "Windfalls!" ejaculated Uncle Gard Thurman. "Wal, the boy's locoed," said Henry. Then an old aunt of Cal's spoke up. "You croakers ought to be ashamed."

At last there was only one present left, and Cal meant this for Georgiana. He had not been unaware of her curiosity, even though she sat in the background and had no share in the hilarity. The moment was fraught with anxiety. Suppose she refused it! But this was Christmas, and she could not do that. Mary Stockwell had opened her lips to reproach Cal for his extravagance, but when she saw what the present was she could only utter her delight. Cal felt that he could safely trust to human nature on Christmas Eve, even if the subject was the wilful and haughty Georgiana.

So he stood with the box behind his back and called out gaily: "Come, Georgie, get yours."

She came forward readily, not at all formidable. Indeed she was smiling, a little wistfully, yet expectantly, and there was something of childhood in her expression. She came right up to him and the light of the blazing logs in the open fireplace shone on her face. It was the closest he had been to her in a month. Cal trembled, and found it hard to keep to his role of gay dispenser of gifts. He almost forgot.

"I'll say you're some little Santa Claus," said Georgiana.

"Guess what it is," suggested Cal.

"Oh, I couldn't. I haven't an idea."

"I'll bet you'll be tickled," he went on tantalisingly. "I was just lucky. This sure was a windfall."

"Well, give it to me then—if it's so wonderful," retorted Georgiana. She was not to be convinced. There was something of pleasurable anticipation in her face, but no enthusiasm.

"Huyler's candy—from New York!" announced Cal triumphantly, and handed over the box.

"Oh! *Really!* How perfectly lovely!" cried Georgiana, suddenly radiant, as she eagerly received the gift.

"Georgie, I wish you a Merry Christmas—an' a Happy New Year here—in the Tonto," added Cal, with a strange earnestness taking the place of his gaiety.

Something in his tone and his look must have struck her singularly. A slight flush came to her pale face.

"Thank you. I wish you the same," she replied, with dark eyes on his for an instant. Then she turned to her sister.

Christmas Day and the Sunday following were nightmares to Cal. He managed to do justice to the sumptuous Tonto dinner, including wild turkey, but the rest of the festivities and social intercourse of the holiday were blank for him. Not until Tuck Merry rode away late Sunday afternoon did Cal regain anything of balance. Then his queer, trance-like vacillation gave way to an intense nervous restlessness. Not much sleep did he get that night!

As luck would have it Monday turned out to be a beautiful bright sunny day. Nature had smiled upon his enterprise. About the middle of the forenoon he saddled his horse, and riding out the back way he circled over a brushy ridge and came down above the ranch, at a point where the walnut swale joined the road. Here back a few rods he tied his horse and returned to the house. Donning the roughest clothes he had—in fact, ragged old garments he had cast aside—he made a bundle of the things he had taken off. He packed a big gun at his hip. And with his old slouch sombrero he imagined he made a rather hard-looking individual. If he had not been so deadly serious about this plan, it would have been funny. He went out and hid in the brush above the house, and with eyes that ached he peered from his covert. He would have an interminable wait. Endless hours before she would come out for her walk! Or she might not come at all, and then he would be forced to go after her. The excitement, the thrill, the zest of the thing had vanished. There was a lump in his throat; his skin felt clammy and cold; and his restlessness increased until it became almost unbearable.

All at once his roving eye caught sight of a horseman riding down a brush-lined trail across the valley.

"Who's that man?" muttered Cal grimly. "I'm not goin' to let him spoil my party. Maybe he'll ride on."

The horseman kept to the brush, disappeared for a few moments, then reappeared farther down, and came off the slope at the end of the Thurman line of cleared ground. Here he kept under cover until he got out to the road, where he was careful to look in all directions. Cal began to breathe hard. The horseman trotted briskly down the road, and turned into the clump of walnut trees in the mouth of the swale where Cal had hidden his horse.

"Bid Hatfield!" gasped Cal, and slowly sank back in his hiding-place.

He was expecting Georgiana to go out for a walk. So was Bid Hatfield. Confronted by this problem Cal pondered over it. At the same time he peered again from his shady nook under the manzanitas. Suddenly he stiffened in his tracks. Georgiana had appeared at the gate, and her quick apprehensive glance up and down the road was not lost upon Cal.

"Ah, hell!" he groaned, and it was as if he had been stabbed. Georgiana knew Bid Hatfield was to be there. She was on the way to meet him. One moment Cal endured pangs the like of which had never before torn his breast, Then swift as light his whole mood changed.

"Ahuh!" he muttered hoarsely. "I'll meet him too, Georgie—an' you can take your choice."

Slipping down like an Indian through the brush, Cal halted just before he came to the road. Georgiana was walking rapidly towards the curve of the road, around which was the opening where Hatfield must be waiting. Cal let her get out of sight. Then he ran along, threading a way through the aisles between the clumps of brush, and turned to climb a low ridge that formed the western bank of the walnut swale. He knew every foot of the ground, and how he could slip right upon these two at their rendezvous. He was in the grip of passion, yet he had self-control left to let the meeting decide his course of action. Bitter and rancorous as he was, he could not give up hope altogether. His faith in Georgiana would not die.

Through an opening in the trees below he caught a glimpse of Georgiana, still hurrying. He glided after her, keeping clumps of brush in front of him. Presently, he caught the brown gleam of Hatfield's bay horse, and next he saw Hatfield sitting on a log, waiting. He saw Georgiana coming. How eager his attitude! Cal ground his teeth in jealous rage. Perhaps the fellow had reason to look happily expectant. They had chosen the thickest part of this swale for their meeting-place. Again Cal saw Georgiana moving along, not so resolutely now. She was lagging. Cal crouched down and covered considerable ground before he looked again. He was now close enough to make up his mind what to do. With tense eyes he peered out.

When Hatfield attempted to take the girl in his arms and she repulsed him in a manner unquestionable, Cal experienced another terrible commotion in his breast. But different from the first! He did not need to see any more to understand that Georgiana was not Hatfield's sweetheart. Cal's keen eyes searched Hatfield's person for a gun. None was visible. "If he's packin' one somewhere, we're in for it—an' I'm ready," muttered Cal to himself. "An' if he isn't, his meetin' Georgie here is great luck for me."

Drawing his gun, Cal glided on, keeping to cover, stepping stealthily. But he need not have taken so much precaution. Hatfield was appealing in poignant tones: "Aw, Georgie, you don't mean it."

"Yes, I do," replied Georgiana almost sharply. "I've been out of my head—long enough. It's wrong to meet you. It'd be wrong if I loved you—which I don't. I'll never——"

Cal called out stridently: "Stick 'em up, Bid!—*Quick!*"

Hatfield's back was turned to Cal. Up went his hands and he stood stiff. Georgiana wheeled to see Cal and let out a startled scream.

"Shut up, you!" ordered Cal, in a voice like a whip.

Then, running round in front of Hatfield he shoved the gun full in that worthy's face. A sweeping glance assured Cal that his rival was unarmed. This immediately lessened Cal's tension, and gave him the force to make the best of his opportunity.

"Reckon I'll kill you!" he hissed out, with all the fury he could summon. He must have done it well, for Hatfield turned a sickly pale hue, and Georgiana screamed in terror.

"For God's sake, Cal—don't—don't kill him!" she begged frantically.

"Why not? You're meetin' him here—sneakin' away from the house where you're a guest—insultin' every Thurman in the Tonto—disgracin' your sister. You must love him."

"Oh, Cal—I swear I don't!" cried the girl, with ashen face. "I've been lonely—miserable. . . . I met him first by accident. He coaxed me, and I was just—just bullheaded enough to come. I was foolish —but I don't care for him. I never even thought so."

"You met him—like this—an' that's enough for a Thurman," replied Cal harshly.

"But Hatfield is not to blame," cried the girl. "*I* am to blame. . . . Put down that awful gun."

In her earnestness she pressed forward as if to take hold of Cal. With one swing of his left arm he swung her off. She staggered against the log and all but fell. Her hand went to her breast; her lips parted and her eyes grew wild.

"Hatfield—get on your horse an' beat it," ordered Cal. "Don't give me any of your chin. I'm lettin' you off because she squared you."

With quick, long strides Hatfield got to his horse and, leaping astride, he reached both hands down for the bridle. Finding that, he straightened up, bent a pale, vindictive face upon Cal, and goading the horse he plunged away under the trees. Then came the swift clatter of hoofs on the hard road.

When Cal turned to Georgiana his stern resolve almost melted. But weakness and tender-heartedness were not to be tolerated now.

"Reckon if you're to blame, I'll take it out on you," he began, striding up to her.

"Why—Cal!" she faltered. "You never were like this—before."

"I never knew all about you before," he returned bitterly.

The little head shot up and a flame of spirit flashed back to the white face.

"You can't talk to me that way," she said. "I'm sorry for what I've done, but I'm not ashamed. Be careful you don't insult me."

Cal decided the fewer words exchanged the better. He thrust his gun back into its sheath, and then with a swift action he fastened his left hand in the front of Georgiana's coat and blouse.

"You come with me," he said.

"I'll do nothing of the——" she responded, but owing to the sudden force he exerted she failed to conclude her statement.

Cal began to stride back into the glade, pulling her with him. For a few yards she went unyieldingly, as if in amaze. Then she began to resist. She held back, fought his arm, and beat at him. But she could not dislodge his hold.

"Let go—I say," she panted. "Are you drunk or crazy? Cal Thurman, I won't go with you. Why, you're worse than Hatfield."

At that he gave her a violent jerk and shake which upset her equilibrium, and she would have fallen, save for his arm. He dragged her on. At sight of his horse she suddenly grew limp.

"What do—you mean?" she whispered.

He made no reply. Untying the bridle with one hand was not easy, but he accomplished it. Then shifting his hold on her, he essayed to mount the horse. This was even more difficult. Finally he let go of her, mounted in a flash, and reaching down secured her again before she had made a step. The horse was trustworthy, yet spirited, and his nervous steps made Cal drag the girl off her feet. Exerting all his strength, he swung her up so that he could reach her with his free hand. Then he lifted her up in front of him, across his saddle. He had tied a blanket over the pommel so that he could carry her there without injury. As the horse started off the swale, Georgiana screamed. Cal clapped a rough hand over her mouth. At that she began to fight. She bit his hand like a wildcat and tore and clawed at him.

"Damn you—Cal Thurman!" she burst out furiously. "Am I an Indian—to be packed off—like this?"

For a moment she made it extremely uncomfortable for him. Wrestling in his arms, beating at his face, she made it almost impossible to hold her and guide the horse under the branches. He was struck several times, once being nearly knocked off. Then a branch hit the struggling girl on the head, hard enough to take the fight out of her. When she sank down into his arms, Cal experienced the most wonderful sensation of his life. He could not understand what it was. But the mingled fear, wrath, and shame with which he had been battling, suddenly changed to a singular deep, vague joy, as if he had plumbed to an old emotion, deep set in his bones. He held her closely.

Then, as her head fell back upon his shoulder he realised that she had fainted. He could only ease her posture and hold her. Over the next ridge there was water, and if she did not come to before he reached it, he would stop there to revive her. Fortunately, the trail had led out of the low-spreading trees, up a brushy slope. Once more out in the sunlight! He noted that she had lost her little felt hat. There was no time to go back for it. Her loosened hair fell over his arms and locks of it yielded to the breeze.

"It's done!" he breathed, as if to the loveliness of the hills. As he neared the summit of that ridge he saw all about him the soft grey-green of the brush and the red of the rocks. Some strange kinship seemed to lie between them and him. They saw him with eyes of Nature. He was in a transport, and yet his heart quaked at the whiteness and stillness of her face. A scratch on her brow showed tiny drops of blood. Cal kissed them away, and suddenly he bent to her lips. Coward and thief he felt himself, yet he had to kiss them. Not the first time, but so differently! She was his now.

It was a brush-overgrown trail, and try as he might he could not save Georgiana from being torn and dragged. He managed, however, to protect her face.

She lay quiet so long that he began to be concerned. Yet he could not convince himself that she had been hurt. Still, a bruise had appeared on her brow, slowly swelling, and blood welled from it. Perhaps the bough had struck her harder than he had imagined. How strangely calm he seemed about this possibility of hurt to her! He did not understand how he could pass over it lightly.

But when he had ridden down the slope of the hill, into a wide, well-wooded valley, with a rocky stream-bed winding through it, he turned off his course to find water. Finally, he came to sycamores, still holding golden-brown leaves, and here he found a clear rock-bound pool of water.

He had to slide out of the saddle while holding Georgiana on the horse. Then he lifted her off, and laid her in the shade of the trees. She appeared to be stirring, but her eyes were still closed. Running down to the water, he saturated his scarf, and hurried back to bathe her pale face. Presently she regained consciousness. Her eyes opened wide, dark dim blue, full of vague dread. At sight of Cal kneeling there she seemed to connect him with what had happened. He was aware of her instinctive shrinking. Words of love, regret, shame, trembled on his lips. But he bit them to keep silent. She lay there watching him for what seemed a long time. Then she gazed at his horse, at the strange place in the woods, and back at him again. Some kind of comprehension showed in her eyes.

"You knocked me—senseless!" she whispered, in wonder, and almost horror.

Quickly Cal read her tone and look. She believed he had struck her while she was fighting him. It was almost impossible to keep from blurting out that she had been stunned by a blow from a sweeping branch. But he could tell her that some other time. His quick intuition grasped the fact that she was regarding him in utter amazement, awe and dread. Yet there was no hate in her expression. He expected her to flay him with scorn for being such a brute. Indeed, she was not reacting to this situation as he had imagined.

"Can you sit up?" he queried gruffly.

"I guess so," she replied, and with his help she rose to a sitting posture. But she did not recover from faintness as promptly as he had hoped. His heart smote him. Where were Miss Georgiana's temper and spirit now? She kept gazing at him so steadily that he found it difficult to hide confusion. Wringing out his scarf, he tied it round his neck.

"Cal, tell me—would you have—have killed Bid Hatfield—if I hadn't taken the blame?" she asked very low.

"Ahuh! Same as I would a hydrophobia skunk," replied Cal, in the hard, deep voice he had assumed.

"Oh, my heavens! What have I done?" she cried out, as if suddenly stricken in conscience.

"Reckon you've done a lot."

"This is no joke—no Tonto trick—to—to——"

"I should smile not," he declared in dark, grim humour.

Then her gaze strayed away from him, and she seemed to look into the woods without seeing them. Cal had his chance to scrutinise her closely. Then he was to grasp the fact of her decline in health. The brown, and the contour of cheek, and the richness of health, won during the early part of her stay at Green Valley, all had vanished. It seemed to Cal that his pity and fear and love would make a fool out of him. If she began to cry and beseech him, he would be lost. But she did neither.

"Get up now. I don't want to lose any more time," said Cal.

She stood up without any assistance from him.

"Where are you taking me?" she asked.

"Time enough to tell you—when we get there," he answered, and stepped to his horse. Mounting, he held out his hand to her. "Put your foot in the stirrup—an' I'll pull you up."

He did not believe in the least that she would comply with this order, and was prepared to chase her into the woods. But thought of escape had evidently not occurred to Georgiana. With his help she climbed up in front of him, and sat as on a side-saddle.

Soon he turned up out of the ravine, and climbing a low hill, proceeded on to the road. This led to the clearing where the cabin specified by Tuck was located.

All this while the girl had maintained silence. Cal did not know what to make of this, but he welcomed it. She would burst out presently. At sight of the cabin his heart gave a leap, and then, when he espied two horsemen riding in from the far side of the ranch, he realised the crisis had arrived.

"I see two riders," spoke up Georgiana, for the first time showing excitement.

"Ahuh!" replied Cal.

"For Heaven's sake, can't you talk?" burst out the girl at last. "You'll drive me mad. What are you going to do next? . . . Those men! I'll call for help."

"Go ahead. It won't do you any good," replied Cal desperately. If she did call he would have to stop her somehow. But as all his part in this unheard-of adventure was pretence, he thought he might as well see how far he could go. She made no outcry. But her languor had vanished. She was now erect, keen, strung with excitement, and unconsciously holding on to his arm. They rode through a grove of beautiful pines to the clearing. The cabin was now close at hand. Two horses were tethered to pine saplings. Their riders had manifestly entered the cabin, for a thin column of blue smoke was rising from the stove chimney.

Dismounting, he lifted the girl off, and then kept hold of her.

"Haven't you—hurt me enough?" she asked, wincing under his grasp. Her dark-blue eyes flashed. She was only subdued for the moment, not conquered.

"I'm takin' you into that cabin, an' you've got to do as I tell you," he said in suppressed passion.

"Who's there?" she faltered.

"Friends of mine. Tuck Merry an'—Parson Meeker." Cal's voice helped him carry on. He felt that he wanted the earth to open and swallow him. Yet the gaze he bent so darkly upon Georgiana seemed to see her as a girl to be overcome.

"Parson Meeker!" she whispered.

"Yes. . . . An' you're goin' to marry me. Do you get that?" She only stared.

"I said—you're goin' to marry me," he repeated hoarsely, giving her a shake. He sensed then that she was physically afraid of him, and this through a false impression. She was white again, and one shaking little hand sought her breast.

"Cal—you can't *make* me say—yes," she said.

"No. But it'll be worse for you an' me if you won't."

"I can tell Parson Meeker you dragged me up here—when I resisted you knocked me senseless. Then he wouldn't dare marry me to you."

"But you're not goin' to tell him," declared Cal fiercely.

"Why am—I not?"

"Because I've gone too far. I don't care what happens. I'd just as lief throw a gun on Parson Meeker. . . . If you tell him, I'll carry you off anyhow."

"Where?" She gasped. "Not to your homestead. Why, your own family would rescue me!"

"I'll take you somewhere deep in the woods—until you do consent to marry me."

"Cal—have I driven you—mad?" she faltered in distress.

"It's too late. Do I marry you or not?" he rasped out.

"Cal Thurman—I'll never go with you *alive* unless you do marry me," she retorted.

"Ahuh! So—it's—settled," panted Cal. "Come on. Let me do the talkin'."

He led her towards the cabin, and all the will he could summon did not halt his riot of emotions. He was in a dream one instant, and the next he was poignantly alive to the girl whose little hand he held closely in his. She was walking beside him willingly.

"Come—on—Georgie," he said huskily, and pushed open the door, to lead her across the stone threshold.

It was dark and smoky inside. Cal closed the door. For a moment he could not see. Then Tuck towered over him, eagerly and joyfully.

"Here you are," he boomed out. "Right on time—Buddy, it's great. . . . Georgie, I'm sure glad to see you. Looks like you must have rode some. Well, elopin' from big sister is some stunt, I'll say. . . . Parson Meeker, this is the little lady, Georgiana Stockwell."

The parson, a tall grey man, bent low in the dim light to shake hands with Georgiana and peer into her face.

"I'm shore glad to meet you, miss," he drawled, in the unmistakable Texas accent. He did not seem to consider the event unusual.

"Thank you," replied Georgiana in low, nervous voice.

"Howdy, Parson," broke in Cal heartily, and wrung Meeker's hand. "It's sure good of you to rustle up here quick. You see—Georgie an' I have been up against a—a little trouble over this marryin'. We had to ride the brush to avoid meetin' anyone, an' I'm askin' you to hurry."

"Right-o," gaily replied Tuck. "Grab her hand there, Buddy, and we'll soon arrange this little matter."

It was then that the dark, smoky little room whirled round Cal, and all he seemed to be sure of was the shaking little hand in his. He heard the preacher and his own voice, and Georgiana's whisper, all strange and far away.

Then Tuck was pounding him on the back, wringing his hand, and talking at a great rate. Parson Meeker, too, shook his hand. His mind seemed to clear with the marvellous fact that he had married Georgiana.

"Ho! Ho! I guess I got to kiss the bride," quoth Tuck Merry as he bent over the girl, "Georgie, I always had a hankering to kiss you just once. There! That's for good luck. . . . And listen, I've a little sister of my own. If she was in your shoes to-day, I'd be happy. Get that! You've married a real man, my dear. God bless you."

The preacher had kind words of congratulation and hope for both Cal and Georgiana. Tuck Merry, however, was the dominant figure there. Perhaps he was the only one with a true perspective of the situation.

"Cal, old scout, we'll be rustling along," he said. "It's all over now and you're the luckiest boy in the Tonto. I'll go back to the ranch and break the news. Won't they be surprised? Too late! Nobody can change it now or stop you. Georgie and you are married. Can't you realise it? Well, Georgie does. You bet no girl could be married without being wise to it. To-morrow I'll have Mary pack all of Georgie's things and I'll bring them up to Rock Spring Mesa. The new homestead, Cal. . . . Georgie, remember my prophecy. You will love that homestead."

If Cal had been in a strange state of locked suspension on his way to that cabin, he was in a stranger one leaving it, leading Georgiana back to the edge of the clearing, where he had tied his horse.

Cal unhaltered his horse, and began to shorten the stirrups. Georgiana stood close by, watching him. How keenly he felt her eyes upon him! He did not look at her. This miserable pretence of his would not last much longer.

"Are you going to walk?" she asked.

"Yes. It's a hard trail uphill, an' you'll have to ride," he said.

"Is what Tuck Merry said true—about you taking me to your homestead?"

"Wait an' see," he replied, trying to assume the former gruff voice.

Cal untied the blanket from in front of the saddle, and then motioned for her to mount. She had difficulty in getting up, but he could not trust himself to help her then. He was afraid even to look squarely into her face. Her skirt, which was short and tight, was going to make riding uncomfortable. Cal folded the blanket lengthwise and threw it over the saddle in front of her, so that it would afford some protection from the brush. Then he took up the bridle, and started off at a brisk walk, leading the horse.

The afternoon, with its short winter sun, had begun to wane. A chill had come to the air. The deep shadows of the pines hid what little sunshine filtered down.

"Are you cold?" asked Cal, turning once.

She was huddled down in his saddle, a forlorn little figure.

"Pretty cold," she replied.

Cal slipped out of his coat. "Here, put this on," he said, stepping back and handing it up to her.

Their eyes met. He saw there weariness and pain, and a shadow he took for fear.

"No," she said.

"It won't soil you," he retorted, with resentment.

"I refused it because I thought you needed it, not because it's dirty and ragged," she replied haughtily.

"Ahuh! You're wonderful considerate of me all of a sudden," he said sarcastically. "Well, you put it on pronto, or I'll yank you out of there an' throw you into it. Savvy?"

Her eyes dilated, even while a blaze rose and died in them, and her lips trembled. She lost no time putting on the coat.

Cal picked up the bridle and resumed his walk. Any exchange of words between them could lead only to scorn, anger, hatred. If she had never hated him before, she surely must hate him now. A melancholy resignation came to Cal. Most certainly, in spite of Tuck Merry's superlative language, Cal had expected to gain only two things by this venture—one was to make Georgiana his wife, and the other to put an end to her dangerous trifling with the young men of the Tonto. Marvellously to behold, he had succeeded in both. Absolutely he had not a hope beyond that. When it occurred to Cal that Tuck had mentioned packing Georgiana's belongings up to the homestead, he had to indulge in a bitter, silent laugh. Georgiana would be gone before Tuck could reach there.

At last the summit of the mesa no longer seemed an unattainable height. Soon Cal led his horse up on the level, in under the great, gnarled, grey-coloured chequer-barked junipers, through the brown-matted aisles, to the new clearing.

There, across the open field, where the blackened stumps still smoked, stood the new cabin. Sight of it gave Cal a sudden pang, as if a blade had pierced his side. His homestead! What mockery was this bringing home a bride! In the gloaming the cabin seemed to presage the loneliness that must always belong to it.

A few more steps, a few more false words, and then the farce would be ended.

Cal dropped the bridle in front of the porch. Turning to Georgiana, he found her sitting up, peering curiously at the cabin. She did not look much the worse for this second long ride. Then her dark gaze fell upon him. In the twilight her face appeared small and wan. Pulling the blanket from round her, he threw it upon the porch.

"Get down an' come in!" he said. The old cordial welcome of Westerners to any visitor! Here it did not ring true.

Georgiana neither moved nor spoke. Her head appeared tilted back a little. Cal expected one of her stinging slang remarks that would make him hate himself worse than he did already. His nerves were all unstrung.

"Come on—my bride!" he called hoarsely and laid a heavy hand on her.

Suddenly she slapped him violently across the face. It was such a shock that he almost staggered. The blow burned him. He had not meant to insult her. To himself he could have explained that facetious mocking allusion.

Then a kind of bursting passion made a savage of him. One powerful pull brought her out of the saddle, sliding into his arms. He held her there, hard and tight, so that her feeble resistance was futile. He kissed her, almost as violently as she had struck him. All his wrath and love and agony then found terrible expression in the kisses he pressed upon her eyes and cheeks and lips. She became limp in his arms. Had she fainted again? He drew back. Her dark eyes were open wide in her white face, and in the gulf of them he seemed to see his own soul.

Mounting the porch, he carried her to the door of the kitchen and opened it. Going into the dark room, he felt around until he found a corner with a built-in couch, and there he deposited her. Everything was in readiness for him to put his hand on. He lighted the lamp. It was a large new one and gave forth a bright light. His hands ceased their trembling and that cataclysm of his heart slowly subsided. Without a glance at the girl he proceeded to start a fire in the stove. The splinters of dry hard juniper began to blaze and sputter. He added larger split pieces, and soon there was a cheerful blaze. Then he closed the stove. In his right hand he still held a billet of wood. This he clutched tightly, as if somehow it might inspire or incite him to the delivery of Tuck Merry's ultimatum.

Wheeling suddenly, Cal looked for the girl. She was sitting up, with her hands clutched in his coat, which she had removed. Her gaze was fixed strangely on him. All about her seemed strange, not what he had anticipated or feared. Even in that moment her sweetness and beauty filled him with despair. But nothing could hold back the climax of this tragic comedy.

"Now, Mrs. Cal Thurman!" he thundered, and then beat the stove with the billet of wood. It clanged loud. Georgiana gave a fearful start. *"I want my supper!* . . . I'm not goin' to beg for it an' I'm not goin' to serenade you to get it. . . . *But I want it!"*

Then Cal had the surprise of his life. She dropped his coat and rose to her feet. This was not the Georgiana he knew. Yet it was, too—her face, the wide eyes, now darker and more strained, the dishevelled hair. She came right up to him. Something was gone from her.

"Yes—I—I will get your—supper," she said tremulously.

"Ah——!" Cal's favourite exclamation broke off in the middle. Yet it served as an acceptance.

"Have you—things here?" she asked.

"Everythin' ready for you," he replied thickly. "I—I'll go put my horse away an' do some chores."

He stamped out, closing the door behind him. The cold night wind fanned his heated face.

"Whew!" he whispered, as he leaned against a porch post. "Scared her into the middle of next week! . . . Damn that Tuck Merry! I'll lick him for this. .

He unsaddled his horse, and hobbling him, turned him loose in the clearing. Then he carried the saddle and put it on a pack under the porch. Next he carried some pieces of wood, and thumped them down near the door of the cabin room that stood across the porch space from the kitchen. Opening the door, he went in. This was the living-room. Cal lit a lamp, and then proceeded to kindle a fire in the open fireplace. This leisurely done, he surveyed the room. It was cheerful. He and Tuck had made elaborate efforts to utilise all Cal had bought. A red blanket on the bed lent a touch of colour. What would Georgiana think of the bedposts that reached to the ceiling? There was even a mirror and a white pitcher and bowl. Cal feared it was somewhat luxurious for a pioneer. Then, suddenly, as grim, cold realisation returned, he felt his castle of dreams fall asunder for ever. Georgiana would never share this homestead with him.

He strode out, leaving the door wide, and the broad flare of light followed him across the intervening space of porch to the kitchen door. Vigorously he opened that. Georgiana was setting the table, and his entering so suddenly startled her.

Cal faced her now, feeling like a man for the first time in a long while. She had been frightened, and she had experienced a rough ride, but she had not been harmed. He was the one who must suffer. He was the one upon whose head ridicule and scorn must fall. She had been saved, at least from the Tonto. All his pretence and his former morbidness fell away from him like dead husks.

"Reckon I'd like some hot water, Georgie," he said cheerfully.

She poured it out of a steaming tea-kettle. Cal was aware of her scrutiny, but he paid no heed, and went to splashing in the basin. He washed his face thoroughly, as if to remove with the brush-dirt all of the villainous expression he had counterfeited.

"How about supper?" he asked as genially as if this was really natural.

"It's ready," she said, "the best I could do. . . . My fingers are all thumbs to-night."

Cal was hungry, and he wished to spare her and himself any further pain. He did not speak again except to ask her if she could not eat.

"I'm afraid I cannot," she replied.

Soon he had finished and then he rose. "Jollyin' aside, Georgie, it was a good supper. Reckon there's no danger of my forgettin' it. I'll wash the dishes."

"Cal, you're different—like your old self!" she exclaimed suddenly.

"Well, Georgie, you never did get me, an', worse luck for me, you never will. . . . Come now, I want you to see the other cabin."

"Other cabin?" she echoed.

"Sure. This is only the kitchen. Come on!"

As she made no move to accompany him, and stood with eyes dilating, he possessed himself of her hand and led her out of the kitchen. The shaking of her hand, its clammy touch, told him much. He had to urge her, drag her a little to get her into the other cabin.

How bright, rosy, cheerful, and cosy! It was warm, too, and the burning juniper sent out a fragrance.

"Isn't this nice?" he asked, without looking at her, and he released her hand.

Georgiana did not reply.

"Reckon you're all in," he said hurriedly. "Here—see the bar that locks the door. Uncle Gard said a grizzly bear couldn't get in here with the door barred."

Then he drew his gun from his belt and laid it on the table.

"Reckon you won't need that, but there it is," he said, and moved back to the door.

Suddenly he flung up his head, with pride and finality, and looked at her with piercingly sad and revealing eyes.

"Good night," he said, and wheeling he went out and closed the door behind him.

As the door slammed behind Cal, not violently, but decisively, Georgiana's nerve-racked body gave a little leap. For a moment she stood there, trembling, passing from uncertain dread to certain relief, gazing at the door where Cal had disappeared. Then, answering to instinct, she ran to lift the heavy bar and place it in position. That seemed to make a vast, strange difference.

Her legs threatened to give way under her, and again she was visited by that lightness of head. She got to the bed, and falling upon it lay there for a long time, with only dull, vague thoughts. This stupor passed, and at length she sat up, conscious of bodily weariness and a headache, but otherwise gradually returning to herself.

What was it that had happened? Gazing around this log-cabin room, so new, so redolent of freshly hewn pine, at the rough slanting shingled roof, at the red clay hardened in the chinks between the logs, at the few articles of crudely fashioned furniture, strong and serviceable, at the several deerskins on the solid plank floor, at the small windows opening to the inside like doors, at the great open fireplace, made of white stone, with its glowing red fire on the hearth—gazing at these, and then at her ragged dress, Georgiana Stockwell established something of the reality of her situation.

When her roving eyes fell upon the big blue gun Cal had left upon the table, a thrill ran through her. That was the gun he had levelled at Bid Hatfield, and with which he might have killed him. Georgiana shuddered. She closed her eyes. But that did not blot out a picture of Cal Thurman, wild-eyed, villainous of mien, suddenly revealed in his true character.

She hated him. She would go away from this place to-morrow as soon as she dared. Someone would come to whom she could tell her story. But what if she raised that devil in him again? The thought made her absolutely weak. How cold-bloodedly savage he had been! In such a mood Cal Thurman was capable of anything. Yet, why had he suddenly become transformed, back seemingly to the Cal she had liked so well? Why had he told her to bar the door of this room and had given her his gun, and then stalked out like an outraged prince? It was this which perplexed and troubled Georgiana. There seemed no way to connect it with his earlier conduct. He had two sides to his nature, then, both of which were new to her.

After a moment's deliberation she extinguished the lamp, and without removing even her shoes she lay down on the bed and pulled a couple of blankets up over her. The room now seemed wonderfully changed. The red embers threw ruddy shadows on the floor and sent long streaks to her eyes. Suddenly she became aware of a low, moaning sound. It startled her. She listened. Only the wind under the eaves of the cabin. It had the strangest, loneliest, most haunting sound she had ever heard. Lower she crept down under the blankets. She had begun to feel warm and comfortable and a languor was stealing over her.

She wanted to put Cal Thurman out of her mind, as much out of her mind as he would be out of her life after to-morrow.

"Yes—very well—but you are his wife!"

Georgiana spoke these words aloud to her own ears. They brought her upright in bed, transfixed and thrilling.

Somehow it seemed a terrible realisation. Not that it changed her future action in the least! But how would she be regarded in the Tonto? She had not been any too well liked, except by a lot of those sentimental mooning riders. Cal Thurman, however, was liked by everybody, even by Bid Hatfield. What had Bid said once? "Cal's a square shooter." And from Bid, who had been insanely jealous of Cal, that was equivalent to a eulogy.

"It'll have to be annulled," said Georgiana. "I can put him in jail. . . . Won't his life be one long round of bliss after I tell what he did to me? . . . He won't be so darn' popular then."

As the night wore away Georgiana lay there refusing to go to sleep or listen to a still small voice that seemed to be knocking at the gate of her conscience. Yet she grew drowsy, and her reflections lost clarity as weariness gradually overcame her. At last, when she was thinking how dark it was and cold and strange, she fell asleep.

Georgiana awakened with a start. Her eyelids almost refused to come open. Her body felt in a comfortable, immovable state. A bright sunlight was streaming into the room. One glance around brought instant establishment of time, place, situation. After all, she had slept. The sun was high. Now she became aware of a knocking on the door.

"Georgie, are you all right?" called Cal in a tone of anxiety.

Georgiana felt like telling him that he had an awful nerve. What did he expect? But she lay quiet.

"Georgie, are you dead?" he yelled, and pounded hard on the door.

"It's no fault of yours that I'm not dead," she replied. "What do you want?"

"Aw!" She heard him exclaim in relief. "If you'll let me in I'll start a fire for you. It's cold up here under the Rim."

"I don't need any fire," she answered presently.

"But you want breakfast?"

Georgiana pondered that a moment, then replied. "I'll get breakfast for you, but I don't want any."

"I have your breakfast ready," he went on.

Georgiana sat up in the bed and slowly pulled down the blankets. Cal's tone was acquiring a little of the ring that affected her nerves. She was about to say that she did not feel hungry, when he spoke again.

"You get up an' hurry, before your breakfast's cold. I've work to do. I can't wait any longer."

"What time is it?"

"Reckon it's nearly noon. . . . Georgie, I must rustle over to my Uncle Gard's ranch. Won't be back till late." Here he paused and coughed. "I—you—see here, what I want to say is—you're free to do as you like."

Georgiana listened to this with mingled surprise and doubt.

"Do you hear me?" he queried sharply.

"Yes, I hear you, Cal Thurman, but I don't get you," she retorted. "You think I'm a liar, don't you?"

"Wal, since you tax me," he drawled, in capital imitation of his relatives' Texas accent, "reckon I do. An' I shore think yore a hell of a lot more!"

Blank silence followed. Georgiana could not understand her impulsive, reckless outburst. But she wanted to laugh, and yet she knew she was angry. What a fool Cal was!

"Ahuh!" he ejaculated. She heard his deep breath. "Reckon that'll be about all."

His heavy footfalls crossed the porch and crunched the gravel beyond. Georgiana slipped to the window and peeped out. He was mounting his horse. Now—he was riding off. Most likely it was a ruse to deceive her. Presently he disappeared in the edge of the woods. After a moment's reflection Georgiana decided there was really no reason for her to imagine he had not ridden off. But the fact that he had gone at all was most welcome.

Whereupon she bethought herself of personal matters of the moment. She had slept fully dressed, and thought she looked as if she had. Her hair was in a condition she could not remember as ever equalling it. Her face showed tear streaks through the black stain of brush-dust she had accumulated. And a big black and blue bruise showed above her temple. Luckily she could hide it with her hair.

"Good night!" muttered Georgiana, as she surveyed herself, especially this disfiguration of her pretty face. "Fancy me ever coming to this!"

The water in the pitcher was so cold that Georgiana could not use it. Hurrying to the door, she opened it, and with a furtive glance to right and left, she ran across the porch and went into the kitchen. It was warm. An odour of ham pleasantly assailed her nostrils. Georgiana suddenly discovered she was ravenously hungry. The kitchen table was set for one. Its neatness and cleanliness surprised her. The biscuits were hot, the coffee-pot was vying with the tea-kettle in emitting the fragrant vapours, the skillet with two crisp slices of ham sat back on the stove.

"What do you know about that?" queried Georgiana.

Then she washed her face in hot water, and, finding a comb and brush under a little mirror, she worked her rebellious hair into some semblance of its former well-groomed condition. Her mind seemed to be both active and trance-like. Her fears were for the moment in abeyance. It pleased her to note that, despite the lump on her brow, when she brushed her hair down over it she looked more interesting than for a long time. Not so pretty without the paint and powder, but pale, intense, interesting! She wanted to look that way when she told her tragic story.

There was then nothing to do but wait for somebody to come. Georgiana could not wait very well for anything. She must occupy herself, or a nervous restlessness would soon possess her.

"I suppose it'd be decent to wash his old dishes," she muttered. "To give the devil his due, I've got to hand it to Cal Thurman as a housekeeper. He's got me skinned to death—well, men might as well learn that, and to take care of kids. For it's certainly coming to them."

Georgiana washed the dishes and utensils, and had just finished making the kitchen tidy when sound of voices and the pound of hoofs made her heart beat quickly. Had Cal returned? She peeped out of the kitchen window, to see a number of packed burros, the very first of which was Jinny, and she had a trunk on her back.

Georgiana stared. She recognised that trunk. It belonged to her. Then into her amazed sight came her sister Mary, riding Enoch's bay pony, and after her Tuck Merry and another rider.

Georgiana fell back from the window. She felt at once delivered and cornered. She wanted to rush out, and realised that she could not.

"But it doesn't cut any ice with me—because they packed my clothes up here," she muttered. "I didn't tell them to. And I'll darn' soon read the riot act to Mary."

Footsteps on the porch!

"Ho, homesteaders!" called out Mary's rich, happy voice. It struck deep to Georgiana's heart. When had Mary spoken like that? Georgiana threw open the door.

Mary was right there, on the porch. She wore a short, heavy riding-coat with furry collar turned up. There was frost on it. Her sweet face was rosy from cold and exercise. Her grey eyes were alight with love and happiness. And the smile that came so radiantly when she saw Georgiana was beautiful. It halted Georgiana's speech, whatever that had been.

"Oh, Georgie—little sister!" cried Mary, with a half-sob of joy, and she enfolded her, and hugged and kissed her until Georgiana had scarcely any breath left to talk with. More than that, Georgiana found herself with swelling heart and dimming eyes. Something was disarming her. Mary's joy at sight of her had struck to the depths. Georgiana suddenly realised that she needed her mother, and that Mary stood in the place of mother. She clung to her sister, silently, passionately, and in that contact she bridged any estrangement which might have intervened. Then she wanted to burst out, before Mary misunderstood any more, but she seemed tongue-tied.

"Georgie—dear child—don't cry," Mary was saying, and squeezing her as she spoke. "I'm not angry. Do you understand? Your elopement made me the happiest woman in the world!"

"Made you—happy! . . . Mary?" faltered Georgiana, composed and astounded.

"Of course you don't understand," replied Mary, "but you will, dear, shortly. Let us go inside. I'm nearly frozen."

She drew Georgiana back from the threshold, and then called to the men outside: "Unpack and carry the things here on the porch."

Closing the door, she once more enfolded Georgiana. "You darling! You sly little minx! You atrocious little flirt! All the time it was Cal! . . . Oh, Georgie, I'm so happy! I'm nearly out of my head!"

"You talk—sort of nutty," replied Georgiana tremulously.

"What a cosy, fine kitchen!" exclaimed Mary, sweeping a woman's keen eye all around. "I must see everything. But let's talk first. . . . Where's Cal?"

"Gone off to work," replied Georgiana, and she was nerving herself to blurt out Cal's perfidy and her wretched situation when again she was silenced.

"Georgie, your marriage saved my happiness," declared Mary in sweet gravity.

"Oh, what—do you mean?" replied Georgiana.

"Come, let us sit here," replied Mary, drawing Georgiana to the couch and still keeping her in a close embrace. "I can tell you now. For you're married and out of danger, thank God! Oh, Georgie, that boy Cal Thurman saved you, and me, too. . . . Listen, and please do not be hurt now at anything I say. You never realised just what the true situation was here. I tried to make you see long ago how dangerous it was for you to—to trifle with these boys. You never saw how your accepting Cal's attentions and making him crazy about you was a most serious matter with all the Thurmans. They took to you at first, in spite of your immodest dresses and your slang. But when you began to flirt with other boys and poor Cal showed his misery—then they began to grow cold. There's no need to tell you all I know about that. But after the October dance, and your cool indifference to Cal when you should have appreciated his loyalty, then even Enoch turned against you. He wanted me to send you home. I couldn't do that, for then you hadn't any home except with me. . . . Well, day before yesterday the climax came. Dear, I hate to tell you."

"Go on," said Georgiana in smothered voice. She was smarting as under a lash. "Don't mind me."

"Enoch came home from town, perfectly furious about something he had heard about you—remarks credited to Bid Hatfield, according to the gossip. Enoch said you would have to get out. You had made Cal the laughing-stock of the Tonto. Worse, if that gossip got to Cal's ears he would *kill* Hatfield. I—I was shocked. . . . Well, I told Enoch I was going to stand by you, come what might. You were not so well and I considered it my duty to keep you with me. Then we quarrelled. Whew! I didn't know Enoch could be so—so—I don't know what. Don't you ever make Cal really mad. I told Enoch pretty plainly where to get off, as you would say. Then he raved and swore it was all on account of that 'damned little hussy of a sister.' I shut him up pronto, and I told him I would give him a couple of days to reconsider, then if he did not, I would break our engagement and take you with me—away from the Tonto."

"Oh—Mary!" cried Georgiana.

"It was hard, Georgie dear," went on her sister. "But I could not see any other way. I grew more wretched. Enoch kept away from me, and I know he never would have weakened. It's strange you didn't see something was wrong. But then your mind was full of your own love-affair. Only, if you had guessed how my heart was breaking, you would have told me. . . . I didn't get home until late last night. Enoch met me. He didn't explain. He just hugged me—like—like a bear. Right before everybody. Then I saw that he seemed tremendously happy. So were all the Thurmans, especially old Henry. He beamed upon me. 'Thet air boy Cal shore is a smart one. Reckon he knowed what he was about, drivin' us near crazy runnin' up his cabin.'

"I asked what it all meant, especially Enoch's disgraceful conduct, and everybody shouted at me. 'Cal and Georgie are married!' You could have knocked me over with a feather. But when I realised it was true I was the happiest one there. Tuck Merry had brought the news. He was a hero. Anyone who can participate in an elopement in this country earns distinction. I didn't get a chance to talk to Tuck then, but I had it out with Enoch. He was simply beside himself with joy. 'Aw, Mary, it's for Cal's sake an' yours that I'm so glad.' How he loves Cal! . . . Well, I was not disposed to fall into Enoch's arms because he was satisfied—that is, I mean I didn't want him to see it. So I had a few things to say. I just scared him good. Made him think I couldn't forgive his mulishness. He pleaded with me. It was very, very nice after the way he had talked and acted when we quarrelled. He said he was awfully sorry he hadn't waited a few days, then we need never have had the quarrel. . . . Well, to make a long story short, we made up, and we are going to celebrate your marriage by getting married ourselves."

"When, Mary?" whispered Georgiana huskily.

"Enoch begged to make it a week from your wedding-day, but I held out for a month . . . and so, darling, you've made us all happy. You have saved Cal in the very nick of time, not to mention poor me and yourself! I met old Gard Thurman this morning at Green Valley. I was a little afraid of him. But he was fine.

'Wal, I reckon gals will be gals, an' them Eastern ones don't take the bridle easy. But all's well that ends well. She's a Thurman now.' . . . And, Georgie, that means everything to these simple-minded people."

"Mary, tell me, did Cal know you quarrelled with Enoch?" asked Georgiana, feeling the rising tide of an irresistible flood in her breast.

"Indeed he did! Enoch told him. I didn't know this till last night. Cal was fighting mad, Enoch said. He swore if Enoch drove you and me away he was through with the Thurmans. Oh, they had it hot and heavy. Honestly, I believe Enoch was as happy to have all right between him and Cal again as he was to get me back."

Suddenly Georgiana collapsed against her sister's breast, and clinging to her she sobbed out incoherently. "Oh—Mary—Ma—ry! I've been—just what Enoch—called me . . . and oh, I—I want to die."

"Why, Georgie!" exclaimed Mary in distress, as she folded her sister in a close embrace and bent over her tenderly. "What are you saying? You poor child! Oh, I hope I haven't failed as a mother to you! But, dear, you just wouldn't be mothered. You had to have your fling . . . and that's over now, thank goodness! I'm glad you *can* cry. Just let go and cry all you want. Oh Georgie, I was worried sick about you. But never mind. I won't say any more. I'll just hold you and remember how you used to come to me, years ago, with your baby troubles."

Georgiana did not soon wear out that spasm of weeping. The dammed-up flood burst, and for a good while she was in the physical throes of collapse. When at length she began to recover somewhat she seemed to be the victim of an enormous dread.

"Mary, you still—love me?" she asked brokenly.

"Georgiana, what a question? You haven't given me a chance to love you. Oh, maybe all this trouble will be good in the end. It must bring us closer, sister dear."

Then Georgiana lay silent, her head pillowed on that loving, heaving breast. She had sustained a terrible shock. It seemed that Mary's revelation had transformed her very life. But how she could not tell. Only two things took concrete shape in her whirling mind—her lips were locked, and there seemed just reason why she should despise herself. For an hour all she could do was to force herself to be woman enough to spare her sister, to hide her shame and misery, to accept her strange destiny for the present, and for the sake of others put aside her own selfish wants until a more favourable time. She stood alone now. There was no one to help her, no one to get her out of this muddle.

"Sister, all I can say is, I begin to see—and if I had the last few months to live over I'd do different."

Mary kissed her with most earnest warmth. "Georgie, that is all I needed to-day to make my happiness perfect. Oh, I never lost my faith in you."

But scorn of herself could wait, as also the hour to face her problem. Just now she must force herself to pretend to be what Mary believed her. So she braved it out. She submerged herself. She dried her tears, and wrought the miracle of a smile when her self-abasement and wretchedness were exceedingly poignant.

It was five o'clock in the afternoon and the sun was tipping the distant mountain range. Mary had been gone two hours. Two whole hours Georgiana had sat motionless, racked between emotion and thought!

"What can I do—what must I *do*?" she whispered, rising out of that cramped inactivity. She paced the room, sweeping her eyes over the vast improvement Mary had wrought. What an ordeal she had endured in helping Mary drag her trunk and bags and boxes, all her possessions, into this living-room, in watching her and listening while she unpacked everything, and hung and arranged and draped until the cabin interior was transformed! Here all of Georgiana's pictures and pennants and trifles, so dear to her heart, and which had no place down at Green Valley, were united in making a colourful and beautiful room.

Georgiana gazed around in her extremity, as if these belongings of hers could speak in wisdom that would enlighten her. But they spoke of pleasure, happy memories, the comforts of home, all of which seemed mockery here.

The fire she and Mary had kindled shone red and warm on the hearthstone; and it likewise seemed a lie.

"I'm here. I haven't gone away. He'll return soon. . . . And I'm his *wife*!" She cried out in her distraction.

It came to her then that she had to stay now. Her one hope of escape had failed. She might have courage enough to run off, anywhere away from this hateful homestead. But she was afraid of the forest at night. Of what avail would it be to starve and freeze? Besides, she was compelled to stay for Mary's sake, at least until Mary was safely married to that iron-jawed Enoch.

"I've got to stay," Georgiana admitted, and in the admission her hand covered her mouth, a gesture almost of despair. "If I run off now they'll say I *deserted* my husband a day after the marriage. My heavens! That would ruin Mary. I'm stuck here. I've got to pay for my—my cussedness."

It seemed then that the decision to stay did not make the situation any easier. As a matter of fact, no decision had been needful, simply because there was no alternative. What distracted Georgiana then was the dire necessity of finding some way to save her pride. It was vanity and she knew it.

"What can I say to him—when he finds me still here?" she asked. "I've got to dope out some plan."

Making believe had been Georgiana's pastime as a child, and as a girl it had become a dominant characteristic. All at once a flash of divination seemed to illumine the dark perplexity of her mind. Why not try honesty? In less than a day she had come to fear Cal Thurman more than she had ever feared anything. Here she was racking her brain to find some means to deceive him—to show she was not afraid—to save her pride. To realise it sickened her.

But she had been faced with the havoc caused by her unwitting dishonesty. And she could never again be a liar and a cheat.

"I'll be on the level," she decided, "and I'll take my medicine."

Whereupon she resolutely went into the kitchen and put her mind upon the considerable task of getting supper. The short winter day had ended and twilight had mantled the mesa. She lighted the lamp. Then she bethought herself of her pretty aprons. Running back to the living-room, she found one and donned it, tarrying a moment to catch a glimpse of herself in the mirror. Upon returning to the kitchen she rekindled the fire in the stove, and then busied herself in preparations for the meal. Busy with hands, preoccupied in mind, she forgot what she dreaded until she heard a step on the porch and a knock on the door.

"Who's there?" she called.

"It's Cal," came the reply in a weary voice.

"Come in."

He entered, haggard and dirty, covered with brush-dust, and he limped as he walked. His clothes gave forth the odour of the dry pine woods.

"I met Mary down at the school-house. You didn't tell her," he said.

"No," she replied simply.

"Why?"

"You know the trouble she and Enoch had on my account?"

"Ahuh! Enoch is an old porcupine. Did they make up?"

"Yes. And I—I just couldn't tell her."

"Reckon it would have been tough. . . . An' that's why you're still here?"

"Mostly. But I—I've no great desire to be handled as I was yesterday."

He studied her with sad, knowing, dark eyes. It seemed the hours of that day had worked a change in him, as they had in her. Without more words he turned away to the bench, and filling the wash-basin with water he stooped over it. Georgiana watched him out of the corner of her eye, while bustling round table and stove. When at length he turned again to the light she glanced concernedly at his face. His ablutions had removed the stains of labour, but had rather augmented the haggard intensity. Cal showed the inroads of mental distress. All in a day he seemed years older. The boy had gone. Yet there was something proven about him.

"Can I help you?" he asked, as if suddenly becoming aware of her work.

"It's about done," she replied, and now that she was aware of his scrutiny she no longer looked at him. Presently the supper was ready, and they sat opposite each other, silent except for the fewest of words necessary at the table. Cal ate rather methodically without his former gusto, and his brow was wrinkled with ponderings.

When they had finished this strange meal Cal said he would do the rest of the work. Georgiana was glad enough to get out of it. This hour was a strain. She left Cal sitting at the table, his head bowed on his hand. Once safely barred in her room, Georgiana fell victim to remorse.

"Oh, I'm sorry—sorry for him, no matter what he's done to me," she exclaimed. "He knows how hopeless it is. He knows what I'll do . . . and then he'll be ruined. . . . I've ruined him. Oh, if I had only known."

Next day established in Georgiana's mind a true perspective of the state of affairs as they existed then, and would, not improbably, remain for some time to come.

She could not understand Cal Thurman. He talked very little, and seemed anxious to get out of her sight. A brooding, almost sombre preoccupation attended him during the little while she saw him. She decided that he knew full well she would not stay there long, and likewise knew why she remained at all. Strange to see he showed no remorse for his crime. This caused Georgiana surprise and considerable heat. If he had repented she might have thought a little better of him. There did not seem to be any justification in Georgiana's fear that he might have another fit of fury, like the one in which he had carried her off. But undoubtedly, as he had shown such a terrible temper, it was in him and might crop out at any moment. Nevertheless, the day brought relief in the assurance that he would let her severely alone.

Next day, about noon, she had a caller, no other than her father-in-law, Henry Thurman.

"What you-all doin' about heah?" he asked, beaming upon her.

"Cal's building a fence at his uncle's, and I'm up to my eyes in work," replied Georgiana.

He tramped around the kitchen, inquiring about everything, and then performed the same office for the living-room.

"Wal, some folks aboot the Tonto hollered too soon," he said enigmatically. "Daughter, I shore figger that Cal's lucky."

"Thank you," murmured Georgiana, warming under his approval. It was a hollow victory, yet somehow it seemed strangely sweet.

"Georgie, what you want for a weddin' present?" he asked with a broad grin. "Reckon that's why I'm heah. But I ain't said airy word aboot it."

"It's very good of you. But I don't want anything," replied Georgiana.

"Wal, I reckon you do. Young folks jest startin' a homestead need a lot. Come here, daughter; put on yore thinkin' cap."

"If I tell you what I'd like, will you keep it secret—for a while?" she asked.

"Mum's the word, Georgie."

"I'd like a sewing-machine and a lot of dry-goods."

"Fer makin' dresses an' sich?" he queried, with a knowing smile.

"No indeed. For making curtains, sheets, pillow-cases, table-cloths, towels—oh, a whole lot of things."

"Wal, I'll be dog-goned!" ejaculated Henry Thurman, greatly pleased. "Daughter, I'm shore proud of you. Now you jest write out a list of what you want. I'll send it to Ryson. They can phone to Globe an' have it all come on the stage. I'll have it packed up heah pronto. I'll shore do my best to keep anybody from findin' out aboot it."

What with work and sleep the days passed swiftly for Georgiana and though they all seemed similar, there was an intangible something growing with them. If there was any difference in Cal it was the look of wonder and bewilderment he cast upon her in unguarded moments. Following there would come an expression of acute pain, at which times he would go out abruptly or turn away to hide it.

Georgiana had set herself a task almost beyond her strength. But she had set it and she stuck to it. She even chopped wood and carried water, chores that sometimes became necessary when Cal was away.

Georgiana vowed she would not sink under this pioneer work so new to her. She suffered aches, pains, bruises, cuts, burns, and for days the exhaustion of a frail body. Then when she felt she had about gone her limit she found her strength increasing. Her appetite increased to an amusing and alarming capacity. The keen cold winter air, clear and sharp, lost its terrors for her. On that sunny south slope the snow melted almost as it fell, and so one of the dreaded features of winter did not keep Georgiana indoors.

During this time Cal had made additions to his homestead. From his Uncle Gard's ranch he had brought chickens, pigs, two cows and a calf, and also loads of sorghum and corn to feed them. Thus the barn and chicken-coop and pig-pen received tenants, heralding the real beginning of ranchers' activities. Those new-comers did not add to Georgiana's labours, because Cal did all the work of caring for them. Yet naturally they somehow increased Georgiana's responsibilities. Just as naturally, too, she and Cal found it impossible, though estranged as they were, to keep wholly aloof from each other. It was Cal's homestead, and Georgiana, having undertaken a task, could not withhold interest. At night, when Cal came in from his last chores, they talked of the simple facts of the day and the needs and probabilities of the morrow. It seemed that Cal hid every sign of his love and Georgiana gradually forgot her dread. They were never together except at meal-times.

One night Cal came in with a troubled face.

"Enoch sent word we were to come down to Green Valley to-morrow," he said. "He an' Mary are goin' to be married."

"Oh—has it been a month since—since——"

"Reckon it has," replied Cal dryly. "One month to-morrow! Seems like a million years to me. . . . Do you want to go to your sister's weddin'?"

"I'll have to go," replied Georgiana, much perturbed. "Mary would be hurt. . . . And, yes, I want to go. Don't you?"

"I reckon not. But I can stand it if you can. All the Thurmans will be there an' lots of other folks. They'll have a chance at us."

"I—I forgot. It will be embarrassing—won't it?"

"Ahuh! I should think it'll be terrible. That's up to you. If I didn't come, Enoch would be sore. But I wouldn't care."

"Yes, you would. Enoch thinks a lot of you, Cal. He'd miss you. Then we couldn't make any good excuses. I'm scared stiff at the thought of facing all that crowd."

"They think we're happily married," said Cal with a hollow laugh.

That stung her. "Your tone implies an unhappy state you feel you don't deserve," she retorted.

"Ahuh! Are we goin' or not?" he returned.

"Oh, we'll *have* to go," burst out Georgiana.

"All right. Now it's not my doin', please remember that. An' we better put in some tall figurin' right here. . . . We'll have to ride horses and come back home to-morrow night in the dark. That won't be any fun."

"But why?" queried Georgiana.

"You don't seem as bright as you used to be. If we stay all night, mother will give us one room—for both of us. Naturally, since we're supposed to be married. An' we can't stay, that's all."

"I—I didn't think," replied Georgiana hurriedly, and she felt the blood hot in her face. "Of course—we must come back."

"That means you must dress to ride," he went on. "It will be cold, but by bundlin' up an' wearin' your boots I reckon you'll be warm enough."

"But, Cal, I can't stand up with Mary—in a riding-suit—while she's married," protested Georgiana.

"What do you want to wear?" he queried.

She pondered a moment, and then replied hesitatingly: "My white dress—the one you hated. . . . But I've lengthened it quite a good deal."

"Ahuh! I don't care what you wear any more, but I reckon a longer dress would please my folks."

Georgiana maintained silence, conscious of an accelerated pulse and a feeling of pique. So he did not care any more how she looked? She thought that a dangerous remark to make to any woman. Manifestly his love, having nothing to feed upon, had died. How exceedingly constant men were! For an instant the old Georgiana roused to conquest. She could make him love her as wildly as he used to—and more—and there was devil enough left in her to incite her to do it, if he dared to scorn her. But Cal's sad, worn face, his troubled eyes, showing he was trying to forget himself for others, disarmed her rash impulse. Yet a little bitterness rankled in her heart. She had not done anything to make him despise her.

"I'll pack your grip on my saddle," he went on. "Now do you want a hunch from me—somethin' for your own good?"

She eyed him doubtfully. He seemed so earnest, yet impersonal. This marriage day of her sister's had focused attention upon a situation both Georgiana and Cal had avoided. She saw his sincerity. There might indeed be something he could suggest that would make the ordeal less painful.

"Yes," she replied.

"I'm rememberin' the night you pretended to be hurt in the car —you know, when I brought you out to Green Valley. You fooled everybody. An' I reckon you're some actress, as Tuck said afterwards. . . . Well, make the same bluff to-morrow. Go to have a good time, an' pretend to be happy, even if you're miserable. You might fool even yourself. For all my folks an' friends will meet you more'n half-way."

"Thank you. I'll think it over," replied Georgiana, averting her eyes.

The day was an unusually fine one for winter, not cold, but keen and invigorating, dry under hoof, with white clouds sailing the blue sky, and a sun that comfortably warmed.

Georgiana had an auspicious start for this day in which she meant to pretend to be happy. Mrs. Gard Thurman, a woman who showed the hard years of pioneer life, yet was sweet and motherly, struck the right chord in her greeting to Georgiana.

"Wal, lass, I'm glad to see you're pickin' up," she said kindly. "You look fine. An' shore them's real roses in your cheeks to-day!"

Georgiana could not dispel the pleasure this gave her, nor its haunting significance. Not for weeks had she thought of her health. Was it true that she had gained? A throbbing warm wave engulfed her heart. Life was sweet, after all. Could it be possible that out of defeat and travail there might come success and peace? It was a new thought. All she had been concerned with was her vanity, her pride. To be sure, she had stood doggedly by her hard and distasteful task, yet, looked back at now, what it had cost her seemed a reward. Georgiana put the thought aside, to be taken up and pondered over at some other time.

The men rode together, talking and smoking, sometimes half turned in their saddles, in the graceful manner of riders. Georgiana rode behind with the women.

In walk and trot this cavalcade went down the mountain trails, out of the pines into the cedar and juniper, and at last into the brush. It took nearly three hours to reach Green Valley. Georgiana enjoyed it, and only tired towards the very end. The dread of meeting people failed to materialise. Georgiana actually laughed when Tuck Merry strode out into the road, taller and thinner than ever, and showed his pleasure at sight of Ollie Thurman, as well as an unmistakable proprietorship.

"Tuck, this air a bad day to go sweet on a lady," said Henry, with his dry chuckle.

It was he who lifted Georgiana off her horse and he did not neglect to make it an affectionate action. The porch appeared full of people, mostly long, shiny-faced, blue-jeaned riders that Georgiana did not see distinctly. But she saw Mary very clearly, and rushed into her arms.

"Georgie!" exclaimed Mary, after that first embrace, holding her at arm's length and gazing upon her with glad eyes. "You look different. Your face is not so thin. I never saw you so—so pretty. . . Oh, you're getting *well*!"

Georgiana hugged her. "Old dear, it makes me happy to see you and hear you say that. I—I hadn't thought of my health. I've worked. . . . Take it from me, you look pretty good yourself. This marriage stuff must be the dope for women."

Mary laughed happily. She did, indeed, appear very well, younger and free of the line and shadow of worry. Georgiana's keen eyes did not miss that. The evidence went straight to her heart.

"Georgie, when will you ever drop your slang? . . . Come, you must speak to everybody, and, child, curb that terrible tongue."

"Sis, let me babble. Let me rave," implored Georgiana. "To you, anyhow. I haven't spoken thirty words since I saw you. But don't worry. I'm here to be the simple little bride of Cal Thurman. On exhibition; and believe me, I'll put it over this day."

Georgiana had not worn a party gown for over a month. She was so eager to see how much she really had improved during this period that she put on her white dress in the middle of the afternoon. This was in the seclusion of Mary's room. The effect on Georgiana was magical. Deep in her secret heart had been an unuttered fear that she was losing her health, and with it youth and beauty. But never before in her life had she looked so well.

Mary was all smiles, praises, kisses, between which she wondered and marvelled at Georgiana's improvement. Georgiana was no longer thin and frail. This gown revealed that. Yet it was only half as revealing as it had been before Georgiana had changed it.

"When they see you to-night they'll forget how you used to look," declared Mary with gratification, and she did not explain whom she meant by they.

"Cal hated this dress when it was so short," observed Georgiana. "I told him I had lengthened it, but I don't think he took much stock in what I said."

"Goodness! Haven't you dressed up since you were married?" asked Mary.

"Not once."

"Well, you'll make up for it to-night."

"I think I look pretty spiffy myself," replied Georgiana with complacent assurance. "But I've got to hide my hands. Look!"

She spread out the disreputable little members for Mary's inspection. Georgiana had always been proud of her beautiful hands and had cared for them accordingly. But this last month care had gone with pride.

"Wife of a homesteader! They look it. I'll tell the world!" exclaimed Georgiana ruefully.

"You've treated them cruelly, but they'll get well," said Mary. "And now, Georgie, help me a little with my dress."

The sisters spent the happiest hour they had ever known together. Georgiana did not have to play a part. She was intensely human, and excitement, praise, admiration acted upon her like wine. All that had happened to her during the month were but records of her development. Still she did not stop to think. Mary's happiness was infectious.

It took only a few moments for Parson Meeker to make Mary the wife of Enoch Thurman. In the Tonto, neither long courting nor ceremony was in favour.

But the congratulating of the bride and groom was a different matter. Georgiana thought the riders would tear Mary and her husband to pieces. This was their one opportunity and they made the most of it. That hilarious half-hour prepared the way for dinner. This was really a feast. All the Thurman women had a share in it. Georgiana sat next to Mary, and on her left was Cal. Actually she had forgotten him until this hour. Whatever were his true feelings, he wore a genial, manly demeanour that became him in Georgiana's sight.

After dinner came the personal contact with everybody present—

the ordeal which Georgiana had so dreaded. Yet how mistaken she had been! Was the thing to dread within herself? She came second only to Mary in the attention of relatives and friends. Strangely, Georgiana remembered her earlier training. The ultra-modernism had no place here. All was simple, homely, sincere. They rang true. It was not a social gathering. It was the wedding of the chief of the clan. And Georgiana was made to feel something she had never dreamed of—that she counted in the sum of the Thurmans. They all came from fighting Texas stock. If she had been wilful, silly, trifling, even vicious, that was as if it had never been. She had given her hand to a Thurman—to the last of the Thurmans. Life was a strong, precious, splendid thing with these Tonto people. Youth was only a preparation. Marriage was a beginning. Before that hour ended Geogiana was a strangely thoughtful, repentant girl.

The big living-room was cleared of tables, and old Henry got out his fiddle.

They began one of the half-square, half-round, changing-partner dances in which all the young folk and many of the older took part. Never in her life had Georgiana been so whirled and lifted and raced and contended for. She began that dance fresh, excited, in the fun of the hour. She ended it spent, on fire with the life, vitality, intensity of these primitive people. As it chanced, Cal had not met her once in the endless changing of that dance.

"Rest now an' cool off," he said to her. "We've got a long ride an' we must be goin' soon."

Georgiana was glad to leave the gay company and retire to her sister's room to change the white gown for riding-garb Glad—but for a strange reason! Cal's words had broken a spell. She had forgotten him and herself and the hateful reality. It disturbed her suddenly to discover that an abrupt suggestion of departure from that happy circle had brought disappointment. So Georgiana was soberly glad to leave because she found she was having a good time. This extraordinary fact must be delved into.

She and Cal slipped out the back way, just as if they were the bride and groom. A full moon shone white in the pale sky. The hills were black and lonely. An icy wind blew down from the heights.

Georgiana was so bundled up, so booted, chapped, coated, scarfed and hooded and gloved, too, that she had to be lifted on her horse. Once in the saddle, however, she was all right, and she could not repress the sensation of exhilaration.

"We'll ride some till we get to the grade," said Cal, as he swung astride. "Stay close to me an' yell if anythin' goes wrong."

Then he was off at a fast trot. Georgiana's horse needed no urging. Soon Cal took to a lope. Georgiana found herself sailing along the white moon-blanched winding road, with the icy wind in her face. It was sweet, stinging, and so cold that she had to breathe through her nostrils. The dark forest sped by on each side. Now and then Cal looked back to see if all was well with her.

It came to her then that her month of martyrdom had ended with her sister's marriage. She could leave Cal Thurman's home now and go her way. No longer need she and her vexations and troublesome character, her problems and responsibilities, bring peril to Mary's future. Enoch could make no terms now; he had married her, and it was Georgiana's opinion that for a pioneer, sterling and splendid though he was, to win Mary Stockwell for a wife was a piece of supreme good fortune.

Georgiana felt that she must face her problem now. She had no excuse to stay longer with Cal. How easy to name those facts! But a host of considerations, like enemies ambushing her trail, rushed out to confront her. And the very first was a strange stubborn, utterly incomprehensible vacillation. Wait, it whispered. No hurry! Do not face it now. The others trooped after this traitorous weakness. When would she go? Where? How? From what source could she get money to take her away? To whom could she appeal? Was it possible now to confess her trouble to anyone? What might happen to her? And lastly a sickening, humiliating why—why go at all?

She had worked harder in a month than in all the former years of her life. Worked when she longed to faint and fall! By that work and the suffering entailed she saw now a new hold on health, and something nameless, a good not fully understood.

She raised her drooping head to look. Cal rode there ahead, absorbed in his own trouble. She actually felt sorry for him.

At the cabin Cal hesitated just as he was about to help her dismount. He looked up at her. The wide brim of his beaver sombrero hid his face.

"I'd like to ask—are you sorry you went?"

"No. I'm glad, Cal," she replied instantly, somehow wanting him to know.

"Why?" he added.

"Two reasons. Now that I know what it is, I wouldn't have missed seeing Mary's happiness—not for any real or fancied fear in the world."

"Ahuh!" he said, as if he fully comprehended.

"The other reason is that I was wrong," she continued hurriedly. "Whatever it was I—I hated existed only in me. I forgot it. I had a wonderful time. And so I found everybody nice and kind."

"Aw, now that's fine," he exploded. "But I had a rotten time." He removed his sombrero, as if to let the wind cool his fevered head. Then in the moonlight his face appeared pale and sombre. "It was worse for me than I expected. My family, all the old women, the boys—even Tim Matthews, comin' to me, speakin' high of you—tellin' how sorry they were—apologisin' to me for what they'd said of you. . . . You had been only a motherless child. . . . Now all was well an' I deserved such a wonderful little wife—an'—an' they were so glad I was happy. . . . My God!"

"It must have been hell," she replied sympathetically. "I'm sorry you had to endure that for me."

"Reckon I'm glad I went," he returned quickly. "If this was the only time I'd ever have to listen to them. But what kills me is thought of the next time—when—when——"

His voice broke huskily and trailed off. Georgiana understood him to mean when she told the secret of their marriage and left him to scorn and ridicule.

"Cal, I'll stay if it means so much to you—and for Mary's sake," she whispered, impelled beyond resistance. "I'll stay a while longer for your sake and hers—if you'll not expect too much of me."

"Georgie, darlin'," he cried wildly, with a throb in his voice, "I beg you—stay—on any conditions. I'll ask nothin' of you—nothin'. I swear."

"Very well," faltered Georgiana, and slid off her horse. How cramped and dizzy she felt suddenly! She wanted to run, but could scarcely walk. "Good night."

"Reckon you'd better come in the kitchen an' get warm," Cal called after her.

But she stumbled across the porch and entered her room. She did not feel the cold. The darkness of the room was welcome. Anything to get out from under that pitiless, bright, all-seeing moon! She did not light the lamp. Throwing off gloves, hood, scarf, and coats she bent with trembling hands to unlace her boots. Soon she was in bed, creeping deep under the blankets, throbbing and burning.

She did not have to run away just yet. She did not need to face that appalling future to-morrow or next day.

16

Spring! Winter had gone with the fleeting February, and the snow line had vanished from the Rim, and the wild turkeys were gobbling from every ridge. The sun shone warm. Already the red soil of Rock Spring Mesa had begun to dry. One half of the mesa field had been cleared of stumps and rocks, and would soon be ready for spring ploughing. The other half was slowly clearing to Cal's strenuous labours.

Georgiana had stayed on a while longer. She had not been away from the homestead. Mary had visited her once, upon her return with Enoch from Phœnix. A pile of magazines and a shelf of books had been added to Georgiana's room. She worked much the same as on the first weeks of her stay there, only not quite so hard. She spent more time outdoors now.

All had really changed, her illness, her physical being, her spirit, her attitude towards life, yet nothing seemed different because Cal kept his promise. He had asked nothing of her. He let her alone, except those daily hours when their joint labours and mealtimes necessarily brought them together. Georgiana, in her loneliness, in her growing hunger for she knew not what, thought that she might have forgiven him if he had reverted a little to his former self. But he seemed another person now, a boy no longer, a man, kind, serious, preoccupied, but not bitter any more, grateful for Georgiana's presence and help. Yet never by word or action overstepping what he deemed his place. Georgiana resented his humility.

One March day a startling and disturbing and most thrilling bit of news came in the shape of a letter from Mary, brought by a rider. An aunt of the sisters had died, and in her will bequeathed each of them several thousand dollars. Just how much Mary could not determine from their mother's letter, but they would soon receive the heritage. Strange how Georgiana reacted to this news of good fortune! She was not thrilled or overjoyed. She had a feeling of gladness for Mary. For herself there came only the thought that now she could go. There was something inevitable about it. She did not mention the fact of the inheritance to Cal.

Next morning before she awoke, Cal rode off down to Ryson.

Georgiana had the whole day to herself, to think over the un-
limited possibilities open to her. A decision to follow several of
them seemed made, only to be changed.

Cal returned after dark, and the instant Georgiana saw his tell-
tale face she knew something unusual had happened. He avoided
meeting her eyes, and to her timid query he replied briefly:
"Nothin' much."

Georgiana lost her dread, but curiosity and concern remained.
On the following morning, after breakfast, Cal rode up to the
porch and called her.

"Reckon I'd like to tell you somethin'," he said, as she appeared
in the door.

"Yes?" she returned. His cool, easy, dry, rather biting tone roused
her curiosity more than the content of his words. Then she became aware of the piercing gaze of his eyes.

"Georgie, do you remember the day I made you marry me?"

"I'll say I do," she replied in surprise.

"You thought I struck you—knocked you senseless?"

"Yes. Didn't you?"

He gazed down at her in a way that made her feel infinitely
small and narrow-minded.

"No!" he declared ringingly. "I was rough. But I didn't strike
you. My horse ran us under a tree. Your head hit a branch. That's
all."

"Why have you let me think all this time that you did strike
me?"

"Reckon at first it served my purpose to scare you," he admitted. "But after we were married it made me sore to think you
could believe I'd hurt you."

"Ahuh!" replied Georgiana, imitating him. "Well, why did you
tell me now?"

"I'm ridin' over to the Bar XX," he replied coolly, with his intent gaze on her face. He was neither audacious nor reckless, yet
something of both pertained in his tone. Georgiana knew enough
about Thurmans now to realise that this strange, cool, baffling
presence was dangerous.

"Bar XX?" she stammered.

"Yes, an' if I don't happen to get back by sundown you saddle
up an' ride over to Uncle Gard's."

"Will you be—there?" she asked, beginning to shake in alarm.

"No. I won't be there or here," he replied darkly. "But I reckon
I'll be back early. I just wanted to tell you what to do in case——"

"Cal!" she cried piercingly.

"So long, Georgiana May," he called, with all his old bitterness and something of mockery. His last glance seemed full of fiery reproach. Then he spurred his horse, and like a brown flash was off across the clearing.

"Cal!" she screamed after him. But he did not heed. And quickly he was out of sight in the timber.

"Bar XX!" exclaimed Georgiana in distress. "That is Saunders's ranch. Bloom is foreman of the Bar XX. Bid Hatfield is there."

The first hours of that day severely punished Georgiana. She fell prey to morbid dread and fear. But gradually her reasoning began to overcome her intuitive sense that catastrophe threatened. Even if Cal had ridden over to the Bar XX to confront Bid Hatfield, it could hardly mean more than a fight.

About an hour before sunset, when Georgiana was in the kitchen beginning to prepare for the evening meal, she heard the pound of hoofs outside. It startled her. Cal was returning. A strange new thrill of gladness shot through her.

"Whoa thar! Steady!" called out a rough voice that certainly was not Cal's.

Georgiana flew to open the door. She saw a tall rider—Wess Thurman—and two horses, and over the hindmost horse hung the long, limp shape of a man, head down from the saddle.

"Who's that?" cried Georgiana piercingly.

"Wal, I reckon it's all thet's left of Cal," replied Wess. His dark face gleamed and flashed.

"Oh, Heavens! I knew something dreadful was going to happen!" burst out Georgiana, and ran to where Wess was trying to slide Cal off the saddle. "Oh, Wess—say he's not hurt! . . . . Blood! All over him! Oh, how awful!"

"Hurt?" snorted Wess. "Hell, yes, but he ain't daid. Get out of my way."

Wess got both arms around Cal's middle and pulled him over the saddle. Then changing his hold he lifted Cal clear off the ground and carried him into the kitchen. Georgiana followed, wringing her hands. Wess laid the limp form of the boy on the couch.

"Some water, Georgie, an' I'll fetch him round," said Wess. "He's only fainted again."

Georgiana flew to get water and towels. Her nameless terror began to subside. If he had only fainted!

"My Gawd! What a mug for a Thurman to have!" ejaculated Wess in pity and disgust. "Heah, now, you Georgie—don't you look at him."

"I will!" flashed Georgiana, as she ran back to Wess with the basin. And she did look at Cal. . . . Nose and mouth were bleeding. His hair was matted with blood, and his shirt, that appeared torn to shreds, was black with stains.

Georgiana took this all in, and suddenly, horrified and frantic, she fell on her knees beside the couch.

"Oh, he's terribly injured," she wailed.

"Dammit! didn't I tell yuh not to look at him?" growled Wess as he splashed water in Cal's face. "If yore goin' to squeal, get out of heah."

"Tell me, for pity's sake, what happened?" implored Georgiana.

"Cal was jest bulldoggin' a mean steer," replied Wess as he began to bathe Cal's face.

"Don't lie to me, Wess Thurman," cried Georgiana.

"An' he was ridin' a buckin' bronc," went on Wess imperturbably.

"Oh, how can you jest when he lies there so—so awfully battered?"

"An' he fell off Promontory an' rolled aboot a mile," added Wess.

Georgiana forced composure enough to refrain from further useless questioning. Besides, Cal began to show signs of returning to consciousness. His breast heaved. He stirred. He moved his hands. And then Georgiana saw they were bruised, swollen, skinned raw in places.

"Wal, yore comin' to, Cal," drawled Wess.

"You fetched—me home?" whispered Cal weakly.

"I shore did, an' it was a hell of a job."

"Georgie?" asked Cal huskily.

"She's heah, an' actin' fust rate, considerin'," replied Wess, and it was certain he grinned and winked at Georgiana.

"Cal—I'm right by—you," faltered Georgiana. She wanted to take his hands, but feared she might touch the raw flesh and hurt him. "Can't you see me?"

"Yes, now I can. But not very clear," he said. One of his eyes was swollen completely shut, and the other nearly so.

Wess handed the bloody towel to Georgiana and said: "Reckon

thet's aboot as clean as I can git him. Now, Georgie, I'll lift him, an' you pull off thet dirty shirt. Tear it off—it's all rags, anyhow. . . . There!" That done, Wess proceeded to remove Cal's boots, and then his jeans, which, if not so ragged as the shirt, were certainly as dirty. "Wal, you can sleep in yore underclothes, you ole son-of-a-gun. Now I'll cover you over with this heah blanket—an' shore thet's aboot all I can think of."

"Wess, my hands hurt worst of all," said Cal.

Georgiana brought soft linen from her wardrobe, and with Wess's help she began to bandage the injured members.

"Georgie," said Cal, "I couldn't whip him."

"No?" murmured Georgiana.

"He was too big an' strong for me."

"Say," drawled Wess complainingly, "you are shore makin' me out a liar. I had Georgie believin' you fell off Promontory."

"Yes, you had not," retorted Georgiana.

"Wess, if I'd licked him I'd never told her," said Cal.

For Georgiana there seemed to be a world of significance in this statement. Her first fears allayed, she began to find composure.

"I wish to Gawd you had licked him!" returned Wess, with a sudden dark fierceness that struck terror to Georgiana's heart. That was the Thurman of it. If Cal had beaten this enemy, all of the Thurmans might have been willing to let it go at that. But now matters were worse.

Cal turned his disfigured face to the wall and lay quiet. Wess insisted on spending the night there. He helped Georgiana with the supper, and afterwards, but it was not until he was carrying wood for the living-room fire that she had a moment alone with him.

"Now tell me what's happened," she demanded tensely.

Wess deposited the wood on the hearth, and leisurely raked the red coals into a pile and laid some sticks across it.

"Reckon you ought to go to bed," he drawled.

"Wess, you're a Thurman and I like you," replied Georgiana deliberately. "I think you'd be a great friend in the hour of need— like now. But don't try your lazy, easy Tonto spoofing on me. It won't go with *me*."

"Tonto spoofin'!" ejaculated Wess. "Wal, I'll be darned!"

"Tell me," burst out Georgiana impatiently.

"Wal, Georgie, I don't know a heap aboot it," replied Wess; "I was ridin' the Cold pasture when I seen two hosses an' one

rider comin' down the Mescal Ridge trail. We met, an' I seen the
rider was Tom Hall, one of the Bar XX outfit. He was packin' Cal
over the saddle of the other hoss. He says: 'By golly! Wess, it's
lucky to run into you. Cal busted in on Bid over at the ranch, an'
they had a hell of a fight. I didn't see it, but the boys told me.
They wrecked the bunk-house, where Cal got to Bid, an' then they
tore up the ground all over. The boys said Cal more'n held his
own with Bid on a stand-up square fight. But Bid rushed Cal an'
took to rough-an'-tumble. He damn' near beat Cal to death. Our
boss, Saunders, happened to ride in just then, an' he stopped Bid.
Shore he was sore. Cal was knocked clean out. Couldn't get up!
Wal, someone had to pack him home, an' I was the only fellar
willin' to do it. An' I wasn't a-rarin' to run into Enoch or Cal's
dad. Not me! An' heah I am. Cal's bad hurt, an' I'm glad to turn
him over to you!'"

Wess had talked deliberately, evidently to make sure to recall
everything, and the recital had stirred the slumbering depths of
him.

"Wal," he continued, "I thanked Tom for bein' so decent, an'
I took charge of Cal. When we got as far as Tonto Creek, I lifted
him off his hoss an' brung him to. He thought he could ride
home. But he couldn't. He fell off his hoss an' lost his senses again.
I put him back on the saddle an' rustled for home. We didn't meet
no one before we got heah."

"I think it splendid of you—to—to be so good and fetch him
here where no one can see him. . . . Wess, is he badly hurt?"

"Pretty bad used up, I reckon," replied Wess, wagging his head.
"Of course he ain't in any danger. I don't like the way he spit
blood. But mebbe thet's from cut lips or he might hev a tooth
knocked out."

"Will he need a doctor?"

"Wal, we can decide thet to-morrow. I cain't see any reason fer
it now. An' it's a cinch Cal wouldn't like no doctor to see him.
Mother will come over heah, if she's needed, an' she's as good as
any doctor."

"Wess, now tell me why Cal went after Bid Hatfield?" asked
Georgiana.

"Aw, he jest wanted to fight, I reckon," rejoined Wess eva-
sively, and he bent to blow the slow coals into a blaze.

"Don't try to fool me, and don't lie," said Georgiana.

"Times hev changed since Cal an' me was kids. But we Thurmans ain't changed. . . . Cal will hev to drive Hatfield oot of the Tonto or—kill him."

"Oh, my God! Wess, what are you saying?" cried Georgiana, now convinced of the thing she had feared.

"I shore hate to tell you, Georgie, but it's true."

"Why? Why?" whispered Georgiana, clinging to Wess.

"Because Cal has finally heard what we all knew. He was the last one to heah."

"What?"

"Bid Hatfield's talk aboot you."

"Wess, is—is it bad?" she asked, suddenly letting go of Wess and starting back.

"Reckon it couldn't be wuss," replied Wess, much troubled. "Now, heah, Georgie. . . . Don't you look mad like thet. You made me tell you. . . . An' for Gawd's sake don't believe any of us Thurmans take stock in what Hatfield says. Reckon Cal feels as we all do. He shore acted like he does. Wal, we've all talked this over among ourselves, an' we figgered this way. You was new to the Tonto, an' a high-stepper at thet, as the boys say. You liked Bid an' made no bones aboot it. Same way you liked Tim Matthews, an' Arizona, an' of course Cal. You didn't know which one you wanted an' you wasn't in any hurry. Wal, you married Cal, an' thet settled thet. It shore squared everythin'. An' if Bid Hatfield hadn't been a low-down skunk you'd never heerd again of yore foolin'."

"Fooling!" echoed Georgiana poignantly. "I begin to see now. Oh, if I had only known! . . . Wess, I thank you for your faith in me. It is justified. Yet——"

Suddenly the door swung wide and Cal staggered in. He had put on his jeans and thrown a coat round his shoulders. How he could see to walk was not evident, yet he was able to do it.

"Wess, what're you an' Georgie talkin' about—all this time?" he demanded hoarsely. "I heard you."

"Aw, Cal, I was just tellin' Georgie aboot it. She made me," replied Wess.

Georgiana recoiled from Cal as he approached close, but it was from pity and grief at sight of his bleeding and deformed face.

"Cal, I had to know," she said hurriedly.

"What?"

"Why you fought Hatfield."

"Wess could have left that for me to tell," declared Cal hotly, and his white bandaged hands tried to clench.

"Wal, mebbe. But Georgie has a way of her own, Cal, as I reckon you know. I ain't bustin' into yore affairs an' I'm sorry if I hev offended you."

Cal clumsily found the back of the big home-made rocking-chair, and leaned on it for support. He was breathing heavily, almost gasping, and a bloody froth showed on his swollen lips. Sight of him sickened Georgiana, and so filled her with horror at the proofs of her vanity and selfishness that she was stricken to the heart. She had to watch him. It must be part of her punishment. Something tremendous had begun vaguely to dawn upon her consciousness. He owed his present frightful condition, and the torture of mind he manifestly laboured under, to his defence of her good name. For her—who had given him nothing!

"Cal. Don't be angry with Wess," she implored. "I had to know the truth."

"Ahuh! What'd Wess tell you?" queried Cal.

"All he knew. . . . How everybody had heard Hatfield's defamation of my character before you heard it. Hatfield's a liar!" she said in passionate scorn.

"Georgie, that's the whole trouble," responded Cal, a reply which would have been dignified but for his voice and appearance. "He'd lied about you from the first. He bragged about spoonin' with you. I knew then what a liar——"

"But, Cal—that wasn't a lie," interrupted Georgiana impetuously. "I did spoon with him—played choosies, as I told him we called it back East. We held hands and kissed. It happened three times. . . . But that was all I did, absolutely. And it meant so little to me I forgot it until now."

Georgiana could not tell from Cal's battered face what he felt at her disclosure, but the slow droop of his head, until it finally rested on the back of the chair, seemed proof of utter humiliation. She stared at him in consternation and mounting pain. A shock went through her. Never until that moment had she any divination of the staggering consequences which might follow careless flirting with boys. She felt her integrity, even her honour, assailed by Cal's abasement.

"Cal, don't you be a fool!" she cried in sudden piercing voice. This time her hands went to his bowed shoulders, and she shook him gently. "I understand a little better. But *you* don't understand. . . . I've let lots of boys kiss me. And you here in the Tonto—you first, then Hatfield, and Tim Matthews—and Arizona, yes, even ugly Arizona—and last, Hatfield again. But I meant nothing.

What's a kiss? At least where I was brought up it's no more a crime to kiss than to eat chocolates. Anyway, I did it. I let you all kiss me. I'm sorry. But I'm not ashamed. I may have been a silly, vain little flirt—I must have been wrong, but I wasn't *bad*. . . . You must see, Cal—you must not lose your respect for me."

Cal lifted his bleeding, bruised face, and it touched one of Georgiana's hands, burning her with its heat.

"Georgie, that hurts like hell, but I'm glad you had the nerve to tell me," he said huskily.

"You—you believe me?" she asked tremulously.

"Yes. An' I reckon I understand you better. It's a pity you didn't tell me—before——"

"Before what?" she interrupted as his husky voice faltered. "You mean before our marriage? Would that have kept you from marrying me?"

"Nothin' could have kept me from marryin' you—not even if all Bid Hatfield's claims were true."

"Cal!" she cried, shrinking.

"I regret nothin'. As I said, what a pity you didn't tell me before it was too late."

This time she did not ask him what he meant. She knew. And suddenly she was mute. She had brought worse than disgrace upon Cal Thurman. How bitterly she repented! But it was not less too late for her also.

"Cal," spoke up Wess, as he turned from the window where he had discreetly retired, "thet'll be aboot all from both of you. I was heah an' I got ears. Now I'm a-goin' to put you back to bed."

Whereupon he led the sagging Cal towards the door. Opening it, he half turned his face to the girl. "Good night, Georgie. I'll look after Cal. . . . An' you're welcome to know thet I think a heap more of you than ever."

Georgiana was left alone, a victim to the most acute distress of mind and complexity of emotion that she had ever known. For long she sat on the deerskin rug before the fire, peering into the red glow, but seeing nothing.

At length out of the stress of that time she voiced one coherent thought.

"I've got to keep Cal from killing Bid Hatfield, at any cost."

She had been the undoing of a splendid, manly boy. At realisation of what Cal Thurman was, a strange commotion stormed Georgiana's heart. But she did not ponder on that then. She was concerned with a new point of view—how the eyes of the Tonto had seen her.

In her own eyes, she now became guilty of things she never would have confessed to Cal or anyone. Her quick, practical intelligence laid the blame for her character at other feet than hers. But that was no consolation, no help here in this extremity. She had been more than vain, selfish, thoughtless, cruel. She had been blind, weak, wicked. Her relation to the Tonto now enlarged to any community. And the stunning truth came with realisation that in spite of all the arguments she had brought West with her, and which had so distressed Mary, she would not want a daughter of hers to think and act as she had done. That was the climax which bowed her head. Life was life, East or West. What might be done with impunity back in the sophisticated East could not be done at all here in the Tonto. People did not understand. And through the simplicity and primitiveness of these Thurmans it was easy to see how far the so-called Eastern freedom was wrong. There were things women dared not do, unless they disregarded the progress of the world.

She could no longer be a traitress. She could not leave the Tonto. She was chained there by her conscience, by her longing to make amends, by something that brought a flame to her cheek.

17

Out of the pain of the succeeding days; out of the watching by Cal in the dead of night, listening to his muttered dreams; out of the hours when he lay with discoloured face to the wall, and the weak moments when he wept in his misery; out of nursing him and tending his injuries, and reading to him, talking to make him forget; and lastly out of long association alone with him during this ordeal—Georgiana underwent the developing and transforming experience of real love.

It brought her deeper pangs, yet a vision of future happiness. It made her a woman. It relieved her burden. It decided the future.

But when in a week Cal had mended to the extent of walking out-of-doors, when the hideous swellings had left his face so he was not ashamed to be seen by his relatives, and later when he began to brood darkly and to avoid her, Georgiana realised that she must act soon to forestall any second meeting of his with Hatfield.

Her plan had long been made, and now only waited execution. She wrote a note to Tuck Merry, asking him to meet her the following morning at the fork of the Tonto and Mescal Ridge trails, and enclosing this note in a letter to her sister, she rode over to Gard Thurman's and entrusted it to one of the riders going down to Green Valley that night.

Next morning Cal began to show some little interest once more in his homestead. Wess had come over several days to feed the stock, and had sent his younger brother at other times when he could not come. This day Cal assumed the tasks again, and evidently found them slow, toilsome ones, owing to the condition of his hands.

Georgiana donned her riding-suit and boots, and even in her concentration on her purpose she did not overlook the value of making herself look as attractive as possible. Then she went out to the barn, and saddling her horse, which she had been careful to keep in that night, she rode off without seeing Cal or knowing whether he saw her or not. It did not matter. She could not be stopped now.

Tuck Merry was waiting for her, and his homely features expressed considerable perturbation and very much pleasure. It seemed to Georgiana that she had never before really looked at him. What a huge, ungainly, long, and ludicrous individual he was! His cadaverous face, like a lean ham, appeared adorned with many queer things, most prominent of which was his enormous nose. But his smile, the light of his big eyes, belied the counterfeits of physical nature. Tuck Merry loomed up to Georgiana then as the chivalrous and faithful friend she needed.

"Georgie, this is some surprise," he said in greeting.

"Howdy, Tuck! Aren't you flattered to be asked to meet a girl in trouble?" queried Georgiana, as she offered her hand.

"Flattered and proud," replied Tuck with something of sharpness. "But don't waste time kidding me into taking your part. I'm for you. Come out with it. I know it's trouble between you and Cal. And I'm sick."

"Have you folks at Green Valley heard about Cal's fight with Hatfield?"

"Only yesterday," replied Tuck anxiously, "news came from Ryson, and we took it for Bar XX brand. But, anyway, I intended to ride up to see Cal to-day."

Thereupon Georgiana, in strong and feeling language, told in detail of the terrible beating Hatfield had administered to Cal. How curiously and keenly she watched for Tuck's reaction to this narrative! To her amaze his first expression was delight.

"We heard some of that," he blurted out. "Tom Hall's talk. . . . Cal was getting the best of Hatfield in a stand-up fight. Then the burly buzzer rough-housed him."

But Tuck's pleasure was short-lived, as was evident from the swift hardening and darkening of his face.

"What do you want of me?" he demanded.

"I want you to take me to the Bar XX ranch."

"For Heaven's sake, Georgie, what for?"

"I'm going to call that Bid Hatfield to his face," replied Georgiana, and then, in swifter, more fluent words, that grew poignant as she progressed, she told Tuck how Hatfield had besmirched her character, what a miserable liar he was, why Cal would soon hunt him up to kill him, and lastly that she must see Hatfield first and shame him before his own crowd, and make him retract his vile slander.

"Right-o! I get you, Steve," retorted Tuck, with quick, intent, comprehending look, not devoid of admiration. "I'm for you.

We'll brand Mr. Hatfield a lemon. . . . Now, Georgie, ride across the brook to the trail and go down. I'll catch up with you before you're gone half a mile. I want to phone from the ranger cabin and tell Henry I'm going to saw wood to-day, but not at the sawmill."

Georgiana did as she was bidden, thrilling gratefully for Tuck's instant championship. The home of the Bar XX was as picturesque as Green Valley. The trail led into a road, and that rounded the margin of large fields, with dead stalks of corn and sorghum, and up into a beautiful cove between two brushy-sloped hills. Here stood the corrals of felled logs and low, squat, log-cabins. Blue smoke curled from the yellow stove chimney of the larger cabin. One of the corrals was full of dusty, kicking horses. Saddles littered the ground outside. The Bar XX riders were in for their noon meal.

"Somebody in the door, Georgie," said Tuck. "We're here. It's up to you. Don't lose your nerve."

Georgiana gave a defiant little laugh that was eloquent of her equilibrium. If Cal could stand to be beaten into insensibility on behalf of her reputation, what could she not do to save him from the madness of killing?

Several faces appeared back in the darkness of the cabin door. Then as Tuck and Georgiana rode within speaking distance a tall man strode out, bareheaded. He had sandy hair, rather thin, and a drooping moustache, a lean, brown, weather-beaten face, open and strong, piercing light-blue eyes.

"Saunders, the boss," whispered Tuck to Georgiana.

"Howdy! Reckon I've seen you somewheres," he said to Tuck, and then when he espied that Tuck's companion was a girl he bowed with the quaint deference these Tontonians always showed the opposite sex. "Mawnin', miss. Is there anythin' we can do for you?"

"Are you Mr. Saunders?" asked Georgiana.

"I am, at your service," he replied with a pleasant smile, and his keen eyes studied Georgiana's face. He expected the unusual, but it was plain he did not recognise her.

"I'm Cal Thurman's wife," said Georgiana, with a sudden heave of her heart and a rush of hot blood clear to her temples. "I've ridden over here to face one of your riders—Bid Hatfield. Will you let me see him?"

"Certainly," replied Saunders.

"Then, before you call him out I want to tell you what brought me," continued Georgiana swiftly, feeling the interest and sure of the sympathy of this rancher. "Mary Stockwell, the school-teacher at Green Valley, is my sister. She brought me out here for my health. I was a crazy kid. I—I liked the boys and I flirted with them. Bid Hatfield was one of them. I liked him. I let him kiss me—on several occasions. Then he insulted me. I never told a soul. But the next time I saw him I told him I wouldn't meet him any more. . . . After that I married Cal Thurman. Just lately I learned that Hatfield has been talking about me—making me out a vile little hussy. Cal heard it at last, and that led to the fight. Now I'm over here to face Hatfield."

"Wal, wal!" ejaculated the rancher, at once embarrassed and shocked. "Thet's a serious charge to lay on a man in this Tonto Basin."

"Please let me see him," returned Georgiana.

"Wal, I reckon I will—an' I'll see him, too," said Saunders forcefully. Turning away, he took several long strides towards the door of the cabin. This man was thinking hard. All at once he yelled: "Hey, Bid Hatfield, you're wanted out heah."

"Who wants me?" came in a gruff voice from inside.

"Wal, I do, for one," shouted Saunders, peremptorily. "You come out heah pronto."

Then the burly Hatfield appeared in the door, swaggering a little, the same bold-eyed, handsome rider Georgiana had seen so often. But at sight of her his dark face turned livid. He halted short.

"Hatfield," said Saunders curtly, "heah's Cal Thurman's wife, an' she's made a damn' serious charge against you."

The several faces in the doorway behind Hatfield attached themselves to forms that stalked out into the sunlight. This fact was repeated until half a dozen staring riders had lined up outside the cabin.

At sight of Hatfield and the sudden blanching of his face Georgiana sustained a rush of passion that held her a moment in its grip. It was more thought of Cal than wrong to herself that stirred her fury.

Before she could speak, Saunders and all of the riders wheeled quickly to gaze down the road. A cloud of dust had puffed up beyond the curve. Then Georgiana heard the rapid beat of hoofs. Horsemen hove in sight, riding on a run.

"What the hell!" ejaculated Saunders. "Who's rarin' in heah this way?"

"Boss, it's some of the Four T outfit," called a rider.

"Thurman, huh! Wal, you-all stand pat," ordered Saunders.

Georgiana really did not get the full gist of this talk until she recognised Enoch, and then Tim Matthews. She was sure another was Arizona, and another Pan Handle Ames. The sudden shift of her sensations from wrath to amaze left her trembling. She became aware of Tuck's big hand on hers, as if to reassure her. How those riders were pounding down the road! The white foam flew above dust. In a dark compact mass this half-dozen or more horses swept down on the cabin. They were pulled back on their haunches, and scattering the gravel they slid to a halt. But scarcely a second before every rider landed with thudding boots and jingling spurs on the ground. Georgiana saw then she had been right in her recognition, and the others were Boyd, Serge, and Lock Thurman. They made a sombre, menacing group, from which Enoch stalked out, slowly, with his grey eyes glinting. A gun swung at his hip.

"Howdy, Saunders," he drawled.

"Howdy, Enoch," replied the rancher.

"Someone phoned us to come hell-bent for election over heah," went on Enoch. "Reckon we was comin', anyhow, but as we didn't care much aboot that phone call we rode some."

"So I see," replied Saunders dryly, indicating the foam-lashed, heaving horses. "An' damned if I ain't glad to see you, Enoch."

"Ahuh! Wal, what's up?" queried Enoch sharply, as his eyes flashed from Saunders to his men, then back to Tuck Merry and Georgiana.

"'Pears to me there's a heap up," answered Saunders. "Cal's wife is heah, as you see, an' she can shore speak for herself. She's come to make Bid Hatfield prove his brag, or eat his words."

Tuck Merry pressed Georgiana's hand hard and whispered fiercely in her ear: "Now—hand it to him!"

Georgiana lifted her gloved hand and pointed quiveringly at the livid rider.

"Now, Bid Hatfield—say to my face—that I'm not an honest girl," she called out in ringing, passionate scorn. "Everybody can tell the truth. Show me up, if I'm what you say. If you have anything on me tell it now. . . . Tell me to my face in front of all these men!"

Manifestly the situation was a terrible one for Hatfield. The surprise of her confronting him in daring scorn completely unmanned him.

"Aw, Georgie, it was all Tonto gossip. I never said anythin' bad against you."

"You're a liar!" flashed Georgiana. "Everybody knows you've talked. And if you're not a white-livered coward you'll tell the truth. You'll confess you lied to defame me."

"But, Georgie, I didn't say what—what you've heard," he replied hoarsely.

"All right. If you're not man enough to own up you'll do this. You'll answer me before these men. . . . You told that I let you kiss me, didn't you?"

"Maybe I did--when I was drunk or mad," he replied, dropping his head.

"Didn't I stop letting you kiss me—because you tried to go too far—and didn't I quit meeting you?" Georgiana demanded in all the intensity of her blazing anger.

"Yes—you did," returned Hatfield huskily, with face like a white rag.

Georgiana drew up with abated breath.

"That's all *you* need say, Bid Hatfield. But I'm going to say more," she cried, with all the lashing fury now roused in her. "I told Mr. Saunders the truth. I'm not ashamed to tell anybody. I liked you. I let you kiss me—the same as I let Cal and Tim and Arizona. It was all fun to me. I see now that it was wrong. I'm sorry I was so silly. I've had to suffer for it. . . . But a girl deserves to suffer if she lets herself be kissed by a man who's a cad. To kiss and tell! That is the cheapest, meanest thing a man can do. I'll bet every rider here, your best friends, if you have any, will despise you for that. And for the lies you told—I'm calling you to your face—a dirty low-down bum!"

Georgiana was not by any means through with Hatfield, but as she paused for breath, momentarily overcome, the sudden silence was broken by Tuck Merry.

"Aha! Mr. Bruiser," he yelled as he bounced with remarkable agility off his horse; "the lady has got your number. She's called you. Every man here knows you for a dirty low-down bum. And right now is when it's coming to you."

Hatfield had half turned to slink away when Merry opened up in his loud voice. Slowly the burly rider faced around, scowling, with rolling eyes fixing in surprise.

Tuck Merry just then commanded the intense attention of everybody there. He slammed down his sombrero, and slipping out of his coat he slammed that down. His gloves he kept on, and as he began to prance around Hatfield he fingered these gloves in a significant manner.

"Walk away from the ropes. Get out here in the ring," called Tuck with robust heartiness.

"Say, you goose-necked idiot—shut up, or I'll wring off your big head," harshly growled Hatfield. With a man to encounter he presented a different front.

"Now you're talking, Bid. That's music to my ears. Sing some more. You are the most beautiful hunk of flesh to pound I ever saw. You're also a hunk of cheese. Bid, you look exactly like a fat stiff of a German I met in the Argonne. And would you believe it? I killed that Hun with one punch in the belly."

Hatfield was as bewildered as enraged. He had to keep turning round and round to watch Tuck, who was walking with giant strides round and round, working his enormously long arms.

"Say, the fellar's crazy," he bawled out.

Enoch laughed a dry, cackling sort of laugh. "Wal, Bid," he drawled, "he may be crazy, but I shore wouldn't be in your boots for a million."

Hatfield crouched down like a mad bull, about to charge.

"Bid, have you any messages you want sent?" queried Tuck, as he walked faster and faster. "Tell them to somebody while I get exercise. I used to do this when I was boxing-master in the navy. . . . Bid, I'm a fighting marine and I've licked every Buddy who got inside the ropes with me. And say, before I forget, I want to tell you I was Jack Dempsey's sparring partner," shouted Tuck cheerfully. "And take it from me, my lady-chasing Tonto bull-dozer, Jack had a hell of a lot more trouble with me than he had in some of his ring fights."

"You're a bloomin' lunatic," blurted out Hatfield.

Suddenly, then, Tuck seemed to leap and strike in one incredibly swift action. Hatfield fell with a crash. And Georgiana screamed. Fascinated, gripped in a hot fury of delight that sickened as it thrilled, she listened and watched with senses intensely strung. She recorded Tuck's cheerful sally as Hatfield went sprawling, and that picture was photographed on her memory. The rider rolled up and rushed, only to meet a cracking blow that staggered him. He reeled. Tuck danced round him, his arms working like pistons, and his blows raining upon Hatfield. And it seemed he had a strange name for everything. The riders bawled, and jumped around like Indians. Hatfield swung here and there, and then he would jolt stiff and start to fall, only to be held up from the other side by another blow. Tuck Merry was too swift to follow.

Suddenly he ceased these tactics, and drawing back, all about him changed.

"Damn your black heart!" he hissed. "You rough-housed Cal Thurman. Now I'll give you worse than you gave him."

Like a huge panther Merry leaped straight up to fall hard on Hatfield, carrying him down. A terrible wrestling, thudding, howling *mêlée* ensued. The men rolled in a cloud of dust. Then it seemed to Georgiana that it cleared to show Tuck Merry in terrific swinging action. Not so swift now, but heavy! His blows rang hard, then sounded sodden. They were terrible. Hatfield appeared like a sack. Every blow moved him limply. Georgiana shut her eyes, but still she heard the awful blows. Then they ceased. She opened her eyes. Tuck Merry rose to his feet and looked down upon the prone form of the rider, singularly motionless. Tuck took off one glove and slammed it down in Hatfield's face; then likewise with the other.

"That'll—do—you—for—the—rest—of your yellow life!" he panted heavily.

Then he turned to the rancher.

"Mr. Saunders—he's out—good and plenty," he said, gasping for his breath. "And I'm here to tell you—he won't be—much use to you—for a long time to come."

"Hatfield will never be any use to me again," returned Saunders curtly.

The riders stirred, and moved forward to group round Hatfield. One of them knelt. Some of them whispered. Georgiana began to feel the weakening reaction of all this excitement.

Enoch strode over to gaze down upon Hatfield.

"My Gawd!" was his exclamation.

Then Saunders clapped a heavy hand down on his shoulder.

"Enoch, I never had much against you," he said.

"Wal, I can say the same to you aboot that," drawled Enoch.

"Listen. I'm letting Bloom go the end of this month. An' Hatfield leaves this ranch to-morrow if he has to go on a pack-mule. . . . Suppose you an' me shake hands with this plucky little girl an' with each other, an' be friends. The Four T's an' the Bar XX used to run the same range, an' were the richer for it. What do you say?"

"Jim Saunders, I say, *you bet,*" returned Enoch, heartily.

They stalked over to where Georgiana sat on her horse, thrilling through and through at this amazing issue.

"Little lady," said Saunders with something of gallantry, "accept my respects. You're a brave girl, an' Cal Thurman is lucky. You can tell him you made friends with the boss of the Bar XX."

"Georgie, I shore think heaps more of you," said Enoch, and a handshake was not enough to express his feelings.

Georgiana would not let any of the riders, not even Tuck Merry, accompany her any farther than the forks of the trail. She wanted to ride home alone, to think, to plan, to gloat over her wonderful good fortune. She arrived at the homestead scarcely later than the middle of the afternoon, to find Cal pacing the porch.

"Georgie, where have you been?" he asked.

She dismounted before replying, and threw her bridle.

"Cal, what'd you say if I told you I've made friends of Enoch and Jim Saunders?"

Cal flopped down on the porch bench as if the strength had suddenly left his legs.

"You've been over to the Bar XX?" he ejaculated wildly.

"Yep, and, dear boy, it's a cinch you'll never have to go there again."

"What've you done?" he demanded, rising in mingled anger and wonder.

"Darling. I called Bid Hatfield to his face," cried Georgiana, suddenly beside herself with the joy she could impart. "Made him a liar and a miserable low-down bum before his boss and all the Bar XX outfit, and Enoch, too, with Lock and Serge and Boyd, and the boys. Oh, it was sweet—Damn him, I made him crawl! . . . Then, oh! oh! oh! Cal, if you'd only been there to see Tuck Merry beat that boob into a jellyfish! He said he'd rough-house Bid as Bid had done you. . . . Then it was almost too much for me. I screamed. Oh, such blows and thumps! But I was in a frenzy of glee and I wouldn't have stopped Tuck to save Bid's life. Nor would anybody else there. Tuck beat him into a pulp. . . . Then it was all over. Saunders had his say and he and Enoch made up. They shook hands with me—thanked *me*. Little Georgiana May did it. Now what have *you* to say?"

Cal could only stammer his wonder, his gratitude, his incredulous joy.

"Forget it!" she exclaimed. "I've something better than that to tell you. . . . Suppose we run out to the point—to your juniper tree on the mesa rim—where you told me you used to dream as a boy—of all the wonderful things that were going to happen to you. . . . Let me tell you *there*. Come."

She kept ahead of him, almost running, not listening to him, uttering gay, wild laughter. She entered the belt of timber, glided under the cedars and piñons, over the brown fragrant aisles to the rim, where the gnarled old juniper stood. And there with her back to the tree she awaited Cal. He came, and never had she seen him like that. The light in his face seemed to have transformed the stains and discolorations that had been there. Georgiana toyed with her happiness—jealously holding back the rapture she could give.

"Did you know you had married an heiress?" she asked archly.

"Georgie, are you crazy, or am I?" he cried.

"Fact. A good old aunt I always hated died and left Mary and me some money. Lots of money. But that's not what I want to tell you. I'm a changed girl. . . . Are you sure you didn't give me that knock on the head, the day you married me?"

"Oh, Georgie! I didn't lie. It was an accident."

"Well, you *should* have done it. For that's what made me love you."

"Girl! Don't fool with me now," he said hoarsely.

Then she threw her arms round his neck. "Cal, I'm in dead earnest. I love you. I think I've always loved you. I was only wild. . . . Kiss me! All's well that ends well. Let me make up for my wrong to you. I'm happy. You saved me, Cal. . . . And I—I want to be worthy of a Thurman. . . . I want to be your real wife!"

Together they watched the gold and purple clouds mass over the western range and the purple shadows gather in the wild depths of the Tonto.